# "Then **Wayne** Said to **Mario...**"

# "Then **Wayne** Said to **Mario...**"

## *The Best Stanley Cup Stories Ever Told*

Kevin Allen

TRIUMPH
B O O K S

This book is available in quantity at special discounts for your group or organization. For further information, contact:

**Triumph Books**
542 South Dearborn Street
Suite 750
Chicago, Illinois 60605
(312) 939-3330
Fax (312) 663-3557
www.triumphbooks.com

Printed in U.S.A.
ISBN: 978-1-60078-155-1
Design by Patricia Frey
Editorial and page production by Prologue Publishing Services, LLC
Photos courtesy of AP Images except where otherwise indicated

*To my daughter, Kelsey,*
*who speaks both Spanish and hockey fluently*

# table of
## contents

# introduction

Young defenseman Kyle Quincey didn't play a minute in the postseason for the champion Detroit Red Wings in 2008 and yet he ended up a Stanley Cup hero.

When lead singer Joe Elliott of the band Def Leppard was passed the Stanley Cup by Detroit player Darren McCarty during an NHL-sponsored season-opening rock party extravaganza, the British heavy metalist shocked Motown fans by sitting the Cup upside down on the stage.

Aghast at the sight, a peeved Quincey marched in front of the band and righted the Stanley Cup as concertgoers roared their approval.

"It was so disrespectful—it was like someone throwing a flag down and trampling on it," Quincey said.

Quincey's emotional reaction to the defiling of the Stanley Cup was keeping with NHL players' history of deep adoration for a championship trophy that dates to 1892, when Frederick Arthur, Lord Stanley of Preston and son of the Earl of Derby, then Canada's governor-general, donated a bowl to be used to crown the Dominion of Canada's amateur hockey champion.

A battalion of psychologists would be needed to fully explore the complex relationship that competitors have with this championship trophy. How can you explain that players speak of the trophy in reverent tones and then fill it with champagne, or Cheerios, or popcorn, or fries and gravy, to celebrate their success? The Stanley Cup is both the Holy Grail and a beer stein. It is both a sacred chalice and a serving bowl.

The Stanley Cup weighs just 34½ pounds, but the sentimentality of winning it can be overwhelming to the point that rugged Dallas Drake admitted that his legs buckled and arms quivered when he finally received his chance to hoist it over his head on June 4, 2008. He had endured a 16-year odyssey that took him from Detroit, Winnipeg, Phoenix, St. Louis, and then back to Detroit to achieve the success he dreamed of when he was a youngster growing up in British Columbia.

At the moment of his greatest triumph as a professional athlete, Drake said his limbs seemed as if they were made of rubber and his muscles were like jelly. It was all he could do to not drop the Stanley Cup.

When Teemu Selanne won the Cup for the first time with Anaheim in 2007, he sat on the bench and wept.

In 1999, when the Dallas Stars won a Stanley Cup on a controversial overtime goal by Brett Hull at precisely 1:37 AM Eastern Standard Time, Stars superstar Mike Modano collapsed in a river of his own tears.

"I don't think Mike ever understood the commitment it took to win until that moment," then–Stars coach Ken Hitchcock said about the memory of Modano unraveling in a flood of joy after the Stars defeated Buffalo to win the Cup. "He had put everything he had emotionally into it. Everything. His body melted, and he reverted back to a little boy."

For a multitude of reasons, the Stanley Cup touches the child in all of us. The sporting world is rich in historically significant symbols, including the Masters' Green Jacket, baseball's Cy Young Award, tennis' Davis Cup, and yachting's Americas Cup, to name just a few. Yet an argument can be made that, because its aura has extended well beyond the walls of its arenas, Lord Stanley's gift to hockey in 1893 has become the world's grandest trophy. The Stanley Cup has become a global symbol of sporting success. Tens of thousands of people have lined up everywhere from Sweden to Tokyo to the Czech Republic to Moscow's Red Square, hoping to bask in its glow and understand its allure.

Only champions can come close to unlocking the mystery of its appeal. The word *close* is apt in this case because everyone who has won the Cup seems incapable of offering words to translate the experience. To a hockey player, a Stanley Cup triumph is nirvana—a place where your mind is overwhelmed by a blend of joy and emotion that is truly indescribable.

Lord Stanley purchased the sterling silver cup for 10 guineas in 1893. That was $48.47 at the time. Today, as a MasterCard commercial has shown us, winning the Cup is priceless. The best guess on the Cup's monetary value is that it might fetch around $3 million if it were ever sold at a Sotheby's auction. But anyone who has won the Cup, or desired to win it, will tell you that the Cup's value can't be defined in those terms. This is hockey's priceless 35¼-inch chalice—clearly the most exalted trophy in the professional sports kingdom. The Vince Lombardi Trophy is dime-store hardware compared to Lord Stanley's legacy. Can you even name the World Series championship trophy or the hunk of metal awarded to the National Basketball Association champions?

Lord Stanley had become smitten with hockey during his tour of duty in Canada. His two sons played the game, and his daughter, Isobel, was among the first girls to play the sport in Canada. Lord Stanley's objective was to promote hockey through a national championship trophy, but it's unlikely he could have envisioned the impact his gift would have on the game and its people.

The Stanley Cup has become a symbol of passion and success even for those who don't follow the sport. Even some folks who can't name a single National Hockey League player know that the winner hoists the Stanley Cup.

With an identity all of its own, the Stanley Cup has been a guest on *The Tonight Show* multiple times and starred in its own television commercial. It's been a regular visitor to the White House and has been welcomed by Presidents Bill Clinton and George W. Bush.

"This is really the people's trophy," said former Minnesota Wild president and general manager Doug Risebrough, who won four Stanley Cup championships as a player with the Montreal Canadiens and one as an assistant coach with the Calgary Flames. "It's a huggable trophy. It doesn't sit up in an elite cabinet. It doesn't look fragile. It looks like you can hug it."

The Stanley Cup is awarded to the champion, but those who have their name inscribed on it say it's about so much more than a championship; it's about fathers and sons, vision quests, camaraderie, personal commitment, national pride, and a multitude of other ideals that are personal to each player. How else do you explain why New York Islanders captain Bryan Trottier once slept with the Stanley Cup beside him, or why Dallas Stars center Joe Nieuwendyk felt obliged to make sure a blind Cornell professor—his favorite instructor—could feel and touch the Cup? And what words can explain why Detroit Red Wings All-Star Brendan Shanahan and Dallas Stars veteran Guy Carbonneau both needed to take the Cup to their fathers' graves in recent years?

Part of the Cup's mystique is its tie to the past as well as its immortality. When a player wins the Cup, he knows his name will forever be engraved on one of the Stanley Cup's silver bands. It will stand in perpetuity as a reminder of his success. The quest for the Cup almost seems pure and unpolluted by the rapid flow of money that runs through the sports world. Hockey players seem to want to win the Cup with the same passion with which climbers want to conquer Everest.

The adventurous spirit that fueled Modano's quest for hockey immortality in 1999 was undoubtedly similar to what the feisty players of the Yukon Territory felt in 1904 when they challenged the Ottawa Silver Seven for the Stanley Cup championship. Starting out December 4, 1904, from Dawson City, legend has it that the Yukon players started their trip on dogsleds and covered about 4,000 miles by boat, train, and on foot to arrive in Ottawa on January 12, 1905. The boisterous Yukon players lost the two-game series by a composite score of 32–4, but their trek added another layer of history to the Cup and another colorful story to a trophy that has far more tales than it has champions.

Today, players don't travel by dogsled in their quest to win the Cup, but the journey isn't any less arduous. The players who have won the Cup may feel like they have completed an Iditarod. To win the Cup, a team must win 16 times over two months with pressure blowing through at hurricane velocity. "You play 82 regular-season games and then you have two more months of work in order to become a champion," St. Louis Blues general manager Larry Pleau said. "Doesn't that discourage you right off the bat?"

Given the amount of physical contact in hockey, players argue that no other sport comes close to matching the torturous grind of the NHL playoffs. It's like a two-month gauntlet during which players are clubbed, cut, and worn down by exhaustion. Modano said the two-month march to the Cup in 1999 was "the most emotional and physically draining experience I've ever had."

The grind takes its toll on the mind as well as the body. Bill Clement, who helped the Flyers win back-to-back Stanley Cups in 1974 and 1975, apologizes for using a war analogy, but says that it's the only thing he knows that can sum up the bond he felt with his teammates. "It was a foxhole mentality," he said. "You couldn't describe the bond we had. When we won, it was like the war was over."

When the Cup is won, tradition dictates that players should indeed celebrate like it's V-J Day. With emotions colliding and jubilation uncorked, players have celebrated Stanley Cup victories with unbridled passion and zeal. If the Stanley Cup were allowed to tell its tale, it would be a story filled with raw emotions and zany twists. It would be a sweet narrative with many hardships erased by a happy ending. It would also be a comedic yarn of trips to strip clubs, booze-fueled dips into hotel pools, and a night spent alone on a street corner in Montreal. To many players, having the Cup for a day is almost as rewarding as winning it.

An important aspect of the Stanley Cup's legend are the places it has been and the tales of its travels.

"Every year we hear a couple of stories about where the Cup has gone that seem to add to its aura and mystique," said player-agent Steve Bartlett, who has watched his clients celebrate Cup successes for the better part of two decades.

He has been witness to the euphoria that players experience as they party with a trophy that has a tradition dating to the 19th century.

"For years people didn't believe me when I told them the Stanley Cup ended up in Mario Lemieux's pool," said Bartlett, who was at that party in 1992. "I think my first reaction was shock, and then it was, 'Should I jump in and rescue the Cup?'"

Bartlett has attended Stanley Cup celebrations in recent years, and notes, "There is a little more security for the Cup these days."

In days gone by, players only touched the Cup on the night they won it—on the ice and perhaps at the usually raucous postgame party. In 1995 NHL Commissioner Gary Bettman decreed that every player, coach, and member of management would be allowed a period of 24 hours in which to have the Cup in their possession for the purpose of celebration. But even before players were officially allowed to take the Cup home, it unofficially made party stops in many different locales over the years. That's why New York Islanders great Clark Gillies was able to allow his pooch to enjoy supper out of the Stanley Cup in 1980. That's how it ended up in the bottom of Mario Lemieux's swimming pool in 1992. That's why Pittsburgh Penguins player Phil Bourque was able to sit in his living room and take the Cup apart to determine the source of a rattle.

Where a player chooses to take the Cup is a personal decision that may say more about the athlete than do his season statistics. Colorado Avalanche center Peter Forsberg was so smitten with the championship glow in 1996 that he took the Cup to Sweden. He was the first NHL player to party with the Cup overseas. Igor Larionov, Slava Kozlov, and Slava Fetisov took the Cup to Moscow one year later and stood in Red Square like conquering warriors displaying their plunder.

Wanting to share the Cup with fans, Detroit's Darren McCarty took it to Bob's Big Boy for breakfast, then to a cigar store, a golf course, and a corn roast for dinner. Dallas Stars center Joe Nieuwendyk sweet-talked the Hockey Hall of Fame into giving him an extra half-day so he could split time between his hometown of Whitby, Ontario, and his summer home in Ithaca, New York. In Whitby he drove downtown with his brothers hanging out of the back of his Chevy Tahoe with the Cup in hand. In Ithaca he held a private reception at Cornell, where he let blind professor Dan Sisler lay his hands on the Cup.

To hockey players, winning the Cup means owning a piece of history that can't ever be lost or forgotten. The Cup has frequently runneth over with champagne and fine Canadian ale. That explains why the Stanley Cup has more battle scars than do veterans of foreign wars, and why Stanley Cup celebrations have stumbled into the wee hours and beyond.

Tradition demands that, at public gatherings, the Stanley Cup must be treated with a reverence and dignity that would usually be reserved for religious artifacts. The keeper of the Cup wears white gloves when he brings it onto the ice, and it is always placed on a table covered with cloth. The Hockey Hall of Fame makes sure that the Cup's silver gleams with polish when it's on public display. Tradition also demands that winners have earned the right to treat the Stanley Cup as if it were an old washbucket.

In many celebrations through the years, the Stanley Cup has been treated with some irreverence or been at the center of horseplay. In 1905, for example, the Ottawa Silver Seven drop-kicked the Stanley Cup into the Rideau Canal. The following year, the same Silver Seven were invited to dine with Lord Minto, Canada's governor-general, at Government House. Frank McGee, who had once scored 14 goals in a Stanley Cup Finals game against Dawson City, was the only member of the Silver Seven squad who grew up in affluent surroundings. His uncle was D'Arcy McGee, a famous Canadian politician. In addition to being the Silver Seven's most dangerous scorer, McGee was a notorious practical joker. As he prepared his nervous teammates for a fine-dining experience with the government dignitaries, he told them simply, "Watch me and do whatever I do. And don't worry about the forks. You are supposed to just use your hands." Not realizing that McGee was pulling off the best prank of his career, his teammates followed his lead right down the path to embarrassment. When the finger bowls arrived after dinner, McGee picked his up and slurped it noisily like a cup of tea. His teammates did likewise. The governor-general apparently had a heart of gold. Not wishing to embarrass his nation's best hockey players, he picked up his bowl and began slurping away. The name of McGee was synonymous with the Stanley Cup in its early years. His life was cut short when he was killed in action while fighting in France in World War I.

In 1924 Montreal Canadiens owner Leo Dandurand left the Stanley Cup on the curb after he had stopped to change a flat tire. Hall of Famer Red Kelly has told the story about how he put his infant son in the Cup's bowl one year; the child promptly peed in it. In the 1980s the Edmonton Oilers tucked the Cup in agent Mike Barnett's trunk after a night of revelry, and everyone except Barnett forgot where they left it.

The overflowing emotions of the victors may spill as much from a sense of relief as celebration. Those who enter the NHL do so knowing that, rightly or wrongly, players, especially top players, are made to feel incomplete if they haven't won a Stanley Cup. Marcel Dionne was an outstanding offensive player and ranked third all-time with 731 career goals, yet cruelly he is often remembered as the best player never to win a Cup. Although no one speaks about it, players all know Dionne's story; they also know that Gordie Howe, Wayne Gretzky, Phil Esposito, and Bobby Hull all won the Stanley Cup. They know if they win, their names will be forever linked with the Cup.

In Canada in particular, youngsters dream of winning the Stanley Cup more than they do of becoming prime minister. Hockey seems intertwined with the country's self-esteem. In Canada the Stanley Cup may be a metaphor for life and the struggles that accompany it. Gordie Howe, nicknamed "Mr. Hockey" during his glory days with the Detroit Red Wings, can remember growing up in Saskatchewan and going to a neighbor's house to hear the radio broadcast of playoff games. "All you heard about was the Stanley Cup," Howe said. "It became your dream. Playing hockey was part of being Canadian."

xvi "Then Wayne Said to Mario…"

There's a duty, suggests former NHLer Dave Andreychuk, for players to pass along tales of the Stanley Cup, as if somehow that keeps the hockey tribe strong. "All the years I played I heard the stories," Andreychuk said. "Then I finally won, and I started telling the stories."

Although the players' revelry draws most of the news coverage, the real tradition of celebration is the sharing of the Stanley Cup with the rich and poor, the young and old, the sick and healthy. Almost every NHL player works a charity stop into his victory celebration, and usually it requires a stop at a hospital.

Tradition says that no player is allowed to lift the Cup until he has won it. And most players won't even touch it before then—as if the ghost of Lord Stanley might curse them for their act of insolence. (Hockey players are notoriously superstitious, and it would be an easy leap of faith for many to believe that they might not ever win the Cup if they violated this unwritten rule.) In the 1950s Detroit's Ted Lindsay became the first player to lift the Stanley Cup and take it to the boards so the fans could have a closer look. Since then the hoisting of Lord Stanley's chalice has become the official beginning of the championship experience. It's fitting that Lindsay isn't quite sure what inspired him to do that, other than wanting to give the fans a better opportunity to see the Cup. It was just a triumphant, emotional moment.

Lord Stanley had intended that champions engrave their names in the Cup "at their own charge." One assumes that those who did their crude silver-smithing in the early years with a penknife, rusty 10-penny nail, or sharp instrument weren't any less thrilled to win the Cup than today's heroes whose names are engraved professionally by a Montreal silver craftsman. Through interviews with past champions, we discover that, although the game and its trappings have changed dramatically through the years, the emotions have remained a constant that unifies the past with the present. Knowing that game stories and statistical scoring summaries provide an accurate historical record about how each Stanley Cup was won, this book's objective is merely to allow past champions a chance to reflect on how they felt about winning and what they did to celebrate that accomplishment.

Since the 1990s, more than 140 NHL players, coaches, and general managers were interviewed to acquire stories for this book, a cross section from the 1920s to the present. The hope is that a glimpse of their thoughts and their celebrations might give us all a better understanding of why a Stanley Cup victory can reduce stoic men to sobbing boys.

To come close to understanding how players feel about winning the Stanley Cup, you need to accompany an underwear-clad Phil Bourque as he climbed a 25-foot waterfall at Mario Lemieux's home at 4:00 AM. You must know what he was thinking as he stood on that waterfall with the Cup raised above his head like he was king of the world. You must feel his exhilaration as he hurled the Cup into the pool with teammates reveling in the splash that he made. To realize how hockey success feels, you must step atop the glacier on Bull Mountain in British Columbia where Rob and Scott Niedermayer took the Stanley Cup in 2007 to take photographs that would truly capture their ascent to the championship summit.

The Niedermayer photographs may best symbolize the joy of winning because the drive to win a Stanley Cup is often compared to a mountain-climbing expedition.

When the Anaheim Ducks won the Stanley Cup in 2007, then–Anaheim general manager Brian Burke spent weeks researching a plan to prevent his team from being afflicted with "Stanley Cup hangover." That's the name that has been given to the lack of intensity that NHL champions show the following season. In recent years NHL champions have struggled to recapture the inner drive they displayed in their first climb to a league title.

Burke recalls when he called Carolina Hurricanes general manager Jim Rutherford, whose team had won the Stanley Cup in 2006, Rutherford said bluntly there was no preventative cure for Stanley Cup hangover.

"Your players have just climbed Mount Everest," Rutherford said. "Don't expect them to do it again any time soon."

# "Then **Wayne** Said to **Mario...**"

# chapter 1

# Hall of Famers

## Ted Lindsay

*Detroit Red Wings, 1950, 1952, 1954, and 1955*

In the 1950s, when Detroit Red Wings captain Ted Lindsay picked up the Stanley Cup and carried it to the cheering fans at Olympia Stadium, it was the 20th-century equivalent of the king's knight allowing the masses to inspect the crown jewels. It just wasn't done before Lindsay's moment of impulsiveness.

Photographs would seem to prove that Lindsay was the first to raise the Cup above his head in what is now the classic Stanley Cup pose. What did his teammates think of Lindsay's Cup-raising? "They probably thought the idiot Lindsay is off on another tangent," Lindsay said, chuckling.

Lindsay's historically significant act wasn't premeditated. "I really didn't even think about it at all," Lindsay said. "You never know what you will do in your life that will turn out to be important. This was just one of those impulsive things."

After Red Wings owner Bruce Norris and general manager Jack Adams had received the trophy from NHL president Clarence Campbell, it was handed off to Lindsay for the traditional photograph. After that snap, he picked it up over his head and carried it to the boards. There was no Plexiglas in those days, only chicken wire, and fans could actually touch the cold silver of the Cup.

"I was very public relations–oriented," Lindsay said. "I knew who paid our salary. It wasn't the owners; it was the people. I just wanted them to have a closer look. I just went around the rink and let everyone see it.

This is what we dream about, maybe from the time we're born—to be recognized as the best in the world. I wanted to share it with the fans."

Did Campbell say anything? "I don't think so, but I wouldn't have heard him anyway because the fans were pretty loud," he said.

"Terrible Ted" Lindsay was a man of the people, even if he played so aggressively that opponents couldn't stand him. The Detroit Red Wings were a dominant team in Lindsay's heyday, winning eight of nine regular-season championships in one stretch from 1948 to 1957. The Red Wings won four Stanley Cup championships during that period, and it seems somewhat surprising that they didn't win more.

"Oh, we had a great team," Lindsay said. "But every year we had to hope that our farm teams in Indianapolis and Edmonton would go to their championship round because we knew that four, five, or six of those players were going to be brought up. They were supposed to be reserves in case we had injuries, but Adams always became a magician. They weren't good enough to play with us all year, but he would want to insert them in the lineup.

"And you had to give Toronto and Montreal credit at that time. They had good teams back then."

Lindsay had some classic playoff moments in that era, including one in 1955 when he became the second NHL player to score four goals in a Stanley Cup Finals game. He netted four in a 7–1 win against Montreal on April 5, 1955. Lindsay was as respected in that era as any athlete in Detroit, including young Al Kaline of the Detroit Tigers and Bobby Layne of the Detroit Lions. He settled in the Detroit area after the war, starting a manufacturing business with teammate Marty Pavelich. Lindsay has fond memories of winning the championship four times on Olympia ice.

After each championship the team would gather at the Book Cadillac Hotel on Washington Boulevard in downtown Detroit and party until 3:00 AM. "Washington Boulevard was one of the premier streets in America back then," Lindsay said. "It wasn't like it is now. There were no parades. But we just had a very nice party with all of the players, their wives, and their friends. Management became very generous that night.

"We would have dinner and beers. Our parade was we drove home after that."

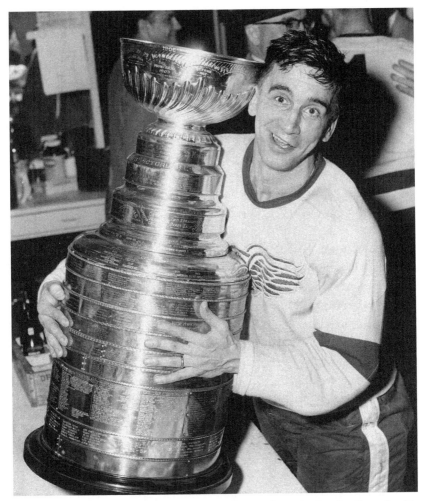

*Team captain Ted Lindsay of the Detroit Red Wings hugs the Stanley Cup after his team defeated the Montreal Canadiens 4–3 in overtime to win the Finals in Detroit on April 16, 1954.*

Players received no rings back then, and the players' lack of what Lindsay considered a fair financial reward became a major source of tension between Lindsay and the team. "When we won the league championship, we got $1,000," Lindsay said matter-of-factly. "When you won in the first round, you were supposed to get $1,000 and $500 if you lost, and when you won the Stanley Cup, you were supposed to get

$1,000. We should have gotten at least $3,000. When I went to school, that's how the math added up. But when we got our checks, they would be $2,365—not after taxes, before taxes. I could never find out where the other $700 or so went. That was one of my gripes that forced me to start up the Players Association. I didn't want people like Adams to control our money."

The Red Wings would eventually end up trading Lindsay, primarily because of his union activism. Lindsay seemed to be at odds with Jack Adams, even when the Red Wings were winning. "When the Red Wings won, Jack Adams would say we won," Lindsay said, chuckling. "When we didn't, he would say, 'It was you guys who lost it.'"

## Guy Lafleur
*Montreal Canadiens, 1973, 1976–1979*
Hall of Fame right wing Guy Lafleur is remembered as one of the most dynamic, crowd-pleasing performers in NHL history. He could steal a game with one dazzling dash up the ice.

But perhaps the slickest, most flamboyant move of his hockey career came the night he stole the Stanley Cup.

It was May 22, 1979, the day after his Montreal Canadiens had defeated the New York Rangers 4–1 to claim their fourth consecutive Stanley Cup championship. The "Flower," as he was often known, had cause to explore his mischievous side. He had run amuck yet again in the postseason, netting 10 goals and adding 13 assists in just 16 games. For the third consecutive season, he had finished the postseason tops in points. In 1979 he and teammate Jacques Lemaire had tied for the playoff lead.

Lafleur's plan for the heist was as well thought out as any move he ever made on the ice. Knowing Canadiens' vice president of public relations Claude Mouton would be entrusted to safeguard the Cup while it was in Montreal, Lafleur schemed to separate Mouton from the Cup while the team was all gathered at Toe Blake's tavern.

Having ridden with Mouton to Blake's establishment, Lafleur pretended to have forgotten something in Mouton's automobile. Mouton didn't suspect anything when Lafleur asked for his key. He hustled outside and gave the key to a friend who had a duplicate made. Later that day, when Lafleur knew the Cup was in the trunk, he put his plan into action.

"Yes, we stole the car," Lafleur said, laughing. "Actually we just borrowed it, but he did have to report it stolen with the Cup in it." The car actually was taken to the parking garage right across from the Montreal Forum, and the Cup went home with Lafleur.

It didn't take all that long for word to filter back to Mouton that Lafleur probably was in possession of the stolen property. Lafleur and friends had taken the Cup to several clubs in downtown Montreal.

According to Lafleur, the late Mouton finally reached him via the telephone, and the conversation went like this:

Mouton: "You've got the Cup."

Lafleur: "Which Cup?"

Mouton: "You had better bring it into my office Monday, or I'm in trouble and you are in trouble."

Lafleur: "I will try to find it and bring it in."

In hindsight, Lafleur was simply 15 years ahead of his time. The motivation for his Cup theft was just to share the championship experience with his family and friends, something players now have the opportunity to do. One of Lafleur's favorite pictures features his then-five-year-old son watering the Cup with a hose on his front lawn.

He also took the Cup to the Thurso, Quebec, home of his parents, Rejean and Pierrette Lafleur.

"It was unbelievable," Lafleur remembered. "Old people were crying and kissing the Cup. They couldn't believe the Cup was there. The Cup means a lot to them, especially when they could see it and touch it. They were never able to approach the Cup before. My sister had had a baby, and she put the baby in the Cup and took pictures. It was something special."

Mouton eventually received his car and the Cup back, and Lafleur has a bundle of memories that players from his era simply don't have. Lafleur was among the few who understood the true significance when the NHL decreed in 1995 that all members of the NHL championship team would be able to have the Cup for 24 hours without resorting to crime to acquire it.

"For the players, it is a great, great prestige and honor to win the Cup," said Lafleur. "When they have the opportunity to show it to friends and family, it means a lot to them."

## Henri Richard
*Montreal Canadiens, 1956–1960, 1965, 1966, 1968, 1969, 1971, 1973*

Henri Richard was only six years old when his brother Maurice played his first National Hockey League game with the Montreal Canadiens, but his father used to tell folks that Henri would end up being the best player in the family.

"That wasn't true," Richard said, laughing. "But it certainly was nice for him to say that, and it gave me a lot of [confidence]."

Although Maurice "Rocket" Richard's stature was legendary, the Richard brothers' father may have been prophetic if one views championships as the only measure of success. Henri Richard's 11 championships as a player stand as an NHL record that may never be broken. To appreciate the immensity of that accomplishment, consider that Mickey Mantle and Babe Ruth won only seven World Series championships each while with the New York Yankees. With 11 titles in 20 NHL seasons, Henri Richard was a champion 55 percent of his career. His brother's championship percentage (eight in 18 seasons) was 44.4 percent. Wayne Gretzky's championship percentage was 20 percent (four in 20 seasons), while Mark Messier's is 28.5 percent (six in 21 seasons). Today, in a league that boasts 30 teams, players hope for just one title in the course of a career. Richard's consistency was at the heart of the Canadiens' dominance in the 1950s and 1960s.

"I just feel fortunate to be on so many good teams," Richard said. "I was in the right place at the right time."

Richard couldn't pinpoint one particular celebratory moment that stands out over the 11 years, although he remembered that winning for the fans of Montreal was almost an honor for a native Quebec son. His favorite Cup triumph may have been in 1970–1971 because it was one of his toughest seasons. He had feuded with coach Al MacNeil, at one point calling him the worst coach for whom he had ever played. "I didn't mean it when I said it," Richard said. "You just say things when you are frustrated."

What made that Cup win special was that Richard scored the Cup-winning goal in Montreal's 3–2 victory in Game 7 of the Stanley Cup Finals in Chicago Stadium. "That was special," he said.

One sad footnote of Richard's championship era is that his championship rings were swiped in a house robbery. "But they didn't get the one that was on my finger," Richard said.

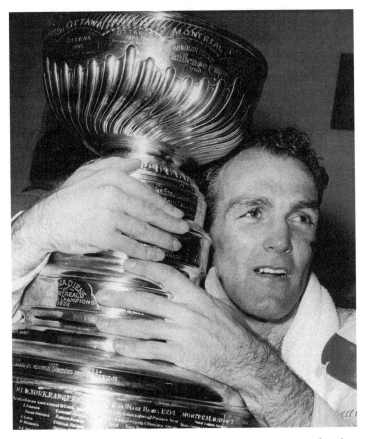

*Montreal Canadiens forward Henri Richard hugs the Stanley Cup after the Canadiens won it on May 5, 1966. Richard scored the game-winning goal in overtime play to give Montreal the 3–2 win over the Detroit Red Wings.*

## Milt Schmidt

*Boston Bruins, 1939 and 1941*
*General Manager, Boston Bruins, 1970 and 1972*

When Hall of Fame center Milt Schmidt thinks about the 1939 Stanley Cup championship postgame revelry at Boston Garden, it's what he heard, not what he saw, that instantly comes to mind.

As NHL president Frank Calder tried to present the Stanley Cup to the Bruins after they had vanquished the Toronto Maple Leafs 3–1 in Game 5, the boisterous, appreciative Boston faithful wouldn't quiet down to allow the event to continue. The reason: their hero, Bruins' defenseman Eddie Shore, had inexplicably left the ice and headed to the dressing room. Schmidt remembers the noise level was deafening until Shore's teammates coaxed him out of the dressing room for the celebration.

"To think about that still gives me goose pimples," Schmidt said more than 60 years after the fact. "Only a couple of other times I dare say someone received as loud and lengthy an ovation as Shore got that night. When they retired [Bobby Orr's] No. 4 and when they retired [Phil] Esposito's No. 7. It was really loud then, especially when Ray Bourque took his No. 7 jersey off, and he was wearing No. 77."

Schmidt was 21 when the Bruins won in 1939. "To win that championship at that age was the greatest thing that ever happened to me in hockey," Schmidt said. "I had various All-Star nominations and the Most Valuable Player trophy, the Hall of Fame. But that championship was the best. When you think of all the great things this game has seen, and so many great players have come and gone, to have won the Stanley Cup championship is the best thing that can happen to you."

Young players, usually somewhat blind to long-range thinking, aren't supposed to savor the Cup's sweetness with the same level of understanding that a veteran player has. But Schmidt appreciated the magnitude of his accomplishment even then. He was indeed mature beyond his years. The Bruins signed him at age 18, but they really had wanted him in the lineup at age 17. He rejected their offer even after attending training camp. "Here I was in 1935 at training camp on the same ice surface with Eddie Shore, Dit Clapper, Tiny Thompson—all the guys I heard about on the radio," said Schmidt. "I'm not ashamed to say they offered me $2,000 to sign. I didn't have an agent back then because your bus ticket would have been waiting for you if you had an agent. But I said, 'I'm 17 and I'm too young. I'm going back to play another year in junior hockey, and I can probably make that money working over the course of a year.'"

They did, however, convince him to join the team in 1936, and he ultimately wound up being part of two Stanley Cup championships. The feeling in the 1940s was that the Bruins might have actually won more titles had Schmidt and others not given up three years of their lives to serve in the Royal Canadian Air Force during World War II.

Schmidt doesn't recall much about the Cup celebrations, other than he was happy just to be part of a group that included Shore, Clapper, and famed goaltender Frank Brimsek. He remembers the people better than the event. "Eddie was kind of a loner. He liked to be by himself on the road, to get his proper rest because he played a lot," Schmidt remembered. "But when it came time to look after the younger players, he did look after us. He would say, 'You are going out to dinner with me,' and we would all go."

Schmidt clearly would like to call Brimsek the best goaltender of that era, but he said he can't "because I never played against him." ("The best I ever played against," he said, "was Montreal's Bill Durnan.") But he remembers Brimsek was highly competitive, even in practice. "He and Clapper were close, and they would play a game after practice," Schmidt said. "Clapper would take shots from 20 to 25 feet, and they would [bet] some kind of ice cream drink. Brimmy would always win."

When it comes to celebrations, Schmidt has more colorful memories of being general manager when the Bruins won in 1970 and 1972.

"We had this big parade, and when we got on the balcony at city hall, John McKenzie found a couple of seconds to pour a can of beer on Mayor White's head," Schmidt said. "That's one of my favorite memories."

Schmidt did end up with the Cup in his possession at 3:00 AM after one night of celebrating in 1970, and he couldn't make up his mind what to do with it in his house.

He and his late wife, Marie, finally decided to tuck it into a baby crib that was no longer in use in their home. "I couldn't think of any better place to put it than the sack," Schmidt said. "We tucked it in, and it slept soundly through the night where it should be." Considering that the Stanley Cup usually parties with players through the night, Schmidt's action may have allowed Stanley the best night of rest it ever had.

## Bernie "Boom Boom" Geoffrion
*Montreal Canadiens, 1953, 1956–1960*

When Gordie Howe used to see Montreal Canadiens great Bernie "Boom Boom" Geoffrion unwind the long backswing for his slap shot, he would joke that "he was going for yardage" until one of Geoffrion's missiles broke his foot.

"The first thing you thought was, *Get out of the way*," Howe said. "But I was dumb. I turned my foot sideways, and he hit it. He had an extremely heavy shot."

When it came to competing for the Stanley Cup, few did it with more zeal than Geoffrion, who still shares the NHL record of competing in 10 consecutive Stanley Cup Finals. He was Montreal's leading points producer in two of his championship series.

In 53 Stanley Cup Finals games, Geoffrion scored 24 goals, ranking third all-time behind Rocket Richard (34) and Jean Beliveau (30). His 46 Finals points ranks fifth behind Beliveau (62), Wayne Gretzky (53), Howe (50), and Richard (47).

Howe recalled that the Canadiens probably also popularized the use of screening the goalie when Geoffrion arrived with his searing shot from the point of the power play.

"Of course, when you shoot the puck 100 miles per hour, it probably goes the 60 feet before you can move anyway," Howe said. "And even if he only got two-thirds of the puck, it would go in because it was so heavy. He scored a lot of goals that the goaltender actually put a pad on but couldn't save. The puck would go off the loose ends of the pads."

A man who loved the spotlight, Geoffrion died of cancer on March 12, 2006, the day his No. 5 was to be retired in Montreal. One of his last requests was that his family attend the ceremony.

No one knows who truly invented the slap shot, but we know that Geoffrion popularized the big wind-up shot and added a layer of perfection to it in the 1950s. He coached in New York and in Atlanta, where he eventually settled. But he is remembered more for his playing ability. He probably owned one of the most intimidating shots in hockey history, especially when you consider that in his era few players used a windup.

"He was effective from the point in those days because of that wicked shot," remembered Johnny Wilson, a former Detroit Red Wings player who had to check Geoffrion. "The coach always talked about him before the game.... You always tried to keep the puck away from him, but he would still end up with it." What Wilson recalls was that Geoffrion's effectiveness was enhanced by the fact that "he had some accuracy."

His shots would find the net with an impressive regularity.

"He could skate, but he wasn't the greatest skater," Wilson said. "He was a goal scorer."

According to the *Canadian Press*, Geoffrion was given the nick-name "Boom Boom" by *Montreal Star* sportswriter Charlie Boire in the late 1940s when he was playing junior hockey for the Laval Nationale. One "Boom" was for the sound of his stick striking the puck; the second "Boom" was for when his rocketing shot hit the boards.

Geoffrion captured the goal-scoring and point-scoring championship in 1954–1955, but it was bittersweet because Canadiens fans were unhappy that he passed the popular Rocket Richard to accomplish that feat. Richard had been suspended for three games and the playoffs for an altercation with a linesman after a stick-swinging incident with Hal Laycoe. Richard had been in the lead when he was suspended, and there had been fan sentiment that Geoffrion shouldn't pass Richard out of respect for the legend. Fans obviously didn't believe Richard's suspension was justified. When Geoffrion received the scoring championship trophy in a ceremony, they booed.

"When he outscored Rocket, a lot of people in Montreal didn't like it," Howe said. "And then he tied Rocket's record of 50 goals. I just thought, *Give Rocket credit because he got there first and he showed us how to do it.* Boomer got there, and I ended up one behind."

In 1955 the Red Wings defeated the Canadiens in seven games, but Geoffrion actually had six goals in the series, compared to five for Howe.

Geoffrion's popularity extended beyond his playing ability. He was a colorful man who enjoyed being on the center stage. During his playing days, he was frequently seen on Quebec television, often singing. Players remember that he liked to go on stage at nightclubs and sing.

"He was comical as hell on the ice," Howe said. "He was a funny bugger. He would hit me, and then say he was sorry. Then he would laugh."

Howe competed against Boom Boom for All-Star selection, but he couldn't work up any amount of hatred for him. Boom Boom was too likeable.

"There are certain players on the ice that you dislike when you play against," Howe said. "He was always one that I liked. Anytime I go fishing with someone, I like him, and I went fishing with him."

## Jean Beliveau
*Montreal Canadiens, 1956–1960, 1965, 1966, 1968, 1969, 1971*
Jean Beliveau's parting gift to hockey in 1971 was the launch of a grand tradition that more than likely will be among the Stanley Cup's most sacred rituals through this millennium and beyond.

Le Gros Bill, as French Canadian fans knew him, is clearly one of the most beloved players in hockey history. He is remembered as one of the NHL's most elegant athletes, a 6′4″ center who played his position with a curious blend of grace, dignity, and dominance. It's almost fitting that it is Beliveau who is credited with beginning the tradition of the team captain skating around the rink with the Cup raised above his head and teammates following behind in an informal parade line.

One irony of the moment was that it came in Chicago Stadium, not in the Montreal Forum. The Canadiens had just defeated the Blackhawks 3–2 in Game 7 to win the Cup when Beliveau unexpectedly began what could be called his "farewell tour" around the ice.

"Why did I do it?" Beliveau asked rhetorically. "What comes to mind today is that I just wanted to bring the Cup closer to the fans."

As Beliveau, then 40, circled the ice, he knew this was to be his last NHL skate. At the end of the 1969–1970 season he wanted to retire, but management had talked him out of it. However, he made it clear before the 1971 playoffs that there would be no change of heart. Beliveau admits that he felt a great sense of satisfaction that night in Chicago, not surprising considering that the Cup triumph was his 10th. In that playoff year he set an NHL record (since broken) of 16 assists in postseason play. He is tied for second place on the all-time list with former teammate

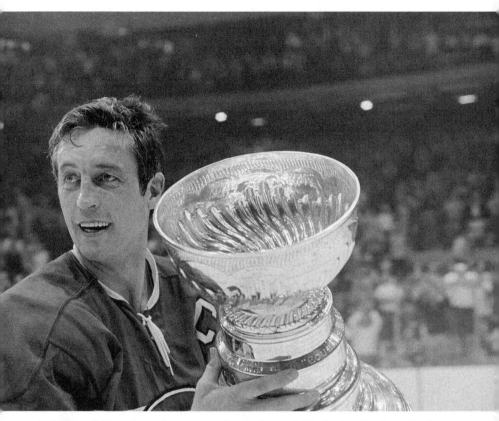

*Montreal Canadiens team captain Jean Beliveau holds the Stanley Cup after his team's 3–2 victory over the Chicago Blackhawks in Chicago on May 18, 1971.*

Yvon Cournoyer; they trail only Henri Richard, who has 11 Stanley Cup victories. When Beliveau stepped off the ice that night, he held the NHL record of 97 postseason assists and 176 postseason points.

"Maybe there was some connection to my [pending] retirement when I did what I did," Beliveau said. "But really I think it was a spur-of-the-moment thing. It was just a natural reaction, and I wanted everyone to enjoy the Cup."

Beliveau wanted the fans, even the rival Chicago Blackhawks fans, to enjoy the trappings of winning the Stanley Cup as much as he always had. Beliveau, always stately in appearance and speech, waxes almost sentimental about the grand Stanley Cup championship receptions at the

Queen Elizabeth Hotel. "They invited all of the Canadiens' employees, the secretaries, all the people behind the scenes," he said.

His other fond memories of that storied era in Canadiens history was Montreal mayor Jean Drapeau insisting that the Canadiens' triumph should be celebrated each time with a parade to city hall. "Sometimes on those parades up St. Catharine Street we would barely be able to move because there were so many people."

Today Beliveau admits he enjoys watching the on-ice Stanley Cup victory celebrations because many memories flood into his mind. He says his first Stanley Cup in 1956 is probably his favorite because he reached the final in each of his first two playoffs, in 1954 and 1955, only to lose to the Gordie Howe–led Detroit Red Wings.

"When you are a little boy growing up in French Quebec, your first goal is to play with the Canadiens," Beliveau said. "Secondly, you want to be on a Stanley Cup championship team. To finally win one after coming close the first two years made it more special."

Beliveau paused as if searching for the right words. "When I look at some of the great players like Ray Bourque, Jean Ratelle, Rod Gilbert, who have never won a Cup—and Bill Gadsby played 20 years without winning one—I just feel fortunate to have joined the Canadiens at the right time," he said.

His decision to carry the Stanley Cup around the ice was perhaps the best possible illustration that Beliveau understood the relationship between fans and their teams.

"Quebec fans identified themselves with the Canadiens," Beliveau said. "When you have great success, it makes it their success."

## Bud Poile

*Toronto Maple Leafs, 1947*

The average player salary is about $2 million in today's NHL, and players receive a $10,000 ring for winning the Stanley Cup. In 1947 Bud Poile received $600, a silver cigarette case, and a cardigan sweater for helping the Maple Leafs capture the same Cup. But it was a damn nice cardigan.

"It was quite an honor to get that button-down sweater," Poile said before he died in 2005. "It had that Maple Leaf crest on it. It really was quite a sweater." Poile donated that sweater to a museum in his hometown of Thunder Bay, Ontario (formerly Fort William). But Poile's pride in the sweater and its meaning may symbolize the Cup's charm and mystique as much as any 14-karat jewelry could.

This was a time in hockey when a fan could still secure a gray seat in the upper reaches of Maple Leaf Gardens for 90¢, and players' wages were more in line with common laborers than entertainment icons.

Poile suggests that it probably cost some players money to compete for the Stanley Cup because players traditionally had summer jobs lined up to supplement their hockey income. "My first year with the Leafs I had to put a deposit on my skates," Poile recalled.

Through the years, Poile, elected to the Hockey Hall of Fame as a builder, liked telling the story that crusty Detroit Red Wings general manager Jack Adams once sold him to the New York Rangers because he needed cash to build a press box at the Olympia Stadium.

With only six teams in the NHL, only the world's 120 top players were afforded the opportunity to compete for the Stanley. Making it in the NHL was the Canadian equivalent of knighthood, maybe even sainthood. To play for the Cup as a member of the Maple Leafs or Montreal Canadiens was the hockey equivalent of praying in the Holy Land.

"Being a Canadian winning the Cup in Canada was like winning the World Series for the New York Yankees," Poile said.

Poile always said he made "a little contribution" to the Leafs' championship. Actually he netted two goals in the six-game triumph against the Montreal Canadiens, and only Teeder Kennedy and Vic Lynn managed to score three goals. One of Poile's tallies came in Game 3 when the Maple Leafs won 4–2 to take a 2–1 lead in the best-of-seven series. The Maple Leafs had seven different scorers producing their 13 goals in that series, and that result may have been a reflection of general manager Conn Smythe's philosophy more than coincidence. Smythe believed that the key to winning is making sure all hands are pulling on the rope at the same time. He was famous for coming into the room and saying, "We can't let another dog hunt in our yard."

The Maple Leafs turned out to be the bigger dogs in 1946–1947, even though Montreal had the better regular-season record.

Poile and his Maple Leafs teammates were celebrities, but he doesn't believe the Stanley Cup hoopla was as crazed, scripted, or lengthy as it is today. For example, he can't remember having his picture taken with the Stanley Cup, except in the team picture that was taken at 12:20 the next day. He knows that because the Garden's clock is in the picture. He does remember being a "big wheel" that summer in his hometown, Fort William, especially at Armstrong's Pool Hall and Dom DePiro's Barber Shop. You weren't anyone in Fort William if you didn't frequent those two locales.

"Today they go to Disneyland when they win the Cup," Poile said in 1999. "If memory serves me, we did what we always did after weekend games. We went to Howie Meeker's house and had a few beers."

## Marcel Pronovost
*Detroit Red Wings, 1950, 1952, 1954, 1955*
*Toronto Maple Leafs, 1967*

Imagine what 19-year-old Detroit Red Wings defenseman Marcel Pronovost must have been feeling and thinking in 1950 when hockey's gladiator, "Black Jack" Stewart, came into the dressing room breathing fire at his teammates.

"If I have to hit players on both teams, I will," Stewart said. "You are going to play better, or you will have to face me."

Defenseman Stewart called that meeting after the Red Wings had fallen behind 3–2 in the best-of-seven Finals against the New York Rangers. Fifty years later Pronovost still remembers the Stewart firestorm as if it happened yesterday. Not even revered captain Sid Abel had immunity from Stewart's wrath. Pronovost's memory is clear on that.

"That bag of bones Don Raleigh is making an ass of you," Stewart barked at Abel. "Do something with him."

In Game 6, the Red Wings trailed early but came from behind to win 5–4 on the strength of Abel's two goals, including the game-winner at 10:34 of the third period.

"Black Jack was one tough son of a bitch," Pronovost said. "He had a bad back, and we had the real hot liniment back then that he splashed on like it was aftershave."

Pronovost's memories of his Stanley Cup championships are rooted more in the camaraderie players shared in the battle than the beers they shared afterward. "I know I was on cloud nine when I won my first one,"

Pronovost said. "But what I tell everyone is that every Cup was special for different reasons."

After winning his first Cup at a tender age, Pronovost discovered all of his championships would be unique. He views them like a parent views his or her children, each one deemed special for a different reason:

**1949–1950.** Winning at such a young age was a remarkable achievement, given that it was rare for young players to even make the NHL unless they were budding superstars. Pronovost got called up from Omaha after the regular season, meaning he made his NHL debut in the postseason.

**1951–1952.** The Red Wings won eight consecutive playoff games to claim the Cup, with goaltender Terry Sawchuk giving up just five goals. Sawchuk gave up just two goals in the Finals, and none at home. "They called us Terry and the Pirates," Pronovost said.

**1953–1954.** Tony Leswick scored a memorable overtime goal to give the Red Wings a 2–1 win against Montreal in Game 7.

**1954–1955.** The Red Wings were three points back with 10 games to go and passed the Montreal Canadiens in the stretch run. That year was memorable because of the Rocket Richard riot. The Red Wings were leading 4–1 in the Montreal Forum when rioting began (because of the fans' anger over Richard being suspended for the remainder of the 1955 season). That game was awarded to Detroit, and they won the next game against the Canadiens to win the regular-season championship by two points (95–93). They won the Finals in seven games.

**1966–1967.** The Maple Leafs were a third-place club when they captured the Cup in 1967. "We were a club going nowhere that year," Pronovost said. "King Clancy came in and coached awhile. And we had a good group of veterans and some good kids. If you remember, that was the year of Expo '67 in Montreal. They were going to put the Stanley Cup in the Quebec Pavilion. We made them put it in the Ontario Pavilion."

Pronovost understood the Stanley Cup's lure before he played for it. He was brought into the Detroit organization at age 16 (he used to say he was "raised by Detroit") and actually was brought in to travel with the team in the playoffs the year before he was called up. He possesses vivid memories about all of Detroit's players in that era, particularly the late Sawchuk, whom he considered to be misunderstood.

"He was a real competitor," Pronovost said. "A lot of people had the wrong impression of Terry. He didn't like the limelight. In order to get rid of the limelight, he got rude. But not to kids, he really loved kids."

Pronovost remembers one night in Toronto when one of his shots rose up just above the short glass and broke a youngster's nose. "They brought that kid into the dressing room after the game, and Sawchuk grabbed his goalie stick and handed it to me and told me to give it to the kid," Pronovost said. "But he said, 'Don't tell anyone that I gave it you.'"

Although Stewart's tongue-lashing is prominent in Pronovost's collection of Cup memories, Stewart isn't on Pronovost's list of the toughest Stanley Cup competitors he knew.

"Ted Lindsay and Rocket Richard epitomized the desire to win," Pronovost said. "Of the people I see play today, there is no one like them."

## Scotty Bowman
*Coach, Montreal Canadiens, 1973, 1976–1979*
*Coach, Pittsburgh Penguins, 1992*
*Coach, Detroit Red Wings, 1997 and 1998*

The Stanley Cup is so intertwined with Scotty Bowman's life and career that it seems appropriate that he and his wife, Suella, named one of their children Stanley.

In 1973 Suella was within a month of her due date when Bowman was trying to capture his first Stanley Cup as the young coach of the Montreal Canadiens. "We decided if we won and had a boy, we had to call him Stanley," Bowman said.

The Canadiens won that Cup by beating the Chicago Blackhawks, completing the task with a 6–4 win at Chicago Stadium on May 10. In June Suella gave birth to a boy named Stanley. At that time, no one would have guessed that Bowman would coach seven more NHL championships, nor could anyone have guessed that Stanley would someday end up sharing the championship feeling with his father on the same ice where his name became official.

Scotty Bowman witnessed his share of championship celebrations. "The first I heard of anyone taking the Cup anywhere was when Guy Lafleur took it home," Bowman said, chuckling. "One story I heard about that was that after the party a neighbor called him to tell him that the Cup was still in his backyard."

Bowman surprised his players and defied convention when he slipped on skates to join the Detroit Red Wings' Cup celebration in 1997. As with most everything else in his life, Bowman viewed the situation with logic. "That's one thing I had never done before," he said. "And I knew teams were starting to go around the ice more with the Cup. Before, they would go around once. Now everyone gets to go around once with the Cup. I didn't feel comfortable walking around the ice. I had the trainer bring me my skates with a minute or two to go in the game."

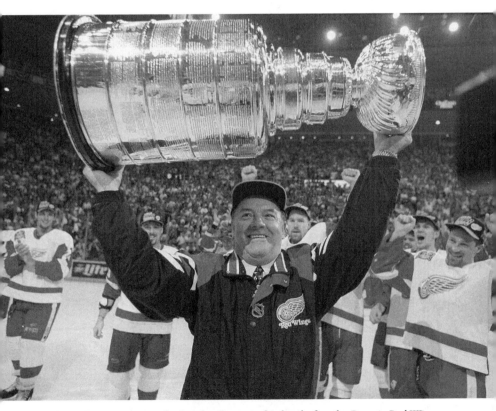

*Scotty Bowman raises the Stanley Cup over his head after the Detroit Red Wings defeated the Philadelphia Flyers to win the cup in Detroit on June 7, 1997. Detroit won the game 2–1, sweeping the series and giving Bowman his seventh Stanley Cup.*

One of his favorite Cup moments was attending the impromptu party captain Mario Lemieux threw in 1992 after the Penguins, coached by Bowman, won their second consecutive championship. Bowman has a fondness for that 1992 championship because his children were older then and were able to share in the success.

Bowman and family members witnessed Phil Bourque set a distance record for the Stanley Cup throw at the Lemieux party. He hurled it into Mario's pool in one of the memorable moments of Stanley Cup history. (That incident will be discussed in great detail later in this book.) "He threw it from way up," Bowman said. "It could have hit the deck. He was lucky."

Winning that 1992 championship had more special meaning for Bowman because it happened in Chicago—the site of his first championship and the place where it became official that his son would be named Stanley.

"Nineteen years later in Chicago he was on the ice after we won," Bowman said. "He was just finishing school and he was able to come to the game."

And there's more to the Stanley Bowman story: today, Stanley serves as assistant general manager of the Chicago Blackhawks, and the elder Bowman serves as a team consultant.

## Denis Potvin

*New York Islanders, 1980–1983*

In Canada, hockey is about fathers and sons as much as it is goals and assists. Denis Potvin understood that, which is why his most emotional Stanley Cup championship moment doesn't involve any of his 56 post-season goals or the wild celebrations accompanying any of the Islanders' four titles under his watch.

On the day after the Islanders won their fourth consecutive Stanley Cup in 1983, Potvin took the Cup to visit his cancer-stricken father.

Armand Potvin had been a high-caliber junior hockey player in the late 1930s for the Perth Blue Wings. He often lined up against Maurice "Rocket" Richard, who played for Verdun. Potvin was talented enough to earn a tryout with the Detroit Red Wings. However, he broke his back in training camp—effectively destroying any hope he had of playing in the NHL.

Neither father nor son had to say anything to know what it meant to both of them to have the Cup in such an intimate setting. Armand had been diagnosed with cancer a year before, and the family suspected that he was fighting a losing battle against his disease.

"That was kind of the ultimate," Potvin recalled. "Just to have my dad be able to touch the Cup, to feel it, to share it with me. He had come to the rink before and seen the Cup. But not like this."

Potvin treasures the pictures he has of him and his father with the Cup. "It was very emotional and very important to me," he said. "To me, the beauty of winning the Cup is the emotion that goes with it."

In that era NHL players were not officially allowed to have the Cup in their possession for individual events. But Potvin, Trottier, Mike Bossy, Clark Gillies, and perhaps others defied convention during their four-Cup run. No one spirited it away to his Canadian hometown, but several Islanders had private moments with hockey's chalice.

"It's always asked of me which is the most important," Potvin said. "I always say obviously the first one is the most important because it is the first one. You never know whether you will get another. So the first is the ultimate because all of the emotions come to the forefront because all of your dreams as a kid are being realized. But then when you win four, it's almost like having children. You love them all equally, and they each have a different story to them."

Potvin's father survived the following 1983–1984 season, but it was clear his time was short during the playoffs. He died while the Islanders were in the midst of defeating the Washington Capitals in the second round. Denis Potvin's uncle Andre relayed that, shortly before Armand died, he had asked whether the Islanders had won their fifth consecutive Cup. He was told that the Islanders did win the fifth Cup, even though the playoffs were far from over.

In fact, the Islanders lost the battle for the fifth Cup to Wayne Gretzky's Edmonton Oilers.

"I never believed in my own heart that my dad actually believed that we had another Cup," Potvin said. "Even though he was at the stage he was losing everything, I still today believe that my dad knew we hadn't won, even though he was told we had."

## Clark Gillies
*New York Islanders, 1980–1983*
When Clark Gillies watched an ESPN commercial in 2000 featuring Dallas Stars center Joe Nieuwendyk turning the Stanley Cup into a Jell-O mold at a fictional family gathering, it was like a flashback to the New York Islanders' glory years.

No Islander ever turned the Cup into a dessert cup, but Gillies remembers the Stanley Cup being a centerpiece of fun during the New York Islanders' dominance of the NHL in the 1980s.

"I remember the night the Cup was at my house, and we were still going strong at 4:30 or 5:00 AM...I saw my German shepherd, and he was looking kind of forlorn that he wasn't part of the party," Gillies remembered. "So I filled the Cup with Ken-L Ration and let him eat out of it."

The Islanders may have been the first NHL team to find the proper blend of reverence for the Cup's symbolism and knowledge of its party value. The Islanders would claim the Cup for a couple of weeks, and some of the players would get some quality time with it. It definitely toured all of the best restaurants and drinking establishments. Players made sure the Cup got to the Cafe Continental early in the victory march because Bruno the owner always made sure the Islanders had a free Christmas lunch at his establishment.

"The Cup was like a barter device," Gillies remembered. "We would get free meals if we brought the Cup along." Gillies said the "Cup got moved around pretty good" in the early 1980s. "It would end up in someone's trunk, and the next morning we would all come back to life, and someone would say, 'Where is it?'" Gillies said. "We would figure out what happened to it, and then we would start again. But we treated it with the respect it deserved. We didn't abuse it. I had heard stories of other teams leaving it all night on their lawn. We never did that."

Clearly the Islanders did respect the Cup because they knew how hard they had worked to get it. In hindsight Gillies believes there were three factors involved in the Islanders' dynasty: first and foremost, this was an exceptionally talented team, with Bryan Trottier and Butch Goring at center ice, Billy Smith in goal, Denis Potvin and Ken Morrow on defense, Mike Bossy, Bob Nystrom, and Garry Howatt on the right wing, and Gillies, John Tonelli, and Bob Bourne on the left wing. Second, the Islanders never had any major injuries during their Cup run. Finally, the Islanders were the luckiest team Gillies had ever seen. Other teams seemed to hit crossbars while the Islanders were always finding the net.

In the third Cup year the Islanders were trailing 3–1 with five minutes to go and facing elimination by the Pittsburgh Penguins. They ended up winning that game in overtime.

"I remember thinking then, *We have something working for us that no one else has*," Gillies said.

Remember, 15 players were on all four Islanders' championship teams; this was a team that was bonded together like brothers. Gillies remembers each celebration as being different, with the first one prominent in his mind.

"That first year had been very emotional for me. Fighting with Terry O'Reilly in the series against Boston and playing Philly in the finals hadn't been easy," Gillies said. "It had been very physical, and when finally we won I got my hands on the Cup and just ran around the ice with it over my head. People asked me if the Cup was heavy, and I said it wasn't at that time. I was full of emotion. The following year Bryan Trottier did what I had done in our first. He lost it, he went running around with his fist in the air. And he wasn't like that. But winning becomes very emotional. It's just so draining."

Gillies also has vivid memories of the Islanders' parade that went down the Hempstead Turnpike. "It was a little different than riding down Broadway," Gillies said. "But in our own little way it was pretty exciting."

The Islanders rode in Model A automobiles in a procession from Roosevelt Field to Nassau Coliseum. The closer the parade moved to the arena, the more people crowded along the roadside. Near the end, it became difficult for the cars to move, and the motorcycle police escorts found it hard not to hit people. Players escaped to a stage that had been erected on the north side of the arena, but even that plan didn't work well. Planners had put up a snow fence to keep back the thousands of fans who had come to salute the Islanders. Soon that gave way, and people fell on top of each other. "It got scary, and we were afraid people would get hurt so we got out of there," Gillies remembered. "We went downstairs [in the arena] and drank beer with the motorcycle cops," Gillies said, laughing.

The other fond memory Gillies has of the fourth Cup celebration was Smith's zany acceptance speech for the Conn Smythe Trophy. It was such a funny bit that Gillies now has it on tape. Two bits of knowledge are needed to understand the humor of the moment. First, Smith had a penchant for malapropisms—figures of speech never came out of his month quite right. For example, Gillies remembers that during one particular snowstorm he turned to one of the clubhouse workers and said, "If you want to get on my good eye, you will come over and shovel my driveway." Of course, he meant to say, "If you want to get on my good *side*." When someone said the wrong thing, it was considered "Smittyness" or a "Smittyism."

During the fourth Stanley Cup run, Smith was embroiled in a handful of physical confrontations with Edmonton Oilers players. At one point he slashed Wayne Gretzky in a game at Edmonton, and Gretzky went down "like he was shot in the head." He also whacked Glenn Anderson on Long Island. "He was looking like a real villain," Gillies remembered.

In Game 4 Smith obviously schemed to change perception. Anderson did something to him, and Smith began rolling around, moaning and groaning, like he had been speared in the throat. Anderson received a major penalty.

After the game, Smith was given the Conn Smythe Trophy as the series MVP with NHL president John Ziegler standing there and *Hockey Night in Canada*'s Dave Hodge conducting the interview.

According to Gillies, while live on the air, Smith said during the game Gillies had shown that "two can play at that game," presumably meaning that good acting helped turn the Anderson whack into a major penalty.

"Then he says people all over Canada must be turning over in their graves after that," Gillies said. "It was priceless."

# Red Kelly

*Detroit Red Wings, 1950, 1953, 1954, and 1955*
*Toronto Maple Leafs, 1962, 1963, 1964, and 1967*

Hall of Famer Red Kelly doesn't mind letting the world in on a Kelly family inside joke connected with one of his championship celebrations with the revered Stanley Cup.

In 1964 Kelly was playing for the Toronto Maple Leafs and sitting as a member of the Canadian Parliament. The Maple Leafs defeated the Detroit Red Wings 4–0 in Game 7 of the Stanley Cup Finals, and Kelly had to be carried out of the dressing room after passing out from pain. He had suffered a knee injury in Game 6 when he was crunched simultaneously by Gordie Howe and Bill Gadsby. The injured knee had been frozen to allow Kelly to play in Game 6, but the novocaine had long since worn off. He was standing in the shower when the pain just overwhelmed him. Goaltender Johnny Bower helped carry him out. To add further complication to his life, he had to fly to Ottawa by 2:00 AM the next day to fulfill legislative duties. He got some crutches at the hospital and did his civic duty.

"I never got a chance to celebrate," Kelly recalled. "At the time, [owner] Harold Ballard was a neighbor. I don't know what other owner would have thought of this. He was a strange character in many ways. But when I got back, he brought the Cup to the house with two bottles of champagne."

A central figure in the Kelly celebration that day was Red's newborn son, Conn, whose name is the subject of another inside joke. Famed Maple Leafs general manager Conn Smythe assumed that the child had been named after him, and gave him stock shares of Canadian Pacific as a birth present. It wasn't until later that Kelly told Smythe that Conn had actually been named after the first king of Ireland, who had been credited with winning more than 100 battles. "I told Conn Smythe the story of the king and how the people he defeated often became his friends because he was actually a good leader," Kelly remembered. "He liked that story and began to tell people that's where he got his name, even though I don't think he had ever heard that story before I told him."

Ballard never had a reputation for being overly generous with players. ("You needed a magnifying glass to see the first diamond in our

Stanley Cup rings," Kelly said.) But he apparently liked Kelly quite a bit because he went out of his way to make sure that Kelly's Cup celebration was special. He sent along a photographer so the Kelly family could have pictures of the event. Red put three-month-old Conn into the Cup for the picture, and the infant chose that moment to relieve himself. "He did the whole load in the Cup," Kelly said, chuckling. "He did everything. That's why our family laughs when we see the players drinking champagne out of the Cup."

## Glenn Hall

*Chicago Blackhawks, 1961*

Glenn Hall remembers Noel Picard going around to all the expansion St. Louis Blues team members in 1967–1968 and reminding them that their former teams had discarded them into the expansion pool.

"He was rabble-rousing a little bit, and he would yell, 'These are the teams that do not want you!'" Hall remembered.

Hall understood that sentiment, because in 1960–1961 he led the Chicago Blackhawks to a Stanley Cup championship over the team that didn't want him. In 1957 Red Wings general manager Jack Adams peddled Hall and Ted Lindsay to the Blackhawks for John Wilson, Forbes Kennedy, William Preston, and Hank Bassen. To appreciate what a slap that was, consider that Hall had led the NHL with 38 wins the season before, and the Red Wings had finished first overall. Just two seasons before, Hall had led the NHL with 12 shutouts. This wasn't just a hockey trade; it was an effort to punish Hall, and particularly Lindsay, who had stirred up players to form the Players Association. Before being traded, Hall remembers seeing a pension society report that showed that the Blackhawks had the NHL's smallest payroll at $156,000. The Montreal Canadiens were ranked first in payroll at about $300,000.

"I didn't like Jack Adams any more than he liked me, so it was nice to get away from that situation," Hall said. "I always said my loyalty was with whoever was signing my paycheck."

That thought notwithstanding, Hall admits there was a little more satisfaction in beating the Red Wings for the Stanley Cup in 1961. "It really didn't matter who we beat," Hall said, honestly. "But I suppose it's satisfying to beat the team that didn't want you."

The Hawks downed the Red Wings in six games with Hall playing terrifically in the 5–1 clincher in Game 6. It was a 2–1 game entering the third period. Bobby Hull, in his fourth NHL season, was the Blackhawks' big gun in the playoffs, leading all scorers with eight goals. "He was just starting to become explosive then," Hall said.

Hall remembers receiving a ring for the championship. "I don't know, but that might have been the beginning of the rings," Hall said. "I know the Maple Leafs got them for the Cups they won after that."

He recalls a parade, "or at least they stopped traffic for us." He knows that the Blackhawks didn't open their vault to reward players for their championship performance.

"[Blackhawks player] Reg Fleming told me he asked for a raise, and they said, 'No,'" Hall recalled. "He said, 'But we won the Stanley Cup,' and they said, 'Oh, you've already been paid for that.'"

When Hall went home to Western Canada, local youth hockey groups wanted him to share his championship aura. He says he was more than happy to do it, and he turned down all offers of money from the youth organizations because the Blackhawks had a policy of giving players $10 for their public appearances, and 10¢ per mile. During the spring and summer, he accumulated about $250 worth of appearances. He turned his invoice in to the Hawks, and much to his amazement they refused to pay.

"General manager Tommy [Ivan] said we didn't tell you to go," Hall remembered. "No, they didn't, but that was the agreement. I said, 'Call to make sure I went.' He said that wasn't the point. I said, 'Okay, but see if I ever represent the Blackhawks again.' Even when you won the Stanley Cup back then, they would nickel-and-dime you. They weren't pouring a bunch of money out. Had things been a little fairer then, maybe they would be fairer now. Now it's too bad because it's gone the other way, and the fans are getting stuck. It's the fan being kept out of the arena because of cost."

With Hull and Stan Mikita still young and Hall still in his prime, the Blackhawks believed that championship would be the first of several. But they lost in the Finals to Toronto the following year and haven't won since.

"Remember, Toronto had the best team defensively, and that's how you win the Stanley Cup," Hall offered. "That's how you win any championship, whether it's football, baseball, basketball, or whatever. You win by defense. I believe the Edmonton Oilers [in the 1980s] were the only team to disprove that theory. They had the offense that could overcome their poor defense."

Considered one of the best goaltenders in NHL history, Hall believes goaltenders have always gotten too much credit for wins and too much blame for losses.

"You hear that the team with the best goaltending will win the Stanley Cup, and I disagree totally," Hall said. "The best team will win the Stanley Cup. The goaltending needs to be good. But it's not always the best goaltender that wins the Stanley Cup."

The fact that Hall only won one Stanley Cup supports that contention.

## Stan Mikita

*Chicago Blackhawks, 1961*
Officially, the Chicago Blackhawks won the 1961 Stanley Cup in Detroit with a 5–1 thumping of the Red Wings in Game 6. However, Stan Mikita would argue that the Blackhawks' only championship in the last 60 years was probably won two weeks earlier when Chicago defeated Montreal in the semifinals.

"The Detroit series was anticlimactic as far as we were concerned," Mikita remembered. "We had to play them, and they had some great hockey players. But we didn't think that beating that team was as big a deal as it was beating the Montreal Canadiens."

Mikita's memory speaks to the notion of how awestruck the hockey world was of the Canadiens' championship aura. Remember, the Canadiens had won five consecutive titles coming into that season, and beating them in Montreal was like breaking into the palace and stealing the king's nightshirt. The Hawks had finished 17 points behind the regular-season champion Canadiens that season.

Many consider the Montreal-Chicago 1961 semifinals as one of the real classics with a triple-overtime game won on Murray Balfour's goal in Game 3 and Glenn Hall posting back-to-back shutouts in the final two games of the series. With Jean Beliveau and Henri Richard leading the way, the Canadiens' offensive output was far superior to every other team of that era. "What really impressed me was the play of Glenn Hall in the

*Stan Mikita of the Chicago Blackhawks recalls the semifinal series against the Montreal Canadiens to be more memorable than the Cup-clinching series against the Detroit Red Wings.* Photo courtesy of Getty Images

playoffs," Mikita said. "The way he played in that series, we felt this could go on for quite a while."

Of course the Blackhawks haven't won since. Perhaps an omen of that came the night they won in Detroit but were then snowed in and couldn't fly out. They were stuck in the airport for two hours and then finally went back to the hotel, where they celebrated. But the delay in returning home took some steam out of the city's celebration.

"We had a little victory parade, and I think we rode on fire trucks," Mikita said. "But what I really remember was that we weren't prepared for the weather, and we froze our asses off in the parade. You have to remember, the Stanley Cup used to get over in April, not June, back then, and it was very cold that day."

But whether the celebration was large or small didn't change how players felt about the accomplishment, according to Mikita. "Maybe winning the Cup meant even more back then," Mikita said, "because there wasn't as much moving players around back then. There was more loyalty from the players to management and management to players back then."

## Johnny Bower
*Toronto Maple Leafs, 1962, 1963, 1964, and 1967*
When Maple Leafs goalkeeper Johnny Bower walked into Maple Leaf Gardens for practice for Game 6 of the 1967 Cup Finals, he spied two armed guards posted at the dressing room door.

"I thought there had been a shooting or something," Bower remembered.

But when the guards waved him into the room, instead of a crime scene what he saw was a table in the middle of the room covered with cash. It looked as if someone was in the midst of counting the loot from a successful bank heist. Stacks of every denomination were present, including $100 bills.

According to Bower, when coach Punch Imlach came into the dressing room, he said, "That's $10,000 there, and that's how much money you can make if we win the Stanley Cup."

Bower said, "I headed for that table and I was ready to take that money. If Punch thought it would get us excited, it worked."

Few players appreciate the trappings of Stanley Cup lore more than Bower. Having earned a "second chance" at the NHL at age 34, Bower didn't put on a Maple Leafs' uniform with illusions of becoming a four-time NHL champion and a member of the Hall of Fame. He hadn't even been sure he wanted to leave the Cleveland team in the American Hockey League when the Maple Leafs selected him in the interleague draft. After failing to stick during an NHL trial with the New York Rangers in the mid-1950s, Bower had settled in Cleveland. The hockey was good in the American League, and the fringe benefits were better. Especially after he hit age 30, Bower was very realistic about his chances of playing in the NHL.

"There were very good players in the minor leagues," Bower said. "But there were only six teams, and they carried one goalie. How was I going to beat out [Turk] Broda or Charlie Raynor or Bill Durnan? I had to wait until they got old. But I got old too."

When the Maple Leafs summoned Bower in 1958, he had 13 years of service in the minor leagues.

"When I heard about it, I said, 'I don't know if I can help Toronto or not,'" Bower remembered. "They [Cleveland management] told me, 'If you don't go, they will suspend you.' I didn't want to be suspended. So they put in my contract that if I didn't make the National Hockey League, I could come back to Cleveland. That was what I wanted."

Reasonably sure he would return to Cleveland, Bower went to Toronto without grand expectations. "They only wanted me a couple of years at best because they were developing some young goaltenders," Bower recalled. "Gerry Cheevers was there. And I was going to be their goaltending assistant. But I fooled them. I was thinking, *Punch has a pretty good hockey team here, and I'm not going to give this up.*"

With Bower in goal, the Maple Leafs won three consecutive Stanley Cup championships from 1962 to 1964, and Bower's goals-against averages in those postseason runs were 2.28, 1.60, and 2.12.

He said the 1962 title was the sweetest because "having my name on the Stanley Cup was my dream, and I never thought it would happen."

To play hockey for the Maple Leafs in that era was an honor that is difficult to describe, Bower insists. The thrill of Toronto's winning the Cup for three consecutive seasons was almost matched by the thrill of Montreal's not winning the Stanley Cup in those years. "We were as big as the Montreal Canadiens," Bower said. "I didn't know when I first got to Toronto what a rivalry the Maple Leafs had with Montreal. The Canadiens had won more Stanley Cups than Toronto, and the Maple Leafs' fans were getting pretty perturbed. [President] Conn Smythe hated to lose."

That may be why the Leafs' 1966–1967 championship also has a special place in Bower's memory. The Maple Leafs defeated the Canadiens in six games to win that crown. Bower (teamed with Terry Sawchuk in goal that season) played four games in the Stanley Cup Finals and posted a 1.94 goals-against average.

That 1966–1967 Toronto team had only finished five games above .500 and seemed to struggle at times. Bower remembered the team being a mixture of older and younger players. "We had quite a few meetings," Bower said. "George Armstrong would say to me, 'What's going on with your goaltending?' I would tell him, 'I'm fighting the puck,' or, 'I've lost my angles,' or, 'I am giving up stupid short-side goals,' or, 'I'm in a slump. But I'm working on my negatives.' Then George would go to Allan Stanley and Tim Horton, and everyone would get it off their chest. Then we would go out and have a couple of good practices and we would start to play well again."

What Bower remembers most about the postchampionship celebration was the parade down Yonge Street, in particular all the banners and pennants that flew from the buildings along the route. "I'm glad I didn't have the job of picking up all the papers that were thrown down during that," Bower recalled. "When you win the Stanley Cup, your whole body just goes numb from the excitement. It really is hard to explain."

When the Maple Leafs won the 1962 Stanley Cup, owner Harold Ballard had championship rings made for team members. When the Maple Leafs won again in 1963, he recalled all the rings.

"I wondered what the heck was going on," Bower said. "What he did was he had the diamond removed and put a larger diamond in. And he said when we won again, he would take the diamond out again and put in a little larger one."

Ballard had a reputation for being a skinflint at worst and a man who was tight with his money at best. When the Leafs won again in 1964, Bower dutifully turned in his ring, and when he got it back, he turned to Armstrong and said, "I could swear this diamond is getting smaller."

Armstrong laughingly suggested that Bower should go tell Ballard that. "No, no, you are the captain," Bower insisted. "You go tell him, and don't mention my name."

## Jacques Lemaire

*Montreal Canadiens, 1968, 1969, 1971, 1973, 1976–1979*
*Coach, New Jersey Devils, 1995*

One of the more memorable goals in NHL playoff history isn't on the list of favorite memories for the man who scored it.

Older Montreal fans can all remember Jacques Lemaire igniting a come-from-behind 3–2 win against the Chicago Blackhawks in Game 7 of the 1971 Stanley Cup Finals. It was a crisp shot from center ice that Blackhawks goaltender Tony Esposito whiffed on. The Blackhawks were leading 2–0 and seemed to be in charge until Lemaire unleashed the fateful shot.

"It was a huge goal, but it was a lucky goal," Lemaire said. "It is not all that special to me. I just wanted to get off the ice. I just shot and went directly to the bench. When I was going to the bench, I heard some fans yell. I said, 'What happened?' I didn't know. To me the special moment of winning the Cup came in 1976 when we beat the Flyers."

The Flyers had won Stanley Cup titles in 1974 and 1975, and in 1975–1976 they had the Campbell Conference's best record of 51–13–16. Montreal had the Wales Conference's best record of 58–11–11. They were favored when they met Lemaire's Canadiens in the 1976 Finals.

"I think they were expected to beat us four in a row," Lemaire said. "But we beat them four in a row."

The first three games were one-goal decisions, and the Canadiens completed the sweep when Guy Lafleur and Pete Mahovlich scored third-period goals in a 5–3 win in Game 4.

"I always said that I will never see another group of guys who will stick to a plan the way that we did that year," Lemaire said. "The intensity we had, the way we felt—that's what I remember most."

Even though Lemaire had eight Stanley Cups, he insists he never worked harder to win one than he did when he coached the New Jersey Devils to the 1995 Stanley Cup. "As a player, you think only of yourself," Lemaire said. "As a player, I just worried about doing my job. You worry just about performing. I never worried about making mistakes. As a coach, you worry about 24 guys. Will this guy be okay? Will our system work? You don't want to make a mistake as a coach. You go through every step. You think about the penalty killing, the power play. You must worry about whether there is a certain thing that they could do that would neutralize your team. You must look at everything so carefully. That's why you feel so good when you win as a coach."

## Frank Mahovlich

*Toronto Maple Leafs, 1962, 1963, 1964, and 1967*
*Montreal Canadiens, 1971 and 1973*

Frank Mahovlich's six Stanley Cup championships haven't blurred his perspective about which title was the most memorable of his career.

When the Canadiens traded for 33-year-old Mahovlich in 1971, it was essentially a rescue mission aided by his younger brother Peter's lobbying. Already a four-time champion, Mahovlich knew he wasn't going to return to the winner's circle soon if he stayed in Detroit. The Red Wings were the league doormat that season, and eventually endured the insult of finishing behind the expansion Vancouver Canucks and Buffalo Sabres. Even when he arrived in Montreal, there was no guarantee of success. The Canadiens finished behind Boston and the New York Rangers in the regular-season standings.

The Canadiens beat the odds to win the 1971 championship, and Mahovlich was Montreal's offensive catalyst. He led all NHL scorers in the postseason with 14 goals and 27 points. In the Finals against the Chicago Blackhawks, the Canadiens lost Game 5 to fall behind 3–2 in the best of seven. In Game 6 Frank Mahovlich scored the tying goal and set up his brother for the game-winner in the 4–3 victory that forced Game 7.

But it wasn't the individual glory that Mahovlich remembers most, it was rather sharing the championship with his brother, who was eight years his junior.

"My brother won four Stanley Cups, and I had six. We have 10 between us," said Mahovlich, now a member of the Canadian Senate. "Only the Richards have more [with 19]. I'm proud of that."

## Bobby Clarke

*Philadelphia Flyers, 1974 and 1975*

Boos as well as cheers provide testimony to Bobby Clarke's standing as one of the most exalted playoff warriors in NHL history.

A quarter-century after his last Stanley Cup championship, at the dawn of the new millennium, Clarke went to the podium in Calgary to make a draft choice, and fans greeted him with heartfelt boos. It was the year 2000, and yet to them it was still 1975, and Clarke was still captain and main villain on the league's most despised team—the Philadelphia Flyers. Clarke's greatness rests in the fact that no one, particularly his adversaries, can forget how viciously he played. No one can forget his take-no-prisoners approach to winning. No one can forget the way his intensity burned through opponents like a laser.

He played in four different Stanley Cup Finals and posted nine goals and 12 assists in 22 games. When a title was at stake, Clarke was always at the center of the fray. His leadership savvy will be remembered as much as his goals or assists.

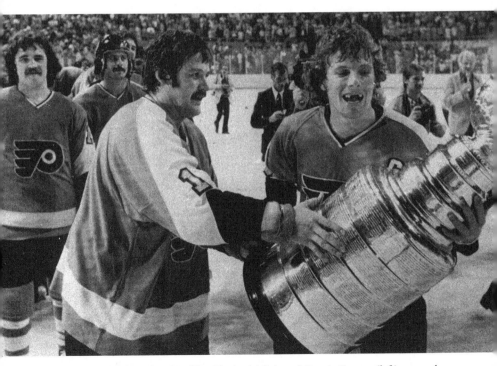

*The Philadelphia Flyers' Bobby Clarke (right) and Bernie Parent (left) carry the Stanley Cup off the ice in Buffalo, New York, on May 28, 1975. The Flyers beat the Buffalo Sabres 2–0 to win their second consecutive NHL Stanley Cup.*

"To be honest, I never really thought about being a leader," Clarke said. "I really never thought about it. I didn't plan anything. Whatever I felt was good for the team, I tried to do it."

He said it's always hard for him to even remember what he did after winning the Cup in 1974 and 1975. He remembered the Stanley Cup being at owner Ed Snider's house for a party, and other than that he had no recollection of being with the Cup. "Back then you were just lucky if you got to put your arms around it or got your picture taken with it," he said, chuckling. "You saw it at the team party, and then you never saw it again."

Clarke does remember the parades. "There were 2 million people there, both years," he said, pride hanging from his words.

But what Clarke remembers most about his championships was a feeling of togetherness that he hasn't felt since, even though he has remained in the game as a general manager.

"I was 23 or 24 when I won, and it was the highlight of my career," Clarke said. "What sticks out in my mind is the commitment that everyone makes to win. It's so hard to get everyone on the same page. That's what you are always trying to do. And it's so hard. You have to get breaks. And you always think you are going to win another, to get back there. And yet I'm still trying."

## Phil Esposito

*Boston Bruins, 1970 and 1972*

Seconds after Bobby Orr scored one of the most spectacular, graceful goals in NHL history, Boston Bruins teammate Phil Esposito enjoyed a klutzy moment that summed up the bedlam of the moment better than words ever could.

As a photographer was capturing the airborne Orr, frozen in time after netting the series-clinching overtime goal against the St. Louis Blues, the Bruins bolted from the bench like they had been sitting on an ejection seat. Esposito remembers that he was so excited that his leg caught on the top edge of the bench. "I felt flat on my head," he said, laughing.

Esposito didn't notice for several hours that he actually had a lump on his noggin from the mishap. He was having too much fun to notice he had been wounded during the Bruins' charge onto the ice, burying

Orr in a pile of teammates. Ken Hodge kept picking up the 220-pound Esposito. "He wouldn't let me leave the ice," Esposito remembered. "He wouldn't leave me alone. It was just so exciting."

The pandemonium in the Boston Garden enveloped Esposito to the point that he remembers being happiest for John Bucyck, who had been with the Bruins since 1957 without winning until then, as well as for Ed Westfall and Ted Green, both of whom had been with the Bruins since the early 1960s.

When the Bruins finally made their way into the jammed dressing room, Esposito remembers that it seemed like a father-and-son banquet. His own father, Pat, was there, and he recalls the fathers of Fred Stanfield, Derek Sanderson, Bobby Orr, and Hodge being there as well. The players wanted to throw the parents into the showers. Bobby Orr's dad went willingly, Esposito recalls.

"But there wasn't anyone big enough to throw my dad into the shower," Esposito said, chuckling. "He said, 'Don't even think about it.' But to be in there with my dad, talking to the players and their parents, that's my fondest memory."

The Bruins hadn't won a Stanley Cup since 1941, and the fans' uncorked enthusiasm poured freely over the Boston players.

The summer-long celebration in Boston seems a bit hazy to Esposito three decades later. "We had a lot of parties," Esposito said. "Sometimes they were two or three days. Sometimes they were four or five days. Sometimes they were a week. I remember waking up in Florida and not knowing how I got there. Eddie Johnston and Bobby Orr were with me."

After a night of revelry, some teammates brought him home just after dawn and essentially dumped him on his lawn. "I fell asleep," said Esposito, laughing at the memory. "The next thing I remember is the sprinkler system coming on around me."

Esposito wears his 1970 Stanley Cup championship ring and stores his 1972 ring. Originally Esposito had given one of his rings to his father. But days before the elder Esposito died in 1984, he summoned Phil for a chat. "Look, Phil," he said. "I want you to take the ring back when I die." Phil didn't want to talk about that, but his father insisted.

"I don't want to be in the casket with that ring," he said. "I'll take the All-Star watch with me because you have plenty of those."

*Phil Esposito of the Boston Bruins remembers the celebrations after the Bruins' Cup wins in 1970 and 1972.* Photo courtesy of Getty Images

Phil agreed he would take care of it.

At the funeral the family was the last to leave; the last thing Phil did before closing the casket was to slip the ring off his dad's finger. It was certainly one of the hardest things he ever had to do.

# Slava Fetisov

*Detroit Red Wings, 1997 and 1998*

Many in the baby-boomer generation grew up wondering and worrying about whether America would someday drop bombs on Moscow's Red Square.

The Cold War made the Kremlin seem like the center of the "Evil Empire." That's why, even though the Communist regime had been toppled for the better part of a decade, it was still a psychological bomb-shell for many hockey fans when Slava Fetisov, Igor Larionov, and Slava Kozlov decided to take the Stanley Cup to Moscow's Red Square after the Detroit Red Wings won in 1997.

"If someone had told me even 10 years before that we would be taking the Stanley Cup to Moscow, I would not have believed them," Fetisov said. "But it was the right thing to do. I had helped to fight to open the doors for Russian players to play in the NHL, and now I was bringing the Cup home."

It needs to be remembered that Fetisov is to Russian hockey what Bobby Orr was to the NHL. He is the most revered defenseman in Russian hockey history. When the Soviets were dominating international hockey, Fetisov was on the blue line along with Alexei Kasatonov. Up front was the famed KLM Line with Vladimir Krutov, Igor Larionov, and Sergei Makarov.

The bond between hockey and Russian culture isn't as strong as the tie that exists between the sport and Canadian culture, but the sport is important to the Russian people. They are keenly aware of what Russian players are accomplishing in the NHL, particularly historic figures like Larionov and Fetisov. The players were cheered loudly when they brought the Cup to Luzhniki Stadium. Russian president Boris Yeltsin was among those who paid homage to their accomplishments.

Regardless of what continent Stanley is on, sooner or later the famed trophy ends up in a bar for post-midnight revelry. In Moscow, the Russian Red Wings showed up at 2:00 AM at a Moscow pub named the Hungry Duck. A Canadian who just happened to be a Red Wings fan as well as a thriving capitalist owns it. They were given a standing ovation.

"I have lots of friends in Moscow and many people who rooted for me. They follow the playoffs. With an eight-hour difference, they would call me in the middle of the night to get a score," Fetisov said. "I thought it would be nice to share the Cup with them."

One of the highlights of the trip for Fetisov was taking a picture with his wife and daughter, the Cup, and his three Olympic medals (two gold and a silver earned when the United States pulled off the "Miracle on Ice" in 1980). The snapshot came in front of Lenin's Tomb.

In another time, under another system of government, victorious Olympic athletes would come to Lenin's tomb and salute him. But neither Fetisov or Larionov entered Lenin's tomb. The site was chosen because the Russian players wanted to show "that the system has changed."

"There is more freedom," Fetisov said that day. "You can feel it."

Fetisov and particularly Larionov had rebelled against the totalitarian Communist regime, particularly with regard to the treatment of their athletes. But Fetisov still has tremendous pride in his country's hockey history. That's another reason why Fetisov wanted to take the Stanley Cup to his native land.

"Soviet hockey school plays a big role in the NHL success right now," Fetisov said. "And not just because of the Russian-born players. Hockey isn't that old in Russia. It started after World War II. Mr. [Anatoli] Tarasov developed his own hockey school. He had no one to learn the game from, and yet others wanted to learn from him."

Fetisov witnessed that firsthand when he was playing for the Soviets in the 1970s and 1980s. "All the specialists from Sweden, Switzerland, Finland, Germany, Czech Republic—they all followed us," Fetisov remembered. "They took the video of our practices and they always invited specialists from Russia to their country. Soviet hockey played a big role in Europe."

He thinks the 1972 Summit Series—won by the Canadians on Paul Henderson's dramatic goal in the eighth game of the series—was the turning point of hockey. "[Canadians] saw a different system," Fetisov said. "We took the best from both systems to get the game we have now."

To reach the NHL in 1989 Fetisov had to fight against the Central Red Army coach Viktor Tikhonov and the Soviet system itself. "We were fighting for human rights back then," Fetisov said during his Moscow Cup trip. "I was born without chances in my life. Now kids have a chance to reach their goals. They can win the Stanley Cup if they wish."

By bringing the Cup to Russian soil, in a sense Fetisov was trying to unify in his own mind the two hockey cultures that have been so important to his life. Presumably, he had aspects of both stages of his career that he liked and disliked, but he feels that each is deserving of respect.

He thought it was important for the youngsters at the Red Army Hockey School "to touch and feel the Cup."

The Red Wings' Stanley Cup triumph in 1997 had an importance for Russian players even beyond what it meant for Fetisov, Larionov, Kozlov, Vladimir Konstantinov, and Sergei Fedorov, all of whom played significant roles in Detroit's first Stanley Cup championship since 1955.

The performance of the Russian Five destroyed the final remnants of the outdated hockey belief that Russian players didn't crave the Stanley Cup as much as their North American counterparts. Even into the early 1990s, it was said behind closed doors that the Russians, because of their upbringing, viewed the Olympics with greater reverence than the Stanley Cup.

No member of the Red Wings doubted the commitment the Russians had toward winning the Cup. The team's feelings about the Russian players were made public after captain Steve Yzerman was given the Stanley Cup in 1997. After he completed the first lap, he immediately looked for Fetisov and Larionov because he had made up his mind that they deserved the next lap.

What even Yzerman didn't know was that shortly before the clock ticked down for the clinching victory against Philadelphia, Fetisov had turned to Larionov and said, "When our turn comes to carry the Cup, can we do it together?"

As Fetisov and Larionov skated together at Joe Louis Arena with the Cup raised between them, the bridge between the past and present was finally bonded together. Tears flowed as freely as the champagne that night.

## Igor Larionov
*Detroit Red Wings, 1997, 1998 and 2002*
When Slava Fetisov speaks of Igor Larionov's courage and spirit, it has nothing to do with Larionov's status as the Wayne Gretzky of Soviet hockey.

Everyone knows that Larionov was a puck-handling wizard of the famed KLM Line, but few seem to know about what kind of human being Larionov has been. Fetisov hasn't forgotten. His eyes tear up when he speaks about how Larionov fought the system on behalf of Russian players. He rebelled against famed Soviet coach Viktor Tikhonov, a man who history has judged to be far more of a bully than he was a great hockey coach. Larionov's playing style is a salute to beauty and grace; off the ice he's been a fighter.

Larionov, a smallish athlete nicknamed "the Professor" because of his scholarly look, refused to follow the Soviet way of doing what he was told without question or complaint. When Larionov saw injustice, he said so. Perhaps he came by it naturally; his grandfather spent 14 years in the gulag prison network for criticizing the tyranny of Joseph Stalin, the Soviet dictator who probably contributed to the deaths of more Soviet citizens than the Germans did in World War II.

Seeing that athletes were treated more like indentured servants than human beings, Larionov demanded freedom. When top Soviet players were denied the opportunity to play in the NHL in the late 1980s, he wrote critical letters to *Sovietski Sport*, a magazine connected to the Communist Party. Tikhonov wouldn't let Larionov travel abroad, even though he was a vital member of the Soviet National Team. When Fetisov was booted off the team for voicing his own criticism of Tikhonov, Larionov organized a player revolt. It was Tikhonov who blinked, and Fetisov came back with an understanding that they would be joining the NHL shortly thereafter. Larionov was allowed to join the Vancouver Canucks in 1989, the same season Fetisov joined the New Jersey Devils. They opened the doors to the flood of Russians that now highlight rosters in North America. It's predicted that one of every five NHL players could be Russian in this decade.

When Larionov and his Detroit teammates planned their trip to Russia, Larionov made sure that the Cup had a stop in his hometown of Voskresensk so it could be displayed at Khimik Arena.

"I wanted to share the Stanley Cup with the people of Russia," Larionov said. "When we played for the national team, we were expected to win. We did. But there was no joy like there is in winning a Stanley Cup. The attitude was: 'Let's go back to work.'"

Voskresensk is a hockey hotbed, producing other NHL champions like Valeri Kamensky (Colorado in 1996), Valeri Zelepukin (New Jersey in 1995), and Slava Kozlov (Detroit in 1997 and 1998).

When Larionov won his first Stanley Cup, he called it the happiest moment of his life. He meant it. "This is the most difficult trophy to win because you have to play at a high level of hockey for two months," Larionov said.

*The Detroit Red Wings' Igor Larionov celebrates his second goal of the first period against the Colorado Avalanche in Game 4 of the Western Conference Finals at Joe Louis Arena on May 22, 1997, in Detroit.*

He had always laughed at the notion that Russian players put more emphasis on international competition. "For us, the main goal is to win the Stanley Cup," Larionov said.

"There's no doubt about that. Nobody was thinking about winning the World Championships when we're in the [Stanley Cup] Final."

Larionov sees the quest for a Cup and Olympic gold as completely different. He loves the run for the Cup "because it's a marathon from the start of training camp."

He says the attitude of young Russian players is different. "For 70 years, North American kids were brought up to win the Stanley Cup," Larionov said. "The Russian kids grew up dreaming to play for the national team, to play for their country in the World Championships and Olympics. Now it's starting to change. The main goal for the [Russian] kids is to try to make it to the NHL and win the biggest trophy—the Stanley Cup."

To no one's surprise, Tikhonov left the Red Army Hockey School an hour before Larionov and Fetisov showed up with the Cup. It didn't matter to Larionov, who hadn't seen Tikhonov in years. He hadn't been looking to resolve anything. He certainly hadn't brought the Cup to Russia to see him. "Like Slava said, we brought it for the kids," said Larionov.

## Patrick Roy
*Montreal Canadiens, 1986 and 1993*
*Colorado Avalanche, 1996 and 2001*

Nothing defines Patrick Roy's career more than his quest for the Stanley Cup. He pursues it the way a renowned artist pursues the inspiration for yet another masterpiece. The Cup is almost like an intoxicant to Roy. "As soon as you win a Stanley Cup, you want to win it again," he said.

No one who has seen his name engraved on the Stanley Cup has appreciated it more than Roy has. As he makes history in the postseason, he has also been studying it. He views the record book with reverence and feels honored to have his name immortalized alongside other heroes of the game. He is a millionaire who collects old hockey and baseball cards. He's a superstar who is also a fan of the game.

"Even when he was a young goaltender he knew all of the stats," said Colorado general manager Pierre Lacroix, who was Roy's agent back then. "He has always been very interested in the history of the game. Actually, I think he would have made a good sportswriter."

Each of Roy's Stanley Cup triumphs reads like a novel, complete with plot twists, antagonists, and a good guy winning in the end.

At 20 years old in 1985–1986, he helped the Montreal Canadiens win. He posted a 1.92 goals-against average and won the Conn Smythe Trophy. "Starting the playoffs, I was the question mark of the team," Roy said. "People didn't know whether I could do the job. Then we beat Hartford, and I will remember the [4–3 overtime win in] Game 3 against the New York Rangers forever. Then beating Calgary in the Final. It was like a dream."

In 1992–1993 he overcame a trying regular season to help the Canadiens win again. A clever promotional arrangement between Roy and Upper Deck trading cards backfired when the Canadiens didn't play well coming out of the gate. Upper Deck launched a "Trade Roy" campaign, which was meant to inspire collectors to trade his hockey cards to one another. But the "Trade Roy" billboards were turned into a rallying cry for those who really wanted him gone. Radio shows conducted polls asking whether Roy should be traded, and the majority said he should be dealt. That was quickly forgotten when Roy won 10 overtime games en route to his second Conn Smythe Trophy. "The season was tough, and to win the Stanley Cup after that was very rewarding," Roy said. "That Upper Deck [campaign] had really turned against me."

In 1995–1996 he spearheaded the Colorado Avalanche's successful campaign for the Stanley Cup. This was after he had vowed that he would never play for Montreal again because Coach Mario Tremblay embarrassed him by leaving him in a game in which he was being shellacked by the Detroit Red Wings. His spirit reinvigorated by a move to Colorado, Roy posted a 2.10 goals-against average in the postseason. "After all the commotion in Montreal, to be able to turn around my season with Colorado was important," Roy said. "I wanted to show a lot of pride that season, to show that I could still reach that ultimate goal."

Roy is a charming, friendly people person, often lionized by the media because of his outgoing, "Technicolor" personality and well-oiled wit. Remember that this is a character who once said he didn't hear opponent Jeremy Roenick's yapping during a playoff game because he had his Stanley Cup rings inserted as earplugs. His passion shows up each time he plays, whether it's through a wink at his opponent, a bold declaration, a glib comment, or his reverence for hockey's history.

Roy has more playoff wins than anyone in NHL history and in 2000–2001 erased Terry Sawchuk's record of 447 regular-season wins.

It comes as no surprise that this Colorado Avalanche netminder devoured David Dupuis' 1998 Sawchuk biography, and that he knows the minutia of Sawchuk's career as well as he knows his own. He seems fascinated by Sawchuk's mental toughness—affording it the same level of respect that a modern rocker might give the Beatles or Elvis Presley.

"How often would a goaltender win three Stanley Cups in four years and then lose his job?" Roy said, his voice unable to mask his incredulity about Sawchuk's career. "With only six teams back then, a goaltender had to play knowing he might lose his job at any time to a guy like Glenn Hall or Roger Crozier. Sawchuk wins in 1955 and then he's traded away to Boston."

The statistical comparison between Sawchuk and Roy shows each with four Stanley Cup championships and three Vezina Trophies. Both Sawchuk and Roy show postseason goals-against averages of about two and a half goals per game. Roy won't venture into a debate about whether his accomplishments—including his four championships and three Conn Smythe Trophies—were accomplished under harsher conditions than Sawchuk's. After all, Sawchuk's titles came in the Original Six era, while Roy is now competing in a 30-team NHL.

"It's just so hard to compare eras," Roy said. "They were playing with no masks, or little masks. Today we have outstanding protection. It's just too hard to compare. The last thing we want to do is to [diminish] how a player performed in his own time."

Roy was 35 when he helped the Colorado Avalanche win its second championship in five years in 2000–2001. Posting a .934 save percentage and 1.70 goals-against average, Roy is the first man to be named playoff MVP three times. After the season, he signed a new two-year contract. Those watching him now say he could easily play into his forties.

Roy doesn't even hesitate when asked to list his favorite Stanley Cup memories. One is obvious: the 1992–1993 season when he turned the Stanley Cup playoffs into his own private playground, winning 10 overtime games in the Canadiens' improbable romp to the Stanley Cup crown. "I especially remember the second game in overtime, when Eric Desjardins scored to win it for us," he recalled.

Another memory is subtler. He remembers the feeling he had in 1986 when the Canadiens beat the New York Rangers in the conference finals. "It was a huge game for us," Roy said. "And I remember facing the media afterward. I could barely speak English. So I made sure someone was beside me to make sure that I didn't say the wrong thing."

Even at the age of 20, Roy's respect for the Cup was so acute that he worried about dishonoring himself or the game with the wrong words.

With all due respect to Roy's reverence for the game, don't think he hasn't howled into the night with Stanley by his side. Let it be known that Lord Stanley's chalice was baptized in St. Patrick's pool in Montreal in 1993. Roy's impishness takes over when he tells the tale about how the Cup accidentally ended up in his pool a few dozen times during the course of the evening.

## Larry Robinson
*Montreal Canadiens, 1973, 1976–1979, and 1986*
*Assistant Coach, New Jersey Devils, 1995*
*Coach, New Jersey Devils, 2000*

One tenet of modern sports philosophy is that great professional players often struggle to become great professional coaches.

The theory is that great players become frustrated watching average players make mistakes they would never have made. As much as Ted Williams loved baseball, he couldn't make managing work for him. Some of Magic Johnson's dunks lasted longer than his NBA coaching career. You could almost see the pain on Larry Bird's face as he watched his Indiana Pacers perform. Most NFL quarterbacks are smart enough to scramble into the broadcast booth rather than roll the dice with a coaching job. Hall of Famers such as Bob Griese and Troy Aikman have more longevity on television than they would have found in the coaching profession.

That's why Larry Robinson's attitude about winning the Stanley Cup as a coach versus winning as it a player is so intriguing. He insists it was a "lot more" satisfying to win it as the New Jersey Devils' head coach in 2000 than it was any of his six times as a player.

"It was great as a player because you were banged up and you had been playing for so long that you said, 'Oh, jeez, it's finally over—my bruises can go away,'" Robinson said. "But as a coach, it's great seeing guys that have never been there before. The euphoria they are feeling—you understand because you were there before. It's great to see the guys jumping around like a little kid. It's a super feeling for a coach."

It's difficult to argue against the notion that coaching is far more emotionally demanding than playing. Top players approach 30 minutes of ice time, while a coach sweats and grinds for every tick of every contest. An inherent frustration is built in because you can't personally make the play on the ice. You can offer a plan. You can diagram it with a magic marker on your coach's board. But you cannot make the play. You are at the mercy of your players.

"The toughest thing about being a coach is that you have to prepare 20 to 24 guys as opposed to just preparing yourself," Robinson said. "You are always thinking of what you can do to prepare them and what you can say and when is the best time."

Until the 2000 glory season with the Devils, Robinson often seemed like a reluctant coach. He had been the Devils' coach Jacques Lemaire's assistant when he won the Stanley Cup in 1995, and then moved to Los Angeles to become the head coach. He coached there for four seasons and often seemed frustrated by his experience. Rightly or wrongly, his tenure was marked by constant rumors that he was fed up with coaching.

When Robinson was let go by Los Angeles, New Jersey general manager Lou Lamoriello invited him to return to New Jersey to be one of Robbie Ftorek's assistants. He agreed to come but he made it clear that he wasn't coming as a head coach–in-waiting. In fact, Robinson was initially eager to move from behind the bench when Lamoriello fired Ftorek with eight games to go in the regular season.

No team has ever won a Stanley Cup after switching coaches so late in the season. The only historical basis for the Devils' optimism was that the 1970–1971 Montreal Canadiens had switched from Claude Ruel to Al MacNeil with 23 games remaining and then won the Stanley Cup. But that certainly wasn't a smooth ride. Remember, that was the season Henri Richard called McNeil the worst coach he had ever encountered. Lamoriello's instincts told him that the Devils weren't going to be able to win with Ftorek in charge. He believed Robinson's style was perfect for the Devils. His instincts proved to be beyond reproach.

During the Stanley Cup Finals, key center Bobby Holik said that the Devils couldn't have gotten that far if Ftorek had remained as coach. What he didn't say, but what insiders were saying, is that veterans just weren't buying what Ftorek was selling.

Nobody questioned Robinson's ideas, and they appreciated his candor. It's widely held that the turning point of the championship season was Robinson's tongue lashing when they fell behind 3–1 to the Philadelphia Flyers. It was a cross between a temper tantrum and an old-fashioned ass-whuppin'. At no point during his presentation would the players have been stunned to see a lightning bolt shoot out of his mouth. They were living in the eye of a Robinson storm.

Robinson has tried to downplay what happened, saying he was simply doing what all coaches do. But when the Devils came back from that 3–1 series, "the speech" became part of Stanley Cup folklore.

Robinson is the 14th person to win a Stanley Cup as both a player and a coach. The list includes Toe Blake, who was Rocket Richard's line-mate and famed coach of the Montreal Canadiens; plus Al Arbour, who gained notoriety as a bespectacled dependable defenseman long before he coached the New York Islanders to four Cups in a row. Jacques Lemaire was also a Hall of Famer for the Montreal Canadiens before he coached the Devils to the crown.

But an argument can be made that Robinson is the best player to ever become a Stanley Cup coach. In addition to his six Stanley Cup championships, Robinson won the Norris Trophy twice as the league's best defenseman, the Conn Smythe Trophy in 1978, and played in the All-Star Game 10 times.

When he was coaching the Devils in the Stanley Cup, the media tried repeatedly to prompt Robinson to discuss his playing career and how it related to his success as a coach. Robinson wouldn't bite that apple.

"I don't look back on my career as it was too damn long ago," Robinson said. "I don't see how it has any bearing on what is happening now. I try to keep my focus on the here and now."

Perhaps that explains why Robinson was able to exorcise the demons that often haunt superstars who venture into coaching. Maybe he has learned not to measure players' reactions to what he was able to do. That's a theory, nothing more.

When it was over, Robinson's jubilation seemed as fresh as if he had never won a Cup before. Patrik Elias insisted that Petr Sykora's jersey be brought on the ice for the celebration because he had been carried off the ice on a stretcher early in the game after being walloped by Dallas defenseman Derian Hatcher's crushing hit. Sykora, Elias, and center Jason Arnott had been the Devils' top line throughout the playoffs. It was Robinson who put on Sykora's jersey to honor the injured Devils warrior.

When the Devils had finished off the Stars in Game 6, Robinson struggled to find the right words to sum up how he felt about the experience.

"I wish I could describe it," he said. "It is an unbelievable feeling. I've had these feelings as a player and I've had them as an assistant. But what went through me in the 2000 playoffs was a fairy tale."

## Harry Sinden
*Coach, Boston Bruins, 1970*
Harry Sinden had one of the best seats in the Boston Garden for Bobby Orr's dramatic, series-clinching goal in 1970, but he wasn't watching.

"My eyes were looking around to make sure that everyone else was in the right place," Sinden said, laughing. "Remember, Bobby came in from the point and Eddie Westfall came back to cover up for him. I was coaching as Bobby was scoring because it was overtime and I wanted to know Westfall was back there."

When the Bruins won that day, it was the franchise's first Stanley Cup championship in 29 years. It was also Mother's Day. "I remember telling everyone to thank their mothers for their first pair of skates because look what it led to," Sinden recalled.

Sinden's memories of the Cup celebration are of the parade and the overflowing crowd that was present on that hot day in May. The players were transported in convertibles, but since the streets are so narrow and there were so many people there, no one could move. Cars overheated, and the Bruins had to walk back to the Boston Garden.

"On the way back a couple of our guys got into a fight," Sinden said, chuckling. "I think it was Wayne Carleton and Ace Bailey."

That wasn't uncharacteristic for this team. Not to suggest that the Bruins didn't get along, but this roster was highlighted by passionate, talented, and colorful characters who all had a penchant for outlandish behavior.

Sinden certainly wasn't shocked when John "Pie" McKenzie doused the mayor with beer during his speech on the wonders of the Bruins team. "He kept saying all these nice things about us, and McKenzie poured it right on him," Sinden said. "He kept talking. He didn't care."

This was Bobby Orr's team; his electrifying talent fueled it. Phil Esposito was a close second to him in terms of impact. But Sinden views Derek Sanderson as one of the unsung heroes of this championship team.

"I think Sanderson got a lot of notoriety off the ice, but he was a tremendous hockey player," Sinden recalled. "He was often overlooked because we had Orr, Esposito, and Gerry Cheevers [in goal]. And we had Ken Hodge scoring goals. But behind Orr and Esposito, Sanderson was probably our best player."

Sanderson's strong play on the ice was often overlooked because of his wild behavior off the ice. He was hockey's playboy, his long flowing hair a calling card that was perhaps the symbol of his free spirit.

"Most of that BS was promoted by Derek himself," Sinden said. "When he first came to the Bruins, he was a saint. He became a bit of a cult figure in town and tried to take advantage of it. I don't think he was nearly as bad as he wants to believe he was."

Sanderson was hockey's Joe Namath. In fact, he actually became Namath's partner in a Bachelor's III club in Boston, modeled after Bachelor's III in New York.

"I'm sure Derek did some wild things," Sinden said. "But on the ice he could play the game."

One thing that has been lost through the years because of all the publicity surrounding the photo of Orr soaring through the air is the fact that there was no drama associated with that goal. The Bruins swept the St. Louis Blues and clearly were the best team in the game.

"Even Cheevers says he was just prolonging the suspense," Sinden said. "There was never any doubt we were going to win that series."

## Mike Bossy

*New York Islanders, 1980–1983*

Mike Bossy may have been one of only a few young boys in Quebec who grew up rooting against the Montreal Canadiens in their glory years; still, he doesn't undersell what that storied franchise meant in the development of his drive to succeed.

"You just got sick and tired of seeing them win all the time, and you rooted for someone else to win," Bossy said. "But one of the reasons I wanted to play hockey was that I had watched them celebrate so much in my childhood. It was always in the back of your mind that you would like to celebrate like you watched them celebrate."

Few players have earned the right to celebrate with the same panache and productivity that marked Bossy's NHL postseason career. During the Islanders' four Stanley Cup celebrations, he netted 61 postseason goals. He captured the 1982 Conn Smythe Trophy after generating 17 goals and 18 assists for 35 points in 17 games. He led the NHL in playoff goals for three consecutive years.

"After we won our first Cup, the confidence level of everyone on the team seemed to leap," Bossy recalled. "We just always knew that there wasn't a situation that we couldn't get ourselves out of it."

That attitude would be useful in 1982, when they had to rally to erase a two-goal deficit in the final five minutes to beat Pittsburgh in overtime on John Tonelli's goal.

"I remember clear as day that in that overtime Pittsburgh had a two-on-one break, and I was the second guy backchecking, and their guy had an open net and shot wide or hit the post," Bossy said. "We came back and scored a minute later. You got the sense that someone was looking down on you."

According to Bossy, "After we got over that hurdle, we did seem to be invincible."

In today's hockey market, it's difficult to keep top teams intact, since older players have so much more freedom to peddle their talents in the league's open market. To appreciate how different the financial landscape was in the early 1980s, consider that Bossy's salary in his second season worked out to about $925 per goal.

"I made $65,000 the second year when I scored 69 goals," Bossy said. "Then my third year I think I got $200,000 and $250,000."

After the Islanders won their second Stanley Cup, Bossy boldly asked for $5 million over six years. "They ended up making it $5 million for seven years," Bossy said. "I gave in on the last year because I knew they weren't going to budge."

Bossy's memory about what happened in the game is sharper than what he remembers about his moments with the Cup. "I really don't remember one being more special than the others with regard to the celebrations," Bossy said. "But I do remember the fourth being very satisfying."

That was the sweep against Wayne Gretzky's Edmonton Oilers. Going into that playoff year, there was a prevailing thought that the Great One and his buddies were ready to take the title away from the champ. As it turned out, the champ wasn't ready to relinquish the crown.

"We had gone three in a row, and they were supposed to dethrone us," Bossy said. "They were a young, brash team with a lot of stars, and they were supposed to be ready to win."

Bossy says he can still remember "the clear disappointment on all of the Oilers' faces at the end of that series." But Bossy has always admired the Oilers for learning from that experience. In 1984 they knocked out the champ in five games. They outscored the Islanders 19–6 in the final three games. That was the first of five Cups the Oilers would win in a seven-year period.

"I have found that no matter what aspect of work you are in, when you make a mistake, the most important thing is to learn from it," Bossy said. "I think they learned a lot from us that year, and what they did afterward certainly proved that."

As Bossy rummaged through his memory banks about the four Stanley Cup celebrations that he experienced, he seemed amused to report that what stands out most in his mind is that his wife slept through the first one.

While all the Islanders and their wives and girlfriends were gathered at the fraternity house–style party at Bill Torrey's house after the 1980 Cup triumph, the usually security-conscious Lucie Bossy was "conked out" on her couch with her door wide open. She had been the victim of lapping up too much of the first celebration at the arena after Bob Nystrom had scored the Cup clincher.

"She was a little tipsy and decided not to go to Bill's house," said Bossy. "She reminds people of that because everyone who knows her knows that it was highly unusual for her to do that. When we first went down to Long Island, the idea of being alone there wasn't her idea of fun. When I would go on the road, I was always finding someone to stay with her or she would go stay at someone's house. So for her to be alone with her door unlocked on that night is funny to us."

Actually there was no reason for her to worry about crime that night. Remember, everyone on Long Island was at Torrey's that night. Or so it seemed.

## Bryan Trottier
*New York Islanders, 1980–1983 • Pittsburgh Penguins, 1991, 1992*
*Assistant Coach, Colorado Avalanche, 2001*

Hall of Fame center Bryan Trottier seems to understand that the difference between playing for a Stanley Cup championship team and serving as an assistant coach for a winner is the difference between piloting an F14 and training someone to fly in combat. "As a player, you can do something about it," Trottier said, grinning. "You can go on the ice, bang bodies, take shots, make passes, defend, attack. As a coach, you prepare the players, tweak, encourage, and push. You just need to do your best to communicate philosophies and experiences that will help the players. But it's really exciting."

That distinction notwithstanding, Trottier wasn't any less enthusiastic when hoisting the Cup as an assistant coach in 2001 than he was as a player almost a decade earlier, when he won back-to-back titles as a role player with the Pittsburgh Penguins.

It is almost unfathomable to him that it has been almost 30 years since he won his first Stanley Cup as the star of the New York Islanders. "When I think about it, it seems like yesterday," he said. "The reality is that it was a long time ago. But the vivid memories are like yesterday."

His most vivid memory? "Probably the Bobby Nystrom [1980 clinching] goal. That was the moment you become a champion for the first time. In Pittsburgh it was like just watching the clock go down. But

*The New York Islanders' Bryan Trottier slips the puck past Minnesota North Stars goalie Don Beaupre in November 1984. Trottier was elected to the Hockey Hall of Fame in 1997 after winning six Stanley Cups with the New York Islanders and Pittsburgh Penguins during an 18-year career. He scored 524 goals and had 1,425 points in 1,279 regular-season games.*

[the Nystrom goal] was like a split-second moment. You become a champion. Everything peaks. Everything you have dreamed of, all the dedication. Your senses start peaking to absorb the moment. To repeat three more times was a great accomplishment, but there is nothing like when you are a champion for the first time."

What makes Trottier's Stanley Cup experiences so unique is that his roles were different for each championship team. During the Islanders' heyday, he was arguably the most multifaceted center in the game. He could score, create offensive chances, shut down the opposing team's top center, and he could bare his teeth if it was necessary. Although

Nystrom's goal is the most famous goal in Islanders' history, it was Trottier who led his team to victory in 1980. He was the NHL playoff leader in goals (12) and points (29), and he won the Conn Smythe Trophy as the postseason's most valuable player.

In the Islanders' four Stanley Cup championships, Trottier had 107 points in 75 games. Known more as a set-up man for premier scorer Mike Bossy, Trottier had 37 goals in those four title runs.

When the Pittsburgh Penguins signed him as a free agent in 1990, he understood that he was agreeing to a supporting role on a team that already had a star in Mario Lemieux. Still, Trottier treasures his Pittsburgh titles because he had reinvented himself. He had only 14 points in 44 playoff games over the two championship runs, yet his role was important to the team's success. "Through the 1980s I was a power-play guy. But with Pittsburgh I was more of a third-line guy, a caboose kind of a guy," Trottier admitted.

But his personal metamorphosis made the championship unique. It made the feeling different when he won. "It was the realization that there were more championships in me after not having won one in seven years," Trottier said. "It was a real good self-esteem moment. I could look in the mirror and say I had something to do with a championship."

The celebration was different as well. He wasn't the central figure in the Cup hoopla as he was on the Island. He sat back and let others take center stage in the festivities.

He does remember the now-famous party in Lemieux's backyard. "In hindsight, we should have rescued the Cup a little sooner," he said. He wasn't a member of the diving party that tried to extract the Cup from the bottom of the pool. "But I remember thinking I should rescue the Cup," he said, grinning. "It's in trouble. It probably needs an air tank."

Despite his triumph in Pittsburgh, Trottier seems to prefer the memories of the Islanders' celebrations. At that time there was no organized sharing of the Cup. When players were in possession of it, they felt as if they were getting away with something. Perhaps stealing moments with the Cup was sweeter when it seemed like forbidden fruit. The Islanders had no guarantee of having private moments with the Cup, and Trottier seems to feel that that made the Islanders' celebrations more memorable than the Penguins'.

"You couldn't plan anything," Trottier recalled. "You couldn't say to everyone: 'Be over at my house at 2:00.' You would ask [GM Bill Torrey] if you could take the Cup until 2:00 PM, and he might say, 'Go ahead and keep it until 4:00,' and those extra two hours seemed so special to you. The fact that we shared the Cup with each other for such a brief time made it more special."

Trottier said all of the Islanders' celebrations were spontaneous, all coming within a few days of winning the Cup. The Islanders didn't have the Cup for very long before it went back to the Hall. "I cherished my moments with the Cup as much as the presentation on the ice," Trottier said. He added, "I think it was more fun in those days because you were able to go up to the general managers and ask if it was all right to take the Stanley Cup home tonight and have some family shots with it. You would zoom it around the neighborhood and take it all over. That was really fun."

According to Stanley Cup lore, Trottier was the first person to sleep with the Cup—or at least the first to receive newspaper acclaim for doing so. "That's an exaggeration," Trottier now says. "No, I didn't sleep with it. I took it home and put it in the bedroom, just in case someone was peeking through the windows. I didn't want anyone to steal it."

## Glenn Anderson

*Edmonton Oilers, 1984, 1985, 1987, 1988 and 1990*
*New York Rangers, 1994*

When Glenn Anderson was finally elected to the Hockey Hall of Fame in 2008, Wayne Gretzky said, "I don't think there was a better playoff-pressure player, other than maybe Rocket Richard."

Anderson's 93 postseason goals ranks fifth all-time behind Gretzky (122), Mark Messier (109), Jari Kurri (106), and Brett Hull (103). He had 17 game-winners, and his five overtime playoff goals ranks third on the all-time list.

In addition to all of Anderson's accomplishments, he might be one of the most daring and dashing Stanley Cup champions in NHL history. In the Edmonton Oilers' 1980s offensive circus, Anderson was the trapeze act. He made the dangerous moves. He kept fans on the edge of their seats. He had a "wow" factor in every performance.

Teammate Craig Simpson recalled that Anderson drove to the net "with reckless abandon.... He had no fear of getting hurt." Seemingly moving at warp speed, Anderson would routinely cut across toward the net with defensemen lined up to knock his block off. "You just knew when we had a big game or a big moment that Andy could make something happen," Simpson said. "He was going to score the big goal, or be part of a big goal, or bring the energy you needed."

"He was going to score," said Detroit Red Wings assistant Jim Nill. "He was going to go through you; his trademark was cutting to the net with his leg out, cutting around the defenseman, going to the net." Nill played with Anderson on the 1980 Canadian Olympic team and then played against him in the NHL. "He could really change a game,"

*Glenn Anderson of the Edmonton Oilers sends a shot past Boston Bruins goalie Andy Moog for a score in the Stanley Cup Finals game at Boston on May 24, 1990.*

Nill said. "He could do it with a big hit or by cutting to the net. People talk about how flaky he was, but when it came time to play, he was all about hockey."

Nill said when Anderson started driving the net "you couldn't stop him. He was going to the net no matter what.… He was a great skater. He wasn't strong physically, but his skating made him strong, and you couldn't knock him off a puck."

What Nill found curious about Anderson was that "he was happy-go-lucky before the game, and in the game he was all business. He would turn into Mark Messier during the game."

Linesman Ray Scapinello, who entered the Hall of Fame with Anderson, called Anderson "one of the greatest skaters who ever performed in the National Hockey League."

Because Anderson's speed was memorable, it's forgotten that Anderson played with a layer of prickliness. Gretzky and Kurri were strictly a finesse pairing, while Messier and Anderson could play with skill but also didn't mind playing like mobsters at times.

"People don't understand the physical part of [Anderson's] game," Nill said. "In the tournament before the [1980] Olympics, he hit [Valeri] Kharlamov so hard, he just about killed the guy. A lot of times skilled players don't have that edge; he did."

It was blend of talents that allowed Anderson to become a six-time champion. He was about winning more than he was about scoring. According to Gretzky, Anderson had trouble with self-motivation when it came to lopsided games.

"You knew Andy would get two goals in a 3–2 game, but if it was a 6–1 game, he might get one point," said Gretzky. "His motivation came from playing in the big games. His numbers probably could have been better if he had the same feeling as I had, or Kurri had, or Messier had, but his attitude was more like, 'It's a big game tonight, we're in Calgary, I'll be ready to go.' If we played a weaker team, he wasn't so much into it. But at playoff time, he was ready to go."

Early in his career, Anderson said his Olympic team's lack of success, plus his Oilers' early struggles, set him back as a hockey player. "I was left wondering if I had the right stuff to be a champion," he said.

That changed when Anderson's Oilers won the 1984 Stanley Cup championship.

"The fact that I hated to lose more than I liked to win is for good reason," Anderson said. "I think it stems back to the hardships of losing early.... I didn't want to do that again. Those were painful wounds."

Based on Anderson's accomplishments, he should have been in the Hall of Fame much earlier than he was selected. It's not known why the Hall of Fame waited so long, but clearly Anderson's off-ice image of being a flighty free spirit didn't help.

An *Edmonton Sun* columnist once nicknamed Anderson "Mork" after the 1970s television character played by comedian Robin Williams. "It stuck, and I was characterized as being from outer space," Anderson said.

He didn't like the name during his playing days, but he is able to laugh about it now. "I guess the question I no longer have to answer is, 'Why aren't you in [the Hall]?'" he said. As a player, Anderson will be remembered as one of the most dangerous playoff scorers in the NHL. But the colorful, flighty Anderson still emerges from time to time, such as when he was on a conference call to discuss his Hall of Fame selection. Not long after giving a serious answer about what he learned from playing for Father David Bauer, the late Canadian Olympic coach, Anderson suddenly had spirits on his mind.

"I heard there's ghosts in the Hall," Anderson said. "And I can just imagine my picture probably looking right at Father Bauer or [former Edmonton general manager and coach] Glen Sather." Anderson jokingly predicted that after his death, and Sather's passing, their ghosts would be together at the Hall of Fame. "I can hear Slats going, 'It's past curfew, you better go to bed,'" Anderson said.

## Raymond Bourque
*Colorado Avalanche, 2001*

It was fitting that defenseman Ray Bourque would be in the Mile High City of Denver, elevation 5,280 feet, when he finally completed a 22-year climb to reach the summit of his Hall of Fame career. When 40-year-old Bourque finally hoisted the Stanley Cup over his head at the

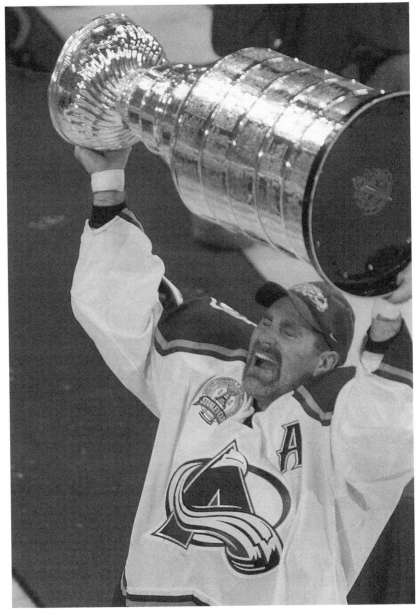

*Colorado Avalanche defensemen Ray Bourque celebrates with the Stanley Cup in Denver on June 9, 2001. The Avalanche beat the New Jersey Devils 3–1 in Game 7 to capture the Cup.*

Pepsi Center on June 9, 2001, no player in NHL history had worked harder to earn that Cup, desired it with greater passion, or deserved an NHL championship more than Bourque.

The Colorado Avalanche allowed Bourque to live his championship dream by downing the defending champion New Jersey Devils 3–1 in Game 7 to win the Stanley Cup title. "I couldn't breathe in the last 30 seconds, and it wasn't because I was tired," he said. "It was just too much, with all of the emotions."

Tradition says that the captain takes the first spin around the ice with the Stanley Cup, but Colorado captain Joe Sakic immediately gave the Cup to Bourque for the first spin around the ice. It was possible to see the relief in his eyes as he raised the Cup.

When Bourque began his Stanley Cup quest as a rookie for the Boston Bruins in 1979, Jimmy Carter was president, the information superhighway was an unpaved road, and Tiger Woods was a toddler.

Had Bourque not won the Cup in 2001, he would not have been the only big star to miss out on hockey's grand prize. Hall of Famer Bill Gadsby played two decades without winning, and Marcel Dionne and Brad Park are among the notable who left the game without a Cup. But no one had played longer without winning than Bourque, whose 1,612 regular-season games ranks third only to Gordie Howe and Larry Murphy, both of whom won multiple Stanley Cups. With 214 playoff games, Bourque trailed only Murphy and Larry Robinson, who was a mainstay of the Montreal Canadiens' blue line during their championship run in the 1970s.

When Bourque finally won, he did what was expected: he shared the Cup first with his family and then his friends. The *Denver Post* reported that at 2:30 AM he brought the Cup to the home of neighbor Bill Heissenbuttel in Littleton. The irony was that Heissenbuttel was from New Jersey, and had rooted for the Devils. But he was Bourque's friend, so Ray wanted to share the Cup with him.

For 22 years, Bourque has been known as one of the NHL's nicest men—a man you want as a neighbor, as a friend, and certainly as a teammate. During a live national television interview seconds after qualifying for the Stanley Cup Finals for the first time in 11 years, Bourque remembered to say hello to daughter Melissa, and in the hectic postgame dressing room scene, he remembered to high-five one of his two sons.

Bourque is a private man who has always believed in public accountability. He never shied away from the spotlight and always accepted blame when things didn't go well. He was a genteel man in a ruffian's sport. "I've been going back to Boston every summer, and no one has ever said a bad word about Ray Bourque," said St. Louis general manager Larry Pleau.

It seemed as if fate were feeling sentimental about Bourque during his final season. Some say the turning point for the Avalanche was in Game 2 of the second round when the Kings, victors in Game 1, seemed poised to take the lead on a breakaway by Glen Murray. His shot, blocked by Patrick Roy, seemed to drift in the air over the goal line when Bourque came out of nowhere to bat it baseball-style out of harm's way. The Avs went on to win that game and the series. "I said to Ray that night, 'You might have made the play of the playoffs,'" Roy said. Coach Bob Hartley also remembered that play as one of the turning points of the postseason. "If that goes in, maybe we don't come back," he said.

Bourque was anything but a passenger on this championship run. He was driving the bus. In Game 2 he scored the game-winner in a 3–1 triumph against the Devils. He became the first 40-year-old player in NHL history to score in the Stanley Cup Finals. "Ray picked the top corner," said Colorado coach Bob Hartley. "I think that is not the first one he scored in his career like that."

Going into the third period, when Colorado players were asking each other who would net the winning goal, Bourque stepped forward and boldly said that he would take care of it. "You don't know anything," Bourque said of the prediction. "You just make the call and you hope you get lucky. What do you have to lose?"

Trailing 3–2 to the Devils in the championship series and faced with a Game 6 in New Jersey, Bourque made a pregame speech. It may not have been Knute Rockne quality, but his message transmitted well. "He just said that it would probably be his last game if we lost, so let's not go out there and give it anything less than our best," Avalanche defenseman Greg DeVries said.

He was plus-2 in the Game 7 victory, and the Avalanche players insisted that Bourque be on the ice when the clock ticked off the final seconds. It looked comical as Blake scurried off the ice and basically screamed at Bourque to get back on. This was Bourque's moment. The Avalanche wanted it that way.

The Avalanche became the first NHL team since the 1971 Montreal Canadiens to win the Stanley Cup by winning Games 6 and 7. They were only the third team since then to need a Game 7 to win the Cup, joining the 1987 Edmonton Oilers and the 1994 New York Rangers.

What makes the Avalanche title run even more impressive is that they played the final two rounds without Peter Forsberg, considered by some to be the best all-around player in the league. He was lost to the team after suffering an injury that necessitated the removal of his spleen.

What made the victory even more special was that the team won it for Bourque, a player who had requested a trade the season before to fulfill his dream of winning a Stanley Cup. It is customary to take only one trip around the ice holding the Stanley Cup over one's head, but when all of Bourque's teammates had received their tour with the Cup, he took a second spin. "There were tears in my eyes many times during this game," he said.

Bourque took the Cup back to Boston, where he had spent the first 20 years of his career. He was traded during the 1999–2000 season. "I have been looking forward to sharing it with the fans here who supported me for so many years," Bourque said after arriving at Hanscom Field in a private jet. "It's a great, great feeling to win the Cup, and everything was great back in Denver for our celebration."

Even though he won the Cup wearing an Avalanche sweater, at a rally attended by 15,000 people, Bourque said that he would always feel like a Bruin.

On June 26, 2001, Bourque officially announced his retirement. Avalanche GM Pierre Lacroix, with Bourque nearby wiping away tears, announced that Bourque's No. 77 jersey would be the first number retired in Colorado Avalanche history. "Frankly, I've always had a strong commitment to myself never to stay too long in the game," Bourque said. "I'd rather leave the game knowing I can still play at a high level than to end with the feeling I should have shut it down sooner."

Bourque was somewhat embarrassed about receiving so much attention after the Avalanche's Cup victory, but his teammates truly wanted it that way. It will be forever believed that the Avalanche rallied from behind in that series because they were winning for him. Throughout the playoffs, Colorado players wore caps that read "Mission 16 W," meaning that the team needed 16 wins to capture the Stanley Cup. Bourque wore that cap more than anyone else. It was like his war paint.

Teammate Roy became the first man to win the Conn Smythe Trophy three times, and yet he shrugged it off as if it was a minor event. "Individual awards are great, but there was nothing better than seeing Ray with that Cup," Roy said. Those words probably summed up the thought of a world of hockey fans. Bourque's mission was finally completed.

## Lanny McDonald

*Calgary Flames, 1989*

As the euphoric Calgary Flames were high-fiving and rebel-yelling in celebration of their Stanley Cup championship in 1989, Lanny McDonald experienced an overwhelming sense of tranquility that probably seemed foreign for such a raucous occasion. But it was an appropriate feeling for an NHL player who endured a long journey to reach his summit.

"When you have finally won the Cup and realized your dream of holding it up after 16 years, it was more a feeling of peacefulness than anything else," McDonald said. "I enjoy looking around the room and seeing everyone whooping and hollering. After 16 years of hard labor, it was peacefulness."

McDonald was 36; he had reached the end of his career when the Flames won the Stanley Cup. In the prime of his career, he was among the NHL's most dangerous scorers. He had scored 40 or more goals for three consecutive seasons in the late 1970s and had totaled 66 goals for the Flames in 1982–1983. But the grand prize, the Stanley Cup, had eluded him, the price he paid for playing the majority of his career with non-contending teams. In two of his prime years he was playing with the

NHL's Colorado Rockies organization that was closer to being a minor-league team than it was to being a real contender.

"I don't think I ever questioned that I was going to win," McDonald said. "The question was whether I was going to have enough time, or whether I was going to run out of time."

It was as if fate had turned sentimental in 1988–1989. Although McDonald was slowing down, he managed to net his 500th career goal before the end of the regular season. McDonald had been scoreless in the playoffs, and Coach Terry Crisp had chosen not to use McDonald in three of the first five games in the Stanley Cup Finals against Montreal. Before Game 6, assistant coach Doug Risebrough had summoned McDonald for a private chat. Not knowing whether he would be in or out, McDonald was relieved when Risebrough simply talked to him about what his role would be on the power play.

With Calgary up 3–2 in the best-of-seven series, clearly there had been public sentiment for McDonald to be returned to the lineup to assure his chance to be involved in the possible Cup celebration. For Game 6, Crisp had to choose among McDonald, Jim Peplinski, or Tim Hunter for his 12th forward spot. Whether Crisp chose McDonald for sentimental reasons or for his offensive knack didn't matter because McDonald's presence turned out to provide an offensive lift as much as a sentimental one.

With the game tied 1–1 in the second period, McDonald emerged from the penalty box and joined a four-on-two break into the Montreal zone. Joe Nieuwendyk threaded a pass through Chris Chelios to McDonald, who lofted a shot over goaltender Patrick Roy for a 2–1 lead. The Flames went on to win the game 4–2.

McDonald remembers the charter flight home to Calgary from Montreal as one of the highlights of his career. Trainer Jim "Bearcat" Murray, armed with wire cutters, had come to McDonald and Peplinski before the plane was loaded to get their blessing for his plan to liberate the Stanley Cup from its locked case in the cargo hold. (Legend has it that Canadian customs officials assisted Murray in this.)

"He was going to store it in the back washroom," McDonald said. "Of course we thought that was an awesome idea."

When the jet was airborne, the pilot came on the intercom and said, "Jim Murray has brought a special passenger on board."

When Murray emerged from the washroom with the Cup, it signaled the beginning of the most joyous four-and-a-half-hour plane ride that McDonald had ever known. "What I remember was that we all shared in that moment," McDonald said. "We had front office, hockey management, players, wives, girlfriends, fiancées, family members. The heart and soul of the organization was all there together."

McDonald remembers looking around and feeling good for someone—defenseman Rob Ramage, who had also known days in Colorado. "Back then you were supposed to be playing to win the Stanley Cup, but after the first week you didn't like your chances," McDonald said.

Then there was Joe Mullen, "who had grown up in Hell's Kitchen, New York, and now his name was going on the Stanley Cup."

He also felt beholden to goaltender Mike Vernon, whose brilliance, particularly in the first-round series against Vancouver, had probably been the most crucial element of the Flames' Cup run. "There were so many stories within the story," McDonald said.

Upon returning to Calgary, McDonald waited for his opportunity and then grabbed the Stanley Cup and whisked it away to his home west of the city in Springbrook for a couple of days. It's still unclear under whose authority McDonald invoked a claim to this rare privilege.

"I wouldn't call it stealing it," McDonald said. "But it was pretty neat to wake up and see the Cup at the foot of the bed."

The McDonalds had the Cup for two days. "But we only drank milk out of it," he deadpanned. Why don't we believe that? "You probably shouldn't," he said, laughing.

Lanny and his wife, Ardell, invited all of their neighbors to come over for coffee with Stanley. He transported the Cup to his children's schools.

"It was just neat to share that experience," McDonald said. "Whether you are five or 55, the mystique of the Cup is phenomenal."

His hockey career now capped in ornate style, McDonald went gently into retirement that summer. Before doing so, he and Joey Mullen tried to impart wisdom to the younger players, such as Gary Roberts and

Joe Nieuwendyk. Roberts and Nieuwendyk were both 22 when the Flames began their 1989 march to the championship.

"We continually kept telling them this doesn't just happen every year," McDonald said. "You think you are automatically going back to the Final. But you don't get back easily. You have to enjoy it when you are there. Nieuwendyk won, but it took him 10 years."

It took Roberts almost 20 years just to return to the Stanley Cup Finals. He did so in 2008, when he was a 42-year-old winger for the Pittsburgh Penguins. But his team lost to the Detroit Red Wings.

# chapter 2

# Championship
# Architects

## Bill Torrey
*General Manager, New York Islanders, 1980–1983*

Bill Torrey knows precisely where he was on May 25, 1980, at about 6:30 AM. He and a friend were floating around in his backyard pool, sipping champagne, while the Stanley Cup floated about on a lounge chair between them. The early morning dip seemed like the fitting poetic ending for what may have been the best party ever thrown in the sleepy Long Island hamlet of Coal Spring Harbor. About 10 hours before, Torrey thought he had invited just his players and their families to his home to celebrate the first NHL championship in Islanders history.

"But I think half of Long Island marched through my damn house that night," Torrey said, chuckling.

He lived on a main street in Coal Spring Harbor, and he had to call the local police to come in and coordinate the flow of automobiles into the area. Traffic was backed up for miles. Early that afternoon, Bobby Nystrom become a permanent figure in NHL playoff lore by scoring at 7:11 in overtime to beat Philadelphia 5–4 in Game 6 of the Stanley Cup Finals. There was a small amount of relief mixed in with pride when the celebration began late in the afternoon. Given that the Flyers had won Game 5 by a 6–3 score, Torrey had packed his bag for Philadelphia before Game 6, figuring it was highly possible that the pesky Flyers could force a Game 7.

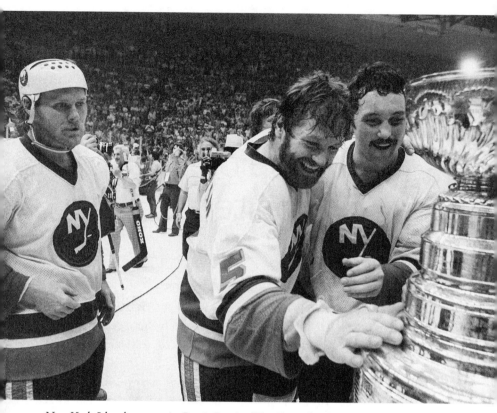

*New York Islanders captain Denis Potvin (No. 5) reaches out to touch the Stanley Cup trophy as teammate Bryan Trottier looks on after the Islanders won the NHL championship at Nassau Coliseum in Uniondale, New York, on May 24, 1980.*

A league party was held at a Long Island hotel, but the Islanders understood their exuberance needed a landing place that had no curfew. "We swiped the Cup and took off," Torrey remembered.

He hadn't anticipated that the party would go all night, and he certainly hadn't figured on seeing so many people in his home that he didn't recognize. He had anticipated it would be crazy; at one point, Clark Gillies put his dog in the Stanley Cup, and at various points "the Cup got very wet."

"But we rescued it right away," Torrey said. "I think we went into the pool to keep ourselves awake. You don't sleep much in the playoffs."

After his early morning Stanley Cup "float-a-thon," Torrey took inventory of his home. There were several items missing, including a handwoven rug with the Islanders' logo in the middle that had been given to him by a Native American woman he had befriended. "I remember walking through the house that morning, and it was a shambles," Torrey said.

The Islanders were ahead of their time when it came to recognizing players' desires to have the Cup in their possession to share with their families. The Islanders didn't return the Cup right away; players didn't get to take it to their hometowns, but it did end up at their Long Island homes. Bryan Trottier reportedly slept with it the night it was in his possession.

Trottier was just one of the Islanders' impressive top players, including Mike Bossy, Denis Potvin, and goaltender Billy Smith. But as Torrey thought back to the Islanders' run of four consecutive Cups, the player he often thinks about was defenseman Ken Morrow, who joined the team after helping the United States win the 1980 Olympic gold medal at Lake Placid.

"People talk about the deal to get Butch Goring as the key, and it was because it opened things up for Trottier and Bossy," Torrey said. "We had a great second line. But I couldn't have done that deal if I hadn't watched Ken Morrow at the Olympics."

On March 10, 1980, Torrey had traded Billy Harris and Dave Lewis to Los Angeles for Goring. Even though Morrow had just joined the Islanders a couple of weeks before, Torrey was comfortable that he could replace Lewis on the Islanders' blue line. "I had noticed that [coach] Herbie Brooks played Morrow all the time against the big Russian line. He was so good defensively. Right from the get-go we used Morrow like he was a 10-year veteran. He was such an underrated player on our team."

That was part of what Torrey shared with his friend as they floated around his pool that morning.

The celebrations of the second, third, and fourth Cups may have matched the intensity of the first, but Torrey can't be sure because they weren't at his home. What he remembers about the second, third, and fourth was the debate about whether the Islanders should get a ticker-tape parade.

"The joke was that we should have our parade on the Hempstead Turnpike," Torrey recalled. "But it was thought that we should get a parade down Broadway because we represented all of New York. We were the New York Islanders, not the Long Island Islanders."

But the Islanders never got the ticker-tape parade in the city. It did actually go up the Hempstead Turnpike. "The mayor said the city couldn't afford it and that New York was Ranger country," Torrey said. "That just made the rivalry that much better."

Interestingly, Torrey almost recalls the heartache of losing the Stanley Cup more than the joy of winning it, the feeling he had when the Edmonton Oilers won the Cup with a 5–2 win against the Islanders at Northlands Coliseum in 1984.

"I remember how depressed I was," Torrey said. "It took me a long time to get over that. When you win 19 consecutive playoff series before losing the 20th, it is an amazing team. I remember how tough that flight home was. That was a huge letdown. I tell this story to show how you feel about winning it. When you have the Cup for that long, you start to think it's yours."

## Ken Holland

*General Manager, Detroit Red Wings, 1997, 1998, 2002, and 2008*
When the Detroit Red Wings won the Stanley Cup in 2008, general manager Ken Holland felt as if he had conclusively proved that it was the Red Wings' wisdom, and not their wallet, that kept the Detroit team successful for more than a decade under his command.

"There was a perception that we won because of money in the pre-cap world," Holland said. "Even when we had a high payroll, obviously we thought we did a good job of building a team…. But everyone was talking like we would go down after the salary cap was introduced, and somehow we managed to stay on top."

Defenseman Brian Rafalski was the only big-money free-agent acquisition on the Detroit roster when the Red Wings beat Pittsburgh in six games to win the Stanley Cup.

Twelve of the roster's 23 players were original Detroit draft picks, and three regulars, Dan Cleary, Andreas Lilja, and Mikael Samuelsson, were claimed off the discard pile. All three played their best pro hockey in Detroit's program.

Defensemen Brad Stuart and Chris Chelios were trade acquisitions.

"It's hard to say that one Stanley Cup was more special than another," Holland said. "They are all different. The first one [in 1997] was the first in many years; and then the second Cup was the [tribute to injured] Vladimir Konstantinov Cup; and then we had all of the Hall of Famers in 2002. But the 2008 Cup was special because we had different players. Players from 2002 had retired. I was happy for guys like Jim Nill and Hakan Anderson and our scouting staff, who had done a good job of keeping our team well stocked with players."

Through the years, Holland's formula has centered on the idea that the franchise has a puck-possession philosophy, and he was going to draft and trade for players that fit into that thinking.

That meant scouts looked often in Europe, where teams place a heavy emphasis on skating and handling the puck. The Red Wings' most respected scout, Haken Anderson, is a Swede, and the Red Wings had seven Swedes on their team when they won the Stanley Cup in 2008. The Red Wings championed the idea that a team could win with a roster overflowing with European talent.

Under Holland's leadership, the Red Wings are patient with their draft picks, keeping young players in the minors, or in Europe, longer than most NHL teams. It's a luxury the Red Wings can afford because of their rich talent supply on the parent club.

Every season, Holland also places extreme importance on a good start, believing that if a team is not in good position by "American Thanksgiving" then it will have a difficult time making up ground.

"I like the idea of banking away points early because you don't know what's going to happen in February and March," Holland said.

But Holland's chief strength is his communication skill and his ability to manage people effectively. He likes to say, "When we win, there's enough credit for everyone." He's the ultimate authority, but he uses a presidential cabinet approach to governing his team. Before he makes important decisions, he relies heavily on input from trusted right-hand man Nill, plus Jim Devellano, the Red Wings' former general manager, who remains with the team as a senior vice president, plus coach Mike Babcock and team vice president Steve Yzerman.

"Kenny Holland is loyal and he has a strong relationship with players," Babcock said. "He sets an atmosphere that you have to work hard, but you can have fun doing it."

Holland was the assistant GM for the Red Wings' 1997 Stanley Cup, and was GM in 1998 and 2002. But the 2008 title seemed to have meant more because it was in the cap world. "It's a level playing field, and we were the champions," Holland said. "It doesn't get better than that."

Holland said he is driven by the thought that he has a responsibility to the team's local and national fan base to maintain the franchise's high performance level. "There are many passionate Red Wings fans around the world," Holland said. "The franchise means so much to so many people that I don't want to screw it up."

Holland has come a long way from the days in 1985, when his playing career was over, and he was considering becoming a vacuum salesman in Vernon, British Columbia. "Vacuums were selling for $320, and up to 20 percent of all sales went to the salesperson," Holland said. "My mom said, 'I need a new vacuum, and I will be your first sale.'" Holland's mother also informed her son that she had talked to her mom and that she was willing to buy a vacuum, as well. "I'm thinking, *This job is great*," Holland recalled. "I haven't even got the job yet and I've sold two vacuums."

He asked his mother whether his Auntie Emma would also buy a vacuum, and his mother said she believed she might be interested. "I was thinking, if I sold one per day, I could make a decent living," Holland said. "Business was booming. Then it hit me—I had run out of family members. Who was I going to sell to on Thursday?"

A week later Devellano called to offer him a scouting job with the Red Wings. It didn't take him long to realize that he would enjoy working in hockey more than he would enjoy being a door-to-door salesman.

After the Red Wings won in 2008, Holland took the Cup back to Vernon for his annual golf outing. But that clearly wasn't his most memorable moment with the Stanley Cup. Holland said that came in 1997

*Once a part of a big red machine, as in the dominant USSR hockey team, Slava Fetisov also became a part of the big red machine in the NHL when he won two Cups with the Detroit Red Wings.*
Photo courtesy of Getty Images

when he took the Stanley Cup to Vernon for the first time and placed it "on my mom and dad's kitchen table."

Holland said he wanted to do that because he remembered his days in youth hockey when Rienie and Lee Holland would rise before 5:00 AM to transport their son to practice. When Holland left home to play junior hockey in Medicine Hat, Alberta, Holland's mom, Lee, told him that his father would play with the radio dials endlessly, trying to tune in a low-frequency Medicine Hat radio station. He was trying desperately to find a play-by-play broadcast of his son's games. "It would be all garbled, but he would just try to get the score," Holland said. "Hockey was a major, major part of our family life when I was growing up. By bringing the Cup home, it was my way of saying thanks."

When Holland took the Cup home, Rienie Holland was already suffering from Parkinson's disease. Ken Holland is glad his father was able to share and feel the Cup's aura before he died in March 1999. What had his father said when Holland brought the Cup home? "He was a man of few words," Holland remembered. "He didn't say much, but I know he was tremendously proud."

## Pierre Lacroix
*General Manager, Colorado Avalanche, 1996 and 2001*

When Pierre Lacroix gave up his agent business to become the boss of the Colorado Avalanche, his beloved wife, Coco, told him she would give him "only five years to win the Cup."

Coco Lacroix simply desired a less hectic lifestyle than they had known during Lacroix's long tenure in the player representation industry. "She told me, 'I won't wait 21 years like I did before,'" Lacroix said, smiling. "We won in our first year, and she loved it so much, she told me, 'Try to win it again. I will give you another five years.'"

That story was frolicking through Lacroix's emotions as he ran onto the ice to join the celebration after the Avalanche defeated the New Jersey Devils in a dramatic Game 7. "When I got the Cup on the ice, I was looking for her," Lacroix said. "I knew where she was sitting, so I turned toward the corner and started moving toward her, saying, 'Mommy, Mommy, Mommy.'"

In the midst of his excitement, Lacroix forgot that trying to lift the bulky and oddly shaped Stanley Cup requires a lot of concentration. "I kissed the Cup, but I forgot how heavy it is, and it came down and, pow, it cut my lip," Lacroix said, laughing. "It knocked me back. I had blood on my lips and teeth. But I was so happy that I didn't care."

Lacroix said past winners had told him that winning the second Cup "makes you go crazy." But he didn't appreciate that notion until he was on the ice, hugging every player on the team. "All you feel is joy," he said.

Even before Lacroix won his first Cup as Colorado's GM, he had experienced the Cup's aura. Among his clients before he changed professions was Patrick Roy, who is now his championship goaltender. "I watched when my former clients won it," Lacroix said. "I said, 'If I changed jobs, the only reason would be to win the Stanley Cup.'"

Lacroix spent most of the evening with team owner Stanley Kroenke, who won a Stanley Cup in his rookie season. Coincidentally, he also won a Super Bowl in his first season as part owner of the St. Louis Rams. "He was still very impressed with how people react to the Stanley Cup," Lacroix said. "It's just not like any other trophy."

At 3:00 AM on the night of the championship, Lacroix was driving home when two cabs crammed with reveling fans pulled up beside him.

When they recognized Lacroix, they followed him to his downtown home. "They rolled down their windows and had their horns going, and I thought they were going to wake up my neighbors," Lacroix said. "But this is why I like waking up every day and going to work every morning."

## Brian Burke
*General Manager, Anaheim Ducks, 2007*

Harvard-trained lawyer Brian Burke is a made-for-television NHL general manager. When the camera light blinks on, words tumble out if his mouth in an entertaining mixture of insight and levity. He boils down complicated issues into polished 14-second sound bites that are the perfect fit for a nightly sports show. He is the league's most quotable personality.

But a couple of minutes after Burke's Anaheim Ducks secured the Stanley Cup championship in 2007, only gibberish escaped from his lips. "I did a 90-second interview with [*Hockey Night in Canada* studio host] Ron MacLean, and I don't think I said one thing that made sense. I was just babbling," Burke said, laughing at the memory.

Named Anaheim GM on June 20, 2005, Burke needed just over 23 months to rework the team into a champion.

"I used the Bill Torrey theory on how to win a championship," Burke said. Torrey was the general manager of the New York Islanders franchise that captured four Stanley Cup titles from 1980 to 1983. "I asked him once how he did it, and he said, 'You have to win four series to win a Cup, and you are going to have to have the versatility and the skill set to play four different styles,'" Burke recalled.

With that in mind, Burke said he has always tried to build his teams with the plan that they had to be big and physical enough to play in a rough-and-tumble series, quick enough to play against a "greyhound" team, savvy enough to play against a veteran team, and trained well enough to play against a team that relied heavily on a defensive system.

"The way Jiggy [Jean-Sebastien Giguere] played, we were the equal of any other team in net and then we had all of the other components," Burke said. "And obviously we spent more cap dollars on the defense than anyone else."

The Ducks hired Burke in the summer of 2005, after the NHL had lost the 2004–2005 season to a lockout. The defense he inherited from the 2003–2004 included Sandis Ozolinsh, Ruslan Salei, Keith Carney, Vitaly Visnevsky, Niclas Havelid, Martin Skoula, Lance Ward, and Todd Simpson. None of those defensemen were on his Anaheim championship squad two years later.

"When I got there, I was pleased that we had the money goaltender," Burke recalled. "That's such a huge piece of the puzzle. But I didn't trust the defense, and I thought we were a little small and passive up front."

The signing of unrestricted free-agent defenseman Scott Niedermayer was Burke's high-profile move, but Burke says it was the re-signing of Niedermayer's brother, Rob, that was actually his top priority. Although Burke presumed that having Rob committed to his program would make it easier to land Scott, he made it clear to Rob that he didn't view them as a package deal. Burke traveled to Rob's ranch in Cranbook, British Columbia, to explain how important he considered Rob's commitment.

"Our strategy was to keep Robbie, come hell and high water," Burke said. "If Scott had signed elsewhere, we still wanted Robbie, and I told Robbie that."

Burke recalled that Rob had reservations about a long-term commitment to the Ducks. "I asked him what was wrong with the team, and he told me," Burke said. "And one thing he said was that we were way too soft. And I told him, 'Give me time to address your concerns.'"

While at the 2005 draft, Burke dialed Rob Niedermayer and told him to watch TSN because he was taking the first step toward toughening up the Ducks.

Burke gave up a second-round pick to Philadelphia to acquire 250-pound tough guy Todd Fedoruk, nicknamed "Fridge." Burke told Rob Niedermayer that was just the first of several moves he would make to improve the team's grittiness. Soon, he had Rob committed, and he turned his attention to Scott.

"I called Scott and said, 'Give me your list of what is important to you,'" Burke said. "He said that he wanted to play in the Western Conference, he wanted a chance to win, some privacy away from the rink, and a chance to play with his brother. I told him, 'There is only one GM that can check off everything on [your] list.'"

On August 5, 2005, Scott Niedermayer signed for $28 million over four years.

But the Niedermayer brothers' presence wasn't enough for the Ducks to win a Stanley Cup the following season. The Ducks were knocked out in the 2006 Western Conference Finals by the Edmonton Oilers in five games.

"We could have won that series," Burke said. "Roloson was great, but the guy who beat us was Chris Pronger."

In hindsight, he also believed that the Ducks didn't yet have enough confidence that they could get past the Oilers. "But after we lost that series, the anger the players had made me believe we would be just fine," Burke said.

In the off-season, Burke asked his staff what the team needed most to win a championship. "Of the eight people I asked, six said Pronger, and two others simply said, 'Stud defenseman,'" Burke recalled. "That is why we overpaid for Pronger. I don't mind overpaying if I think it gives us a chance to win."

Initially, Burke didn't believe he had a good chance to land Pronger. "[Edmonton general manager] Kevin Lowe said to me, 'Why would I trade him in the West?' I said, 'Because I need him, and I'm going to make you an offer that you will have to take.'"

On July 3, 2006, Lowe moved Pronger to the Ducks for forwards Joffrey Lupul, defenseman Ladislav Smid, Anaheim's 2007 first-round draft pick, Anaheim's second-round pick in 2008, plus a conditional first-round pick if Anaheim reached the Stanley Cup Finals within three years. Since the Ducks won the Cup 11 months later, the Oilers received the extra first-rounder.

Burke has said repeatedly that former Anaheim GM Bryan Murray helped him considerably. Before Burke's arrival, Murray had drafted Ryan Getzlaf and Corey Perry, the team's top scorers the season the Ducks won the Cup. "We could not have concentrated the cap dollars on the back end had we not had those inexpensive guys there," Burke said.

With Pronger and Niedermayer accounting for $13 million of the total, the Ducks spent more than $16.4 million on defense.

Burke's aggressiveness also showed in the hiring of Randy Carlyle to be his head coach. Burke had to give up a second-round pick to free Carlyle from his contractual obligation to Vancouver. Carlyle was a former Norris Trophy–winning defenseman with a good reputation as a minor league coach. Carlyle was old school, sometimes gruff, always tough on his players. That meant Burke loved him.

"You want to hire a guy with integrity, balls, and brains," Burke said. "You have to be smarter than your players, or why would they listen to you? You have to have enough jam to stand up to them and curse at them and kick garbage cans at them when things are going poorly, and you have to have leadership skill. He had all of that."

Burke eventually changed the team's look up front, moving out players such as Sergei Fedorov, Petr Sykora, and others, and signing unrestricted free agent Teemu Selanne. "Teemu is a Viking," Burke said. "He's a Scandinavian conqueror. He will do anything to win or score a goal." According to Burke, what he didn't realize when he signed Selanne was the positive impact he would have on the dressing room. "What he does off the ice is remarkable," Burke said. "His success hasn't changed him one bit. He is always happy. We could lose 7–2, and the next morning he would say, 'Let's get the coffee going and go out and kick their butts tonight.' It's never a bad day for Teemu Selanne."

Scott Niedermayer was named captain, but Burke said Selanne's leadership was equally essential. "He was sunshine every day, and those kind of people are hard to find and they are important to the team," Burke said.

According to Burke, another key element of the Ducks' success was their team chemistry. "We were tighter than most people realized," Burke said. "They had lunch together almost every single day, and we didn't pay for it."

A different player paid for lunch every day—and the bills ranged from $400 for Quiznos to $700 for high-end Mexican food. "On most teams, players come out of practice and scatter to the wind, and in Anaheim they ate together," Burke said.

And some of the veterans carpooled together.

On the ice, Burke's gameplan was to acquire players who could hit and fight, and Anaheim quickly became one of the NHL's most intimidating teams. That caused an arms race in the NHL, as other teams tried to match the Ducks' toughness.

"I'm very proud of that," Burke said. "I think the Ducks changed the game for the better. The game is more North American, and I'm talking about style and not who's playing it."

The Ducks defeated the Ottawa Senators 6–2 in Game 5 on June 8, 2007, to become the first modern-day West Coast team to win the Stanley Cup. The Los Angeles Kings had been in the NHL since 1967, the Canucks since 1970, and the San Jose Sharks since 1991, but the Ducks beat them all, winning the Cup in their 14th year in the NHL. Counting the pre–World War II era, the Ducks were the third West Coast team to win the Cup, joining the 1917 Seattle Metropolitans and the 1925 Victoria (British Columbia) Cougars. Those two teams won before the NHL took charge of the Cup tournament.

Although the Ducks were in charge of the clinching game early, Burke said he didn't feel comfortable until Perry had scored the sixth goal in the third period. That's when he went down to the ice level and waited for the celebration.

As the crowd was counting down the final seconds, Burke recalls that Anaheim video coordinator Joe Trotta was in the runway behind him, and as the clock counted down, he yelled out, "And the Chiefs have won the championship of the Federal League!" It was a line from the movie *Slapshot*, and everyone, including Burke, started laughing.

Burke's time with the Stanley Cup that summer has added meaning because he was able to bring it with him when he was inducted into the British Columbia Hall of Fame on July 27.

He also had the Cup for a private party the next night for about 60 people, and he ended up with a rather famous party crasher. Burke had invited Vancouver Giants junior team owner Ron Toigo, and he brought along Gordie Howe, who was in the Vancouver area to fish.

"I was able to sit down and talk with Gordie by myself for about 30 minutes," Burke said. "It was pretty cool."

His time with the Cup was almost more meaningful to him than the night the Ducks clinched in Anaheim. Unlike most champions, Burke didn't celebrate into the wee hours of the morning. "The biggest single emotion I had was fatigue," Burke recalled. "By midnight, I told my wife, Jennifer, 'I'm exhausted and I have to go home.' I was just shot. And I felt the same way the next morning."

## Craig Patrick

*General Manager, Pittsburgh Penguins, 1991 and 1992*

Craig Patrick may not have been born to win the Stanley Cup, but genetics were on his side in his pursuit of hockey's Holy Grail.

Many NHL players have grown up reading about hockey's legends. Patrick grew up with hockey's legends frequently sitting at the dining room table. He is the grandson of Lester Patrick, one of the most storied figures in NHL history. In 1928 then 44-year-old New York Rangers coach Lester Patrick was forced to play goal in the Stanley Cup Finals when Lorne Chabot was injured. "I've heard many versions of that story, but the version I know from my family is that the New York players suggested that Lester go in the goal," Craig Patrick said.

In those days the Stanley Cup was merely the silver bowl that now serves as the head of the trophy. Lester Patrick actually took the trophy to his house one summer and stored it in his basement. Craig was told that his father, Lynn, and uncle, Muzz, played with the trophy like young boys are apt to do. "My dad and uncle scratched their names inside the bowl," Craig said. "On the underside they put their initials."

Certainly the youngsters never realized that they would someday win the Stanley Cup when they were playing for the New York Rangers in 1940. Their father, Lester, was manager of that team. As they defaced the Stanley Cup in 1928, they also couldn't have imagined they would grow up to have a son who would win the Cup as a general manager.

Although the Patrick name was synonymous with hockey for the better part of the 20th century, it was not planned or even encouraged for each generation of Patricks to follow a hockey course. "It wasn't preordained. All the kids were steered away from hockey," Patrick said. "My dad's parents told him to go be a dentist. That's what my parents told me: 'Go do something else.' They wouldn't drive me to practices or games. I had to get rides, my brother [Glenn] and I."

But all of Craig Patrick's friends and teachers could see that hockey was his passion. By simply introducing hockey to their kids, the Patrick elders had fostered an addiction. "My elementary teachers would send home notes or call home and say, 'Can you get this kid to do something else but draw hockey rinks?'" Craig remembered. "Hockey has been in my blood from the beginning."

Patrick played college hockey at the University of Denver with the idea of becoming a pro player. He made it, toiling in the NHL as a journeyman player for parts of eight seasons. He ended up playing in St. Louis in 1974–1975 where his father, Lynn, was general manager. Lynn Patrick didn't like that very much, and the decision to trade for Craig came from Lynn's bosses.

"My dad always said he would never have any of his kids play for him because of what he went through in New York [playing for Lester]," Craig said. "The Blues traded for me against his wishes, and I knew it wouldn't last long." He played 43 games for the Blues before his father dealt him to the Kansas City Scouts.

In '91 and '92 Patrick had done as much to bring a Cup to Pittsburgh as any of the players. He was a bold trader, acquiring Ron Francis and Ulf Samuelsson from Hartford in '91 as the missing pieces. In '92 he added Rick Tocchet, who was the team's leading scorer in the 1992 Finals.

No one was prouder to have won a Cup than Patrick.

"You start playing the game at a young age, and you fall in love with it," Craig said. "As early as I can remember, this has been my life. That's what I wanted to be, a player, a coach, and then into management. I'm living a dream. I feel like the luckiest person."

## Jay Feaster

*General Manager, Tampa Bay Lightning, 2004*

When Jay Feaster was growing up in the mountains of Pennsylvania, he dreamed of a career in the political arena, not the ice arena.

Feaster didn't play youth hockey in the sleepy hamlet of Williamstown, Pennsylvania, population 1,355. As a child, Feaster's only connection to the sport came when his father, the town grocer, braved treacherous wintry roads to drive his son to see the American Hockey League's Hershey Bears. Feaster learned to love the game, but his career vision was to become a lawyer, run for district attorney, and then use that office as a launch pad to win a U.S. Congressional seat. In Feaster's hometown, a city without a single traffic light, he was known as a young man with high ideals and lofty ambition.

He was well on that path when he graduated from Georgetown Law School, but his life plan was altered when his new law firm in Harrisburg

*Executive vice president and general manager Jay Feaster of the Tampa Bay Lightning holds the Stanley Cup above his head after the 2–1 victory over the Calgary Flames in Game 7 of the NHL Finals on June 7, 2004, at the St. Pete Times Forum in Tampa, Florida.* Photo courtesy of Getty Images

began doing the legal work for the Hershey Corporation. The company's holdings included hotels, an amusement park, and the Hershey Bears.

Soon, Feaster went to work directly for the company as an assistant to the president. Shortly thereafter, he received an offer that changed his life. He was asked if he wouldn't mind having "general manager of the Hershey Bears" as one of his titles.

"It took 10 seconds, maybe less, to agree to that," Feaster recalled.

He worked for one year under the Hall of Famer Frank Mathers before taking over the team himself. Originally the Bears were a

Philadelphia Flyers farm team, and they supplied all of the talent for the Hershey team. Bob Clarke was general manager in Philadelphia at the time, and Clarke, an old-school hockey guy, was not one to ask lawyer Feaster his thoughts about hockey. When Russ Farwell took over from Clarke, he was more receptive to Feaster's thoughts on players.

When Clarke came back to Philadelphia, he told Feaster the Flyers wanted out of their affiliation contract with Hershey because the Flyers would have an American Hockey League team in Philadelphia. That left Feaster scrambling to align with another NHL team. At first, Feaster thought he would be able to work out a deal with the Pittsburgh Penguins, but when that fell through, his only option seemed to be to sign a deal with the Colorado Avalanche. That wasn't very appealing to Feaster because Colorado's former affiliate team in Cornwall, Ontario, was Hershey's archrival.

"We hated them," Feaster said. "Our fans even booed their representative to the All-Star Game that year."

Fiery Bob Hartley was coaching the Cornwall team, and Hershey fans weren't fond of him, either. "Every time we played, there would be a donnybrook," Feaster said. "Even the goalies would fight. He had Garth Snow at the time, and it was pandemonium every time we played."

There was tension at the table when Hartley and Avalanche assistant general manager Francois Giguere met Feaster for breakfast to discuss the possibility of Hartley and the Cornwall players moving to Hershey.

"It was uncomfortable," Feaster said. "We almost felt like we were stuck with them because we had no other options."

Knowing he was going to have to climb in bed with the Avalanche, Feaster abruptly turned to Hartley and said, "I have one requirement. You have to promise me that every time we play Philadelphia we have to have a bench-clearing brawl just like we do now with Cornwall."

Hartley smiled. "My friend," he said, "if you pay my fines, you will never have to worry about that."

Feaster's decision to work with the Avalanche would start him down the road that led to winning the Stanley Cup in Tampa Bay.

Feaster and Hartley became close friends. Hartley is godfather to one of Feaster's children. They won a Calder Cup championship together for

Hershey in 1997. More important, Colorado general manager Pierre Lacroix began to believe in Feaster and valued his perspective about hockey matters.

"It's about that time that I started to think, *Could I do this at the NHL level?*" Feaster said. "Because I had never played the game, I would have to pay my dues. I would have to start as an assistant general manager and work my way up."

Feaster's break came when new Tampa Bay owner Art Williams gave coach Jacques Demers the added responsibility of general manager on October 10, 1998. Demers was an old-school coach with no legal background. No one knew at the time Demers was hired, but years later he admitted in his autobiography that he was illiterate. He needed what he called "a contract guy" to serve as his assistant GM.

Originally, Demers' plan was to try to lure away a prominent friend in the hockey community to come in and be a consultant. First, he asked Detroit Red Wings vice president Jimmy Devellano, who had no interest in leaving that powerhouse. He was also turned down by Phil Scheurer, who worked for the NHL.

After exhausting his list, Demers dialed Avalanche general manager Pierre Lacroix and put his problem in the form of a question: "If you lost Francois Giguere as your assistant general manager, what would you do?" Demers asked.

"I would go to Hershey and hire Jay Feaster," Lacroix said, according to Demers' recollections.

At the time, Feaster's duties in Hershey also included managing the company's soccer team, and Feaster was on the team bus when Demers reached him. Feaster still remembers the excitement in Demers' voice.

"Why aren't you in the NHL?" Demers asked.

"Because no one ever gave me a chance," Feaster said.

"Well I want to meet with you," Demers said.

They met in Tampa on a Sunday, and Demers offered Feaster the job during the interview.

By the following summer, the Lightning had been sold by Williams to Detroit Pistons owner Bill Davidson, and Rick Dudley had been installed as general manager. But Feaster was kept as his assistant general manager.

The importance of the new ownership's decision to keep Feaster wouldn't be truly understood until three years later. He played a role in blocking the trade of Vinny Lecavalier and then mediated a peace accord between Lecavalier and coach John Tortorella that eventually led to the 2004 Stanley Cup championship.

"I became general manager essentially because ownership wasn't convinced that getting rid of Lecavalier was the right thing to do," Feaster said. "Duds defaulted. He didn't try to manage the situation and threw his hands up and said, 'This will never work [between Lecavalier and Tortorella].'"

In December 2001 the relationship between Tortorella and Lecavalier was frosty on its best days and nuclear on its worst. Lecavalier didn't appreciate Tortorella's confrontational style of coaching, and Tortorella wanted Lecavalier to be a more complete, passionate player. He didn't believe that Lecavalier cared enough to become the best player he could be.

Although the friction between Tortorella and Lecavalier was significant, it wasn't uncommon for a young star to be at odds with a veteran coach. Mike Modano and coach Ken Hitchcock had issues in Dallas, and it's fair to say that coach Scotty Bowman wasn't completely happy with Steve Yzerman until Yzerman became more of a warrior in Detroit.

Dudley believed in Tortorella, and decided it was in the team's best interests to move Lecavalier. He thought their differences were irreconcilable. Team president Ron Campbell disagreed. Owner Bill Davidson came to Tampa to discuss the situation.

Feaster's recollection of that meeting was that Dudley pointed out that Lecavalier had asked to be traded. "Duds said, 'This isn't going to work, and I can get a lot for him,'" Feaster said.

Then, according to Feaster, Davidson started "rattling off" a list of requirements that had to be met before a trade could be made.

"He said that he didn't want more of the same kind of player we had," Feaster recalled. "At that time, we were very European…he wanted us tougher."

Feaster said that Davidson also wanted the team to save some money on the deal and didn't want any deal that necessitated the team taking back players with high salaries. At the end of the meeting, Davidson did authorize Dudley to "explore" trade options for Lecavalier. Feaster said that Campbell then added, "But that doesn't mean you have to trade him by the weekend."

That angered Davidson, Feaster recalled. "Don't be ridiculous, Ron, he's not going to trade him by the weekend," Davidson said.

Tom Wilson, who was Davidson's right-hand man for the Pistons, then turned to Feaster and whispered, "Don't bet against that."

Dudley was "devastated" by Davidson's list of requirements, feeling as if that handcuffed him in his ability to make the deal.

That afternoon Feaster boarded a charter for a trip to Ottawa, and by the time he landed, there was a message on his phone from Dudley: "Call the NHL, set up a conference call, I've traded Lecavalier." Before doing that, Feaster dialed Campbell to make sure he was in the loop on the deal. Campbell didn't know about the trade and ordered him not to set up the trade call until Davidson could be consulted.

According to Feaster, Campbell also said to him, "Remember who you work for here—it's Mr. Davidson who signs your check."

The meeting with Davidson came the next day. The proposed deal for Lecavalier was to Toronto in a swap that would send puck-moving defenseman Tomas Kaberle and other players to Tampa Bay. When the deal was discussed between Davidson, Dudley, Feaster, Wilson, and Campbell, it was clear that the deal didn't meet all of Davidson's requirements, and Dudley was ordered to rescind his offer.

Two months later Dudley resigned, and Feaster was named Tampa Bay's GM in February 2002. Feaster says Campbell deserves credit for keeping Lecavalier in Tampa. But it was Feaster who negotiated the peace process between Tortorella and Lecavalier. "I remember I told Mr. Davidson, 'I'm not going to try to convince you that I can for sure bring Vinny Lecavalier and Tortorella together,'" Feaster said. "'But I what I can tell you is that we have not tried to manage these two employees in a way that they can work together.'"

Essentially, Lecavalier and Feaster had been NHL rookies together, and Feaster was very comfortable in explaining and selling the idea that Lecavalier and Tortorella had to peacefully coexist. "I said I was not going to trade him on my watch and I wasn't going to fire John Tortorella," Feaster recalled.

Feaster had known Tortorella since their days in the American League, and he made the same speech to him. That's when Feaster's training as a lawyer paid off, as he made a convincing closing argument that the Lightning could be a dominant team if Lecavalier and Tortorella developed a healthy respect for each other's ability.

"Vinny had people around, and John used to call them his 'entourage,'" Feaster recalled. "He had the superstar tag from the beginning, and John always talked like Vinny needed to come back to the team, to come back to the room. And for Vinny it was a case of, 'You will never break me.'"

But once Feaster laid out his version of the law, the reluctant allies began to see value in each other. According to Feaster, Lecavalier started to see that Tortorella was simply trying to make him a better player, and Tortorella began to believe that Lecavalier did care about winning.

"One of my greatest memories is Vinny coming back after playing in Russia during the lockout and explaining why that team in Russia didn't have success. He said, 'We were a team of all-stars, but we had no chemistry and no team concept,'" Feaster said, laughing. "Those were John Tortorella's catchphrases."

Feaster's counseling efforts to save the Tortorella-Lecavalier marriage paid off in the form of a Stanley Cup in 2004. By then Lecavalier had morphed into a warrior as well as one of the league's more dynamic offensive stars. Feaster put his stamp on his team in many other ways, such as becoming a visible spokesperson and serving as a counterbalance to Tortorella's intensity. He supported Tortorella, even when ownership wanted him fired the year before the Lightning won the Cup.

"In the summer of 2003, when we lost Prospal and Torts wanted contract extensions for him and his staff, [Tortorella] was very vocal in the local media and voiced his displeasure as only he can," Feaster recalled. "Mr. Davidson phoned my boss, Ron Campbell, and told him to tell me to fire him. He said Jay doesn't have to put up with that kind of insubordination. Of course, being a manager, I wanted to manage the situation. I always had John's back, and obviously he was the right person to be coaching our team."

Just six months before the Lightning won the Stanley Cup, the team had a mini-slump, and there were people within the organization wondering whether a coaching change was in order. "I had all of my performance stats to back me up and contend that we weren't tuning Torts out but were just hitting some bad luck," Feaster said. "The stats from when we were winning in October and the stats from that losing skid were pretty close in terms of underlying fundamentals. The bottom line was that I believed in Torts."

The big personnel move that Feaster made during the season was bringing in veteran defenseman Darryl Sydor, a solidifying player for his group.

Feaster said Tortorella deserves much of the credit for their 2004 Stanley Cup, particularly for taking the correct approach after the Calgary Flames claimed a 3–2 lead in the best-of-seven Finals with Game 6 scheduled for the Calgary Saddledome.

Feaster said he was concerned, but Tortorella told him not to worry because he had developed a spin that was also a strategy. "When he talked to the media, Torts said there was no pressure on us," Feaster said. "He said, 'All of the pressure is on them. *Hockey Night in Canada*. This is what they have dreamed about their whole life. The Cup is in the building. Their fans and friends will all be there ready to celebrate. All of Canada will be watching. The prime minister will be watching.' He went on and on and on."

Maybe Tortorella was right. In Game 6, Lightning winger Marty St. Louis scored 33 seconds into double-overtime to earn Tampa Bay a 3–2 victory. In Game 7 unlikely playoff hero Ruslan Fedotenko scored twice to give Tampa Bay a 2–1 win for the Stanley Cup championship.

"What we showed in those playoffs is that we were able to play any style of hockey," Feaster said. "We had incredible skill, and we showed that against the Isles and Montreal. But we could also play a physical style when we had to, and we demonstrated that against Philly and Calgary. We could take a hit to make a play and we could hit with the best of them. Roy, Dingman, Sarich, Clymer, Cullimore, Modin, Lecavalier…they could all hit and play a physical style if needed, and all of our skill guys were able to absorb the pounding."

In the Finals Feaster said Calgary players "treated Marty St. Louis like a rodeo horse. They rode him…they didn't just hit him, but they tackled him. They would bear hug him and ride him and throw him to the ice. But he kept getting up, and the entire team kept getting up. That was a huge factor. We had skill, but we also had incredible will, and we could adapt our style to whatever the opponent gave us."

Feaster watched the game with his scouts and staff from a Lightning luxury suite, and when the game was almost over, he was urged to go quickly to the ice. But he stayed.

"I get emotional even now because I wanted to wait for my kids," Feaster said. "For my daughter, Theresa, and my son, Bobby, my two oldest children, they were really into it. They lived and died with the team. So to be able to go down on the ice with them is what I remember most."

Feaster stayed at the arena until 4:00 AM that night, and what he remembers is that his parish priest, Father Pecchi of St. Stephens, stayed at the after-party as long as he did.

There was no doubt when the Lightning won that the Stanley Cup was going to Williamstown. Feaster had moved away from his sleepy hometown, but it remained his home. When he was young, there was a factory in town, but that had closed up years ago. Everyone who lived in Williamstown worked elsewhere, except Feaster's father, who owned the local grocery store. Feaster had stocked shelves there, and it was his responsibility to refill the soda machines in the front of the store. The grocery store offered home delivery, and Feaster had also been the delivery boy.

When Feaster brought the Stanley Cup back to Williamstown, it was as if a conquering hero was returning to his people. Before Feaster brought home the Stanley Cup, the town's only claim to athletic fame was that former Cleveland Browns receiver Gary Collins, who played in the NFL in the 1960s, had come from there. A parade carried Feaster, the Stanley Cup, and his family down the main street as well-wishers waved and shouted congratulations to their favorite son.

Feaster said the favorite moment of his Williamstown day came in the morning when he was able to place the Stanley Cup on the dining room table at his grandma's seat. "I grew up at that table. My mom's parents lived exactly two houses shy of a block away from us, so I was at their place all the time," Feaster said. "Every Sunday, until I went to college, we would assemble at my grandparents' place at noon for Sunday dinner. Every Sunday! You would hear the same corny jokes, the same worn-out stories, the same complaints, the same issues...every Sunday. And I wouldn't trade it for the world."

Feaster recalled, as he was sitting around the table with his grandmother and other family members, "All I could think about is how amazed my [grandfather] would have been to see that Stanley Cup on that dining room table."

Feaster's mom died in the spring of 1997, as the Hershey Bears were in the midst of winning her son's first championship. Feaster's father had suffered a series of strokes before his mother had died. The family house was sold, and Feaster's father had moved to Mechanicsburg, Pennsylvania, to live with Feaster's sister.

"He missed Williamstown until the day he died," Feaster recalled. "So, for him to be back home in Williamstown and have all of these people coming to see the Cup, it was emotional."

Before the American Legion Post 239 opened to the public for the Stanley Cup celebration, Feaster spoke to a gathering of friends and family about his father's influence in transforming him into a hockey fan. They had made the trek to Hershey many times, on slick roads, in the dead of winter, because Jay loved the game.

Feaster had always been a poised communicator. When he was in high school and college, he was a high school football radio broadcaster and wrote football stories for the *Citizen Standard* and *Upper Dauphin Sentine* newspapers. But when he began speaking about his father, his ability to eloquently tie together words was nowhere to be seen.

"I couldn't get through it without crying." Feaster said. "Of course, my dad was crying as well. One of the things the strokes did was make him extremely emotional, and as you can imagine, the sight of the two of us crying while I hugged him, and that big silver chalice sitting there in the room with us, there weren't too many dry eyes at that point."

Feaster's final Cup moment came at St. Stephen's Church in Riverview, Florida. While the Lightning were winning a title, Feaster's wife, Anne, was pregnant with their son, Kevin. When he was born in November, the Feasters asked for and received permission to use the Stanley Cup as his baptismal font.

# chapter 3

# Championship Stories, 1928–1983

## Bill Stewart
*Coach, Chicago Blackhawks, 1938*

Major League Baseball umpire Bill Stewart clearly made the right call when he agreed in the summer of 1937 to become coach of the Chicago Blackhawks.

Massachusetts native Stewart was also an NHL referee, but it was his performance behind the plate during a game at Wrigley Field that prompted showy Blackhawks owner Major Frederic McLaughlin to offer him the job. McLaughlin was at a game and had witnessed a verbal joust between Stewart and St. Louis Cardinals manager Frankie Frisch over balls and strikes.

When Stewart's forceful threat of ejection prompted Frisch to slink back to the dugout, McLaughlin supposedly said, "Anyone who is tough enough to handle Frankie Frisch is tough enough to handle my team."

McLaughlin agreed to pay Stewart $6,500 per season for two years, and gave in on Stewart's demand that McLaughlin not interfere with his personnel decisions. That was almost a deal-breaker for McLaughlin, who liked to tinker with his team.

But McLaughlin wanted Stewart's toughness behind the bench, and perhaps more important, he wanted Stewart's citizenship. The season before, McLaughlin had hatched the idea of bringing in American players to turn the Blackhawks into the "Chicago Yankees." McLaughlin's logic was that bringing in a respected American to coach would add a layer of legitimacy to his plan. McLaughlin wanted to be known as an innovator, not a circus ringmaster.

What Stewart didn't tell McLaughlin was that he didn't think much of McLaughlin's "All-American" gameplan.

"He believed that if you could play, you could play, and it didn't matter where you were from," said Stewart's grandson, Paul, who played in the NHL and then became an NHL referee.

But by coincidence or not, Stewart did end up with a roster made up of roughly 50 percent American-born players. Goaltender Mike Karakas, forwards Roger Jenkins, Elwin "Doc" Romnes, Carl Voss, Louis Trudel, Virgil Johnson, and Cully Dahlstrom, plus defenseman Alex Levinsky were all born in the United States—although Trudel, Levinsky, Jenkins, and Voss had spent much of their younger days in Canada.

Stewart's tough-love coaching style didn't magically transform the Blackhawks into an overnight sensation. The Blackhawks posted a 14–27–7 mark in 1937–1938, and they were only two points better under Stewart's command. But those two points were enough to get the final playoff spot, ahead of the Detroit Red Wings.

What happened in the 1938 playoffs was one of the most remarkable team transformations in NHL history.

The Blackhawks had ended the regular season by losing their final five games while being outscored 24–5. The best-of-three first round of the playoffs began as expected, with Chicago losing 6–4 to the Canadiens in the Montreal Forum. But Karakas then shut out the Canadiens 4–0 in Chicago, and then the Blackhawks stunned the Canadiens 3–2 in Game 3 in Montreal, winning the series on Paul Thompson's overtime goal.

The second round against the New York Americans followed a similar script, with Chicago losing the first game in New York and then wrapping up the three-game series by winning at home and taking the clinching game on the road.

Even after posting two series upsets, Stewart's Blackhawks weren't expected to be a test for Conn Smythe's Toronto Maple Leafs. The Maple Leafs had advanced to the best-of-five Stanley Cup Finals by sweeping the Boston Bruins, who had been the NHL's best regular-season team in 1937–1938.

*Before and after leading the Chicago Blackhawks to the most improbable Stanley Cup championship in NHL history as the team's coach in 1938, Bill Stewart worked as a Major League Baseball umpire. In this August 1941 photograph, Stewart (center) is about to eject the Brooklyn Dodgers' argumentative manager, Leo Durocher, from a game against the Cubs in Chicago.*

To make the situation worse for the Blackhawks, goalkeeper Karakas of Eveleth, Minnesota, had suffered a broken toe in the series against the Americans, and doctors said it was unlikely that Karakas would be able to start the series, although he kept insisting that he was willing to try to play with the pain.

Stewart had his own plan. In that era, NHL rules weren't as buttoned up as they are today, and Stewart arranged to borrow New York Rangers goalie Davey Kerr, who had led the NHL with eight shutouts in 1937–1938. But Smythe was a major-league power broker at that time, and he had developed his own script for how the Blackhawks' goaltending drama should play out.

Smythe believed that the Blackhawks should receive no advantage because of Karakas' injury and allegedly claimed that the Blackhawks should be forced to use the hobbled Karakas or a journeyman goalie named Alfie Moore, 33, of the Pittsburgh Hornets.

The newspaper accounts of the time offer a vivid description of what happened before the opening game of the Finals, and the Stewart family has provided other details, based on conversations with Bill before he died in 1964.

"We get to the Gardens, and Moore walks in to tell us that he's been ordered to play," Stewart told reporters after the game.

Moore didn't have a sterling reputation with NHL players, having failed a tryout with the New York Americans the previous season. The story passed down through the years is that when Trudel saw that Moore was going to be his netminder, he said, "Why didn't you break your leg in Pittsburgh?"

Stewart didn't accept the news graciously. He went looking for someone in the Maple Leafs organization and came first upon assistant general manager Frank Selke, who informed him that the league had decided that Kerr couldn't play.

"You're a liar!" Stewart reportedly shouted at Selke.

The commotion brought many folks hurrying to the scene, including the highly combustible Smythe, who shouted, "You can't call my pal Selke a liar and get away with it!"

According to Paul Stewart, "It was like the battle of Lexington and Concord, and you really didn't know who shot first."

But punches were thrown. Maple Leafs scout Baldy Cotton, Smythe, and Selke were involved in the scuffle and the arguing, along with Stewart and other Blackhawks officials.

The Blackhawks' displeasure with Moore's presence in their net grew exponentially when he surrendered a goal on the first shot he faced.

But the charmed existence that the Blackhawks had known in the first two rounds continued into the Finals. Moore played the finest game of his career and didn't give up another goal as Chicago won Game 1.

Mysteriously, Commissioner Frank Calder then decided that Moore was ineligible because he was under contract with another team. Now the Blackhawks were told that they would have to use farmhand Paul Goodman, who had played in Wichita that season. The screaming between Stewart and the Maple Leafs started anew, because Stewart clearly believed that Smythe's influence had contributed to Calder's ruling.

The Maple Leafs hammered Goodman 5–1, and it looked like the natural order was going to return to the NHL playoffs.

In the second game, the Maple Leafs had also declared war on the Blackhawks. Several of the Blackhawks had been sliced open by Toronto sticks, and a vicious Toronto body check had damaged Dahlstrom's knee. Also, Toronto's Red Horner had used the butt-end of his stick to break Romnes' nose in three places. Romnes acquired a Purdue football helmet to protect his injury for Game 3 in Chicago.

Chicago newspapers, with McLaughlin's urging and cooperation, had published a photo of all of the injured Blackhawks at the hospital.

McLaughlin wasn't trying to incite a riot, just more ticket sales.

The Blackhawks announced that all patrons for Game 3 would be frisked at the doors of Chicago Stadium to prevent them from carrying in objects that could be hurled at the Maple Leafs.

With the spotlight clearly on the game, a record crowd of 18,042 showed up for Game 3, some to hurl insults and beer cups at the Maple Leafs and others just to see what was going to happen that night.

Those fans who came to see violence got their money's worth. Romnes had won the Lady Byng Trophy in 1936 as the NHL's most gentlemanly player, but he came into Game 3 with vengeance in his heart and bloodshed in his plans.

In his first shift of the game, Romnes went after Horner with his stick. The Toronto media reported that he clubbed Horner, and the Chicago media reported that Romnes missed him and that Horner fainted at the attempt. Stewart's son, also named Bill, who was at the game, said in a 1999 interview that his dad said that Romnes "just tweaked his nose, kind of clipped him."

Romnes wasn't finished. Although he weighed just 160 pounds, he leveled Toronto defenseman Harvey Jackson, who outweighed him by 40 pounds. To add insult to the injuries that Romnes inflicted upon Toronto, he scored the game-winning goal.

The physical damage the Maple Leafs suffered that night wasn't severe, but mentally they may have been crippled by the Blackhawks' aggressiveness. In Game 4 the Maple Leafs were no match for the Blackhawks, who won 4–1 to clinch the improbable championship.

"It was the roughest, wildest series I ever saw," Levinsky said years later. "The games were completely out of control, and everyone skated around with their sticks high in the air."

Stewart, carried off the ice by his players, was recognized as the first American-trained coach to win the Stanley Cup. Though Hall of Famer Leo Danderand, coach of the 1924 Montreal Canadiens, was born in Illinois, he wasn't considered a true American because his family had moved to Canada when he was a boy.

Still today the 1937–1938 Blackhawks are the only NHL team to win the Stanley Cup after posting a losing record in the regular season.

In 2006 the Chicago Rush of the Arena Football League took a 7–9 record into the playoffs and then won the Arena Bowl to become the first pro sports team in the U.S. since the 1937–1938 Blackhawks to turn a losing regular season into a championship.

Stewart didn't have much time in Chicago to savor his championship. McLaughlin's meddling was always a source of tension, and Stewart was fired by January of the following season. He returned to major league umpiring and officiated in four World Series (1937, 1943, 1948, and 1953). He was also the home-plate umpire for Johnny Vander Meer's second consecutive no-hitter in 1938. But in the hockey world, he was the mastermind of the most significant championship upset in NHL history.

How improbable was the Blackhawks' rise? When the playoffs started, Levinsky was so convinced that the Blackhawks' appearance would be short-lived that he gave up his Chicago apartment and sent his wife home to Toronto. He spent the entire 1937–1938 playoff run living out of the backseat of his car.

## Murray Murdoch

*New York Rangers, 1928 and 1933*

When then–general manager Conn Smythe first sent Murray Murdoch a telegram in 1926, inviting him to join the fledgling New York Rangers, all he accomplished at first was to make Marie Murdoch suspicious of her husband.

"My wife wanted to know who the hell this Connie Smythe was and why she was inviting me to New York," Murdoch said.

When Murdoch died in 2001, he was 96, and he was believed to be the NHL's oldest living Stanley Cup winner.

He had earned his place in hockey championship lore as a member of the 1927–1928 Rangers. Murdoch had actually moved from the University of Manitoba to Manhattan to join the first-year Rangers team in 1926, right after he and Smythe worked out what seemed like high finances in those days. According to Murdoch's memory, he had Smythe meet him in Minnesota, where Murdoch was playing senior hockey. "He showed up and put 15 $100 bills out there, figuring a small-time boy would be impressed."

Murdoch didn't take Smythe's first bonus offer, although they came to terms soon afterward, and Murdoch ended up playing 11 seasons for the Rangers. To bring his historical significance into context, consider that Murdoch was playing hockey in New York when Babe Ruth wowed the world by smashing 60 home runs during the 1927 season, and he was there in 1929 when the stock market crashed and America plunged into the Great Depression.

"Hockey was well covered in the newspapers back then," Murdoch said by phone from his home in Hamden, Connecticut, a year before he died. "We drew very well. But it was sort of a high-class game in those days. The average public hadn't taken it up. It was a prep school game."

When this interview was conducted in 2000, Murdoch apologized for not recalling all the details of the Rangers' 1928 championship series against the Montreal Maroons or the 1933 series against the Toronto Maple Leafs, and yet his memory of those years was remarkable. He recalled clearly the now-famous Game 2 in which 44-year-old coach Lester Patrick, grandfather of current Pittsburgh Penguins general manager Craig Patrick, had to enter the game to play goal when starter Lorne Chabot suffered an eye injury. During his playing days, Patrick had been a defenseman, not a goaltender. The Rangers were down 1–0 in the series when Chabot was hurt and couldn't afford a loss in the second game.

"They wouldn't give us a goaltender," Murdoch said. "And Lester would play some goal for us in practice, so he decided to go into the net. We didn't have assistant coaches, so some of the [general] managers from the other teams came down to help behind the bench. [Detroit's] Jack Adams was one of them."

The Rangers ended up winning that game 2–1 in overtime on Frank Boucher's goal. "We tried to protect Lester the best we could, but they were shooting long shots at him, and he was stopping them," Murdoch said, recalling that the Rangers defense also tried to block as many shots.

That game was played in Montreal. In fact, every game in that series was played in Montreal because the circus was booked in Madison Square Garden. The circus always took precedence over hockey, even in the playoffs—a tradition that lasted into the 1970s. Clowns and elephants had priority over wingers and defensemen in a ranking that wasn't close.

"You have to remember that the Garden was built for the circus and boxing," said Murdoch. "If you were at the top gallery on the side—unless you were in the first or second row—you couldn't see the complete rink. It was set up to see the center of the circus ring. We knew the circus took over for a month. That was one of the big events of the Garden. Six-day bicycle racing was another big event in the Garden."

Murdoch was a speedy, defensive-minded winger who was often assigned to shadow the other team's top scorers. He often infuriated opposing players because of his knack for covering them as if he were tethered to their torsos. He lined up against all the great players of that era, including Howie Morenz. ("He was a terrific skater, very, very fast," Murdoch said.) Murdoch's longevity seemed apropos, considering that in the 1920s and 1930s he was considered one of the NHL's most durable athletes. He didn't miss a game during his NHL career, compiling a league record of 508 consecutive games that lasted until Johnny Wilson broke it on March 21, 1959.

Murdoch's memory of the 1928 celebration was a little hazy, although he did remember meeting New York Mayor Jimmy Walker. At that point, the Stanley Cup was already 30 years old. "Funny that I don't even remember seeing the Cup," Murdoch said.

He ended up winning the Stanley Cup again in 1933, and he remembered that.

"You never remember all the wonderful plays," he said, laughing. "All I seem to remember is the mistakes I made."

## Clint Smith

*New York Rangers, 1940*

When the New York Rangers won the 1940 Stanley Cup championship at Maple Leaf Gardens, they were acknowledged with a round of silence.

"That's the way it was in those days in Toronto and Montreal," remembered Clint Smith, before he died in 2009. "When they scored, fans would raise the roof two or three inches, and when we scored, you could hear a pin drop."

This was a romantic period in hockey history when fans came to games wearing their Sunday best, and NHL contests were considered high-class entertainment. "When I first got [to the NHL], fans used to come in tuxedos," Smith remembered. "It wasn't unusual to see top hats."

To win a Stanley Cup in a hockey mecca like Toronto added another level of distinction to an already glorious event. Smith doesn't recall the Stanley Cup trophy being central to the Rangers' celebration after Bryan Hextall had scored in overtime to down the Maple Leafs 3–2 in the deciding sixth game. What he remembers is that team president John Reed Kilpatrick, called "General Kilpatrick" by players, came into the dressing room. That probably added as much distinction to the event as did the venue.

"I had never seen General Kilpatrick in the dressing room before," Smith recalled. "He said we were going to have a party at the Royal York Hotel. He said he wanted everybody there. It was like an order, and we obeyed."

Word must have spread around town about the Rangers' party because the room was jammed with bodies, including members of the

*Members of the New York Rangers pose with the Stanley Cup, which they won by defeating the Toronto Maple Leafs 3–2 in Toronto on April 13, 1940. Standing in the center is Rangers coach and manager Lester Patrick; in front of him is NHL president Frank Calder.*

Maple Leafs' team, plus a multitude of gate-crashing people that no one on the Rangers' organization even recognized.

"General Kilpatrick came up to Muzz Patrick and said, 'If I was a younger man, I would take a few of these bottles [of scotch and whiskey] up to my room for later. It won't be long before they are all gone.'"

Smith and Patrick didn't need to be told twice; they squirreled away several bottles for safekeeping. The Rangers' celebrating went well into the night, and it was a haggard looking group of players that trudged across the street to the train station the next morning for their 7:00 AM departure. Given that it was a Sunday, players undoubtedly presumed they would sleep their way back to Manhattan in a no-alcohol environment. They were wrong.

"Everyone had a little hangover," Smith said. "Things were pretty dull. Muzz was the first to bring out one of our bottles. He just wanted to liven things up."

By the time the train chugged into New York, the Rangers' celebration had reached the same level of enthusiasm that had been accomplished the night before in Toronto. "I don't think we had enough liquor left on the train to fill one bottle when we got back," Smith said.

On the train, players talked about making a run at a string of championships. The team was overflowing with dependable, team-oriented players such as Hextall, Babe Pratt, Alex Shibicky, Art Coulter, goalkeeper Dave Kerr, plus Muzz and Lynn Patrick, who had matched their father's accomplishment by getting their name on the Cup. The consensus on the party train that day was these Rangers would win again and again. "I thought we would win two or three more," Smith recalled.

What no one knew that day is that the world would soon realize that Adolf Hitler and Japanese imperialism needed to be stopped, and several of the Rangers would end up in the military. And no one could have dreamed on that day that it would be 54 years before the Rangers would again become champions.

Smith, making about $6,000 to play in those days, recalls that the players received $1,250 from the NHL for winning the Stanley Cup, and the Madison Square Garden corporation "magnanimously" chipped in another $500. But he insists the joke was on the Garden. "We would have played for nothing back then," Smith said.

## Max McNab
*Detroit Red Wings, 1950*

Max McNab can be forgiven for believing that his job security on the Detroit Red Wings always boiled down to how ornery general manager Jack Adams was feeling on any particular day.

With World War II taking two years out of his career, McNab had only played about 20 junior games and part of one season with the Omaha Knights in the United States Hockey League before he was called up by the Detroit Red Wings in 1947. He was a lanky and raw 23-year-old when he played his first game at Olympia Stadium. "I wasn't a guy who played with tremendous confidence," he admits now.

It certainly didn't bolster his confidence that Adams always threatened his players with a demotion after a loss. In 1950 McNab can remember Adams bellowing, "Those kids in Oshawa, [Alex] Delvecchio and [Lou] Jankowski, are going great in Oshawa. Gawd damn it, they are going to be ready! They are burning up the OHA."

McNab was a role player for the Red Wings in that era and lasted parts of four seasons. He killed penalties with Marty Pavelich and served as the understudy for Hall of Fame center Sid Abel, who was the center on the famed Production Line. By 1950 Abel was a 32-year-old playing on a line with a 25-year-old and a 22-year-old.

Ted Lindsay and Gordie Howe were such finely honed physical specimens that they could play 90 seconds without losing their wind. Abel would play more than a minute. "Then I would clean up the last 20 or 25 seconds," McNab remembered. "I would watch the puck cross in front of my nose between Lindsay and Howe."

He learned from watching Abel. "Sid never blew his own horn, but he always knew everything that was going on out on the ice," said McNab. "He took those two kids, Howe and Lindsay, and made them a unit. Sid really couldn't skate with those guys, but he was an engineer. He knew where to go and how to get there. He directed traffic."

With only six teams in the NHL and a host of talented players in the junior and minor leagues, it didn't take McNab long to decide that playing in the league was a privilege. "There were five regular superstars on every team who were irreplaceable," McNab recalled. "The rest of the roster spots went to whoever worked the hardest."

That's why a half-century later McNab still feels honored to have played for the Red Wings when they won the 1950 Stanley Cup championship.

"When you are playing, you really don't understand the impact nationwide," McNab said. "All the people in my hometown of Watson, Saskatchewan, never slept because they got the game on the radio. But I remember the night we won the Cup, it was like a crazy dream."

During a 1999 interview, he recalled the party at the Book Cadillac, including odd details like the fact that the beer-drinking hockey players arrived to find that only champagne was available to drink. "Everyone was totally fatigued, and we were dehydrated," McNab remembered, chuckling. "You couldn't quench your thirst. Guys were popping champagne. Guys got horribly sick. It was an awful night."

But he made it clear that it was really a wondrous evening. He remembers Red Wings scout Carson Cooper sitting at the head of the table poking fun at players who started to show signs of inebriation. "He was joking that the young guys didn't know how to drink," McNab said. "He sat there for a long time and never got up. When he did get up, he just hit the deck. He was out like a light."

As players said good-bye at the "break-up party" a couple days later, McNab said it was a very emotional parting. As a fringe player, McNab had taught himself never "to look beyond the next week when I was with the big club." He certainly knew it was possible that he might not be back in the NHL, but he probably wouldn't have guessed that he would never play another regular-season game in an NHL uniform.

"It's like being in the service," McNab said. "You get close, and then you say good-bye and there are some tears. And everyone says there's going to be reunions and people are going to keep in touch forever. Everyone is going to write. Then everyone gets dispersed all over the country and everyone gets caught up in their own problems. That's the same with a hockey break-up party. For the stars it was like another day at the office. Most of us left there not knowing what the future would hold for us."

The following season Glen Skov won the job that McNab had owned; McNab was demoted to the American Hockey League, where he spent the entire season. He did get into two playoff games with the big club. A back injury dashed his hopes of joining the Chicago Blackhawks the following season, and he ended up spending the rest of his career as a star in the Western Hockey League. He didn't get back to the NHL until he became general manager of the Washington Capitals. He also later served as general manager of the New Jersey Devils.

McNab was earning about $6,000 a season during his NHL career, and his playoff share in 1950 was about half that. In that era players didn't get championship rings.

In 1983 his two young granddaughters, Shanon and Robyn, brought him a present from his family. He opened it up, and it was an NHL championship ring. His son, David (now Anaheim's assistant general manager), had come up with the idea and convinced family members to participate. David had gotten the NHL's cooperation to make sure the ring was like today's championship ring. It included the scores from the 1950 championship games. "It brought tears to my eyes," McNab said.

Shortly thereafter he ran into Tommy Ivan, who had been coach of that team. "My, that's a fantastic ring," Ivan said. "Is it your college ring?"

Impishness took over. "No, it's my Red Wings' championship ring," McNab said. "Didn't you get one?"

McNab died on September 2, 2007, a few months after helping his son, David, celebrate his first Stanley Cup championship in Anaheim.

## Larry Zeidel

*Detroit Red Wings, 1952*

Hanging on the wall of Larry Zeidel's office for many years was a framed copy of a *Hockey News* article that includes legendary Red Wings general manager Jack Adams saying that the 1951–1952 Stanley Cup championship squad was the best team he had in Detroit. Adams had coached three Red Wings teams to Stanley Cup titles in the 1940s and was GM of four Detroit championship teams in the 1950s.

"He complimented the team by saying that we could have played without a coach because there was no jealousy on the team—everyone on the team had a role," recalled Zeidel, who was a rookie on the 1951–1952 squad.

That Red Wings team lost only 14 of 70 games that regular season and only gave up 1.9 goals per game. In the playoffs the Red Wings swept Toronto and Montreal and were miserly in their defensive prowess. Terry Sawchuk had a 0.63 goals-against average, and that probably reflected Detroit's relentless checking as much as Sawchuk's brilliance.

"Offense wins games, and defense wins championships," Zeidel said. "We would practice blocking shots. We would shoot pucks at each other and learn how to handle the fakes."

According to Zeidel, the Red Wings' philosophy was always to have one defenseman cover the front of the net. Zeidel received his chance to play early in the season because Leo Reise was hurt, and he was brought in to play in the playoffs because Reise and Red Kelly were both nursing injuries.

As a young player, Zeidel made sure he stayed in front of his own net every time he was on the ice. "And when I would get back to the bench, the guys would be patting me on the back and yelling, 'Way to cover the front of the net, Larry!'" Zeidel said. "It was like I had just scored a goal."

When it came to leadership, Adams was a dictator who believed that champions were molded by personal discipline and commitment to embracing whatever was necessary to win. Above all, Adams would say, he wanted his players, no matter where they were playing in the organization, to have pride. "He always talked about pride," Zeidel said. "I remember he said, 'People say we are the New York Yankees of hockey. Well, do you want to know something, I think the Yankees are the Detroit Red Wings of baseball. We are a Big Red Machine.'"

Adams would compare his team to a finely tuned machine, and he would compare each player to a part on the machine. He was also like an army drill sergeant, always gruff and usually barking at someone to do something better. "He would be behind the bench, and he would be yelling to get some player off the ice," Zeidel said. "He was an intense guy."

When Zeidel first came to training camp, the younger players, including Zeidel, would actually sleep in the spare dressing rooms. "It was really like going to the Marine boot camp at Parris Island to learn the warrior attitude," Zeidel said. One morning, Adams had paused to get some coffee near the Detroit dressing room and saw Zeidel taking a swig of water in between training sessions. According to Zeidel, Adams started screaming at him. "What are you doing?!" Adams bellowed. "Your stomach is a furnace and you are putting water in your furnace!"

Even later in Zeidel's career, he would only rinse out his mouth with water in a game. "And if I would have a bad shift, I would say, 'I shouldn't have had that water,'" Zeidel said.

Even when Adams wasn't around, his presence was felt because team captain Sid Abel followed the party line when it came to toughening up the Red Wings. Abel would call a team meeting, and according to Zeidel, his speech would always carry an underlying theme that hockey was "war on ice" and that players needed to play through the injuries. "Boys, don't ever give the opposition the satisfaction of knowing they hurt you," Abel would say. "Don't lay on the ice. Get up and get back to the bench." Zeidel recalls that when players went to the trainer or the doctor, there would be suggestions "that they were a hypochondriac."

When the Red Wings would show up for a road game and the crowd hadn't yet been allowed in the building, Abel would pause before entering the dressing room and look out over the vacant sheet of ice. "Boys," he would say, "there is going to be a war out there tonight, and there is nowhere out there to hide."

Zeidel always thought Abel sounded like the late actor Walter Brennan when he did that. If the game wasn't going the way Abel liked it to go, it would be Abel, not coach Tommy Ivan, who laid down the law. "What the hell is going on here?" Abel would say. "The bench is dead." That would prompt everyone on the bench to start yelling, and encouraging their teammates.

"If one of our players would get knocked down, someone would yell, 'Give 'em the lumber!'" Zeidel said.

A well-known storyteller, Zeidel has talked about that phrase so often that, if he walks into a tavern today in Philadelphia, where he lives, someone he knows is likely to ask him to say, "Give 'em the lumber."

The 1951–1952 team had superstars such as Gordie Howe, Ted Lindsay, Red Kelly, and Sawchuk, but Zeidel still believes that what separated this team from other championship teams was their commitment to the less glamorous chores of the sport. "Gordie Howe would attack, then he would bust his butt to get back to get a hit in, and they knew it, and they would be looking over their shoulder," Zeidel said.

Although Lindsay, Abel, and Howe received the attention as the top line, on some nights it was the other lines that did the work. "Tony Leswick was a pest, and he didn't care if you were eight feet tall," Zeidel said. "Marty Pavelich didn't want to be on the ice when the other team scored a goal.... Marcel Pronovost could really motor. He could motor as good as Bobby Orr. He could go through the whole team sometimes." He recalls Red Kelly was an iron man, rarely coming off the ice. "He might have played between 40 and 50 minutes," Zeidel said. "He would turn purple and blue, sucking in wind, trying to catch his breath on the bench."

Injuries to Leo Reise and Red Kelly had given Zeidel his opportunity to play in the playoffs, but he was knocked out of the lineup in the

Finals by a freak injury. In those days, coaches didn't like players to have pucks on the ice before practice because they believed players would injure themselves. But someone would sneak one puck on the ice, and that was the case in Montreal before the second game of the Finals.

"We were all fighting for that one puck, and I happened to have it at that time," Zeidel said. Leswick went to lift Zeidel's stick, and missed the stick and struck Zeidel in the eye. "When Tommy Ivan came out for practice, I looked, and he had two heads," Zeidel said. "In fact, everyone on the ice had two heads. I had double vision. I couldn't hide that."

He couldn't play the rest of the Finals, but 56 years later he still feels like a contributor to that team because of the Red Wings' team philosophy. "They preached guts in Detroit, and that helps me still to this day," Zeidel said. "They preached a winning attitude."

The following season Zeidel played only nine games for the Red Wings and then was traded to the Chicago Blackhawks before the 1953–1954 season. He didn't play another NHL playoff game until 1967–1968 when he was playing for the expansion Philadelphia Flyers.

He still lives in the Philadelphia area, and people know him from his Flyers days. They are surprised to hear that he still feels like a Red Wing because he won a championship there. "The funny thing is that people say, 'You won the Cup. Where's your ring?'" Zeidel said.

There were no championship rings or celebratory parades in those days. Zeidel only received a commemorative plate and a miniature replica of the Stanley Cup. There wasn't even a pat on the back from Adams. Zeidel recalls the day after the Red Wings won in 1952, Adams was quoted in the morning newspaper as saying, "We won't stand pat. There will be changes next year."

Fifty-seven years after that championship, in January 2009, Zeidel received a surprise gift from the Red Wings. It was a 1952 championship ring. Now Zeidel has proof to go along with his memories.

## Vic Stasiuk
*Detroit Red Wings, 1952, 1954, and 1955*
Right wing Vic Stasiuk played 14 seasons in the NHL, and the toughest fight he ever faced was trying to stay in the Detroit Red Wings' lineup from 1950 to 1955. He won three Stanley Cup titles with the Red Wings

in those years, and his stiffest opposition often came in practice. The Red Wings of that era are generally regarded among the most impressive teams in NHL history.

"It was hard to play for the Red Wings in those years, but I kept trying," Stasiuk said. "We had a lot of good players, and we didn't use many of them. The Red Wings were a two-line team."

The top line was the power line of Ted Lindsay, Gordie Howe, and whoever was getting a tryout at that time. "We must have tried a dozen players to fill Sid Abel's spot after he went to Chicago [in 1952–1953]," Stasiuk said. The second line was Marty Pavelich, Glen Skov, and Tony Leswick, and they served as the checking line against the opponent's top line.

"There were four or five us trying to play on the third line, but we seldom saw the ice," Stasiuk said. He was playing quite a bit for the Chicago Blackhawks when the Red Wings acquired him in 1950, but he didn't see the ice for his first 13 games in a Red Wings' sweater. "They had so many good players," Stasiuk said. "They had a guy named Metro Prystai, and I played against him in junior hockey, and if they would have had a draft back then, he would have been the No. 1 pick."

Stasiuk recalls that the Red Wings in that era had such a mystique that his minor league buddies would quiz him incessantly about his experiences when he would come back down after a stint in the NHL. "In training camp, we had a player named Ching Johnson, and he would ask, 'How is it playing up there in the NHL?' Then he would say, 'If I could just play one game with Gordie Howe, I could die happy,'" Stasiuk recalled. Stasiuk was intimidated by Howe's physique and conditioning level to the point that when he arrived in Detroit he joined the YMCA just to get extra work in every day.

According to Stasiuk, Lindsay was "the greatest captain you could ever hope to have. He was a skill guy down the left side and he had a snarl when he talked to you. He always complimented me.… He would say, 'You've got a good shot. Use the goddamn thing.'"

What also set the Red Wings apart from other teams, according to Stasiuk, was Terry Sawchuk's presence in net. "He would have been something to watch if we would have had these shootouts back when we were playing," Stasiuk said. "Back then, Terry would do [breakaway contests] only if you put a case of beer on the line. Then he would be great. If I got one out of 10 against him, it would be lucky. If I got two out of 10, it would be cause for celebration."

Sawchuk was moody, and not always the easiest teammate to be around, but he might have been the most confident goalkeeper in the NHL. "He would say, "Get me a goal, and I might get you a point. Give me two goals, and I guarantee you a point. If you get me three goals, I guarantee you a win," Stasiuk recalled.

In 1952 Stasiuk did play for the Red Wings in the postseason, even appearing in three games in the Finals against Montreal. In 1953–1954

*Goalie Terry Sawchuk is lifted by teammates Vic Stasiuk (right) and Marcel Pronovost (left) after he shut out the Montreal Canadiens 6–0 to give the Detroit Red Wings the NHL championship in Detroit on March 21, 1955. Sawchuk won the Vezina Trophy and $1,000. The star of the game was Ted Lindsay (left of Pronovost), who notched a hat trick.*

Stasiuk played 42 of Detroit's 70 regular-season games and hence qualified as a NHL champion that season, even though he was in the minors for the playoffs. In 1955 he was a significant playoff contributor with five goals and three assists over 11 games. He had three goals and three assists in the Finals against Montreal. "I loved playing in Detroit, and when I was traded to Boston in 1955, I cried," Stasiuk said. He was 26 when he was dealt to Boston, and he quickly developed into one of the NHL's most proficient scorers, playing on the "Uke Line" with left wing John Bucyk and center Bronco Horvath. They earned the nickname because they were all of Ukrainian heritage.

In 1957–1958 the trio became the first NHL line to boast three 20-goal scorers in a single season. The forgotten story about that trio is that all three forwards were with the Red Wings organization and almost ended up playing together for Detroit against Montreal in Game 7 of the 1955 Stanley Cup Finals. Stasiuk was already playing and was surprised when Horvath and Bucyk showed up at the team hotel in Toledo, Ohio. Horvath informed Stasiuk that the three of them were going to play together against the Canadiens. "I couldn't sleep that night…. I was excited about playing with that line," Stasiuk said. "But when we got to Olympia, their sweaters weren't hanging up. As it turned out, they weren't able to play because they would not have been eligible to play for the Edmonton Oilers in the Dominion Cup if they played in that game."

Would history have been different had the Red Wings seen the Uke Line together in the 1955 Finals? "I don't think the Uke Line would have stayed together long enough to make the point the way [general manager] Jack Adams operated," Stasiuk said. "You were never going to break up the Howe and Lindsay pairing, and Pavelich and Skov were the checking line."

## Doug Risebrough
*Montreal Canadiens, 1976–1979*
*Assistant Coach, Calgary Flames, 1989*
Legendary coach Toe Blake retired after the 1967–1968 season, but he shared in the Montreal Canadiens' postseason successes into the 1970s.

Doug Risebrough says a big part of the Canadiens' 1970s Cup celebrations was the ritual of taking the Stanley Cup to the Toe Blake Tavern the day after it had been reclaimed. Blake had won eight Stanley Cup championships as coach of the Canadiens, and players honored his success by bringing him the Cup first. It was like schoolboys showing off their accomplishments to their favorite teacher.

"He had a back room that was full of old hockey pictures," Risebrough remembered. "We would get there around noon, even if we had been up half the night celebrating. Toe would be sitting at a table or desk, and we would talk hockey, laugh, joke, discuss the playoffs for three, four, five, six hours. Toe could reflect back on eight Stanley Cups. There was always a great reflection upon the history of the team. Toe would laugh, 'I can tell you another story about that.' And he would."

Everyone came to Toe's Tavern for a bonding session that none of them has ever forgotten. It was in Toe's Tavern that players truly understood what it meant to be a member of the Canadiens' grand tradition. It was in the tavern that the past was brought together with the present. It was in that tavern that the Stanley Cup took on an even greater meaning, if that was possible.

After spending the afternoon at Toe's Tavern, the party was shifted to Henri Richard's bar. "If anyone had Cup stories to tell, it was Henri," Risebrough said. "He won 11 of them."

A five-time winner himself, Risebrough found that his awareness of the experience grew each time he added another title. "After you have won the Cup a couple of times, you start to feel more happy for everyone who can share it with you," he said. "Your family, who watched you grow up in hockey, your neighbors, the people around the rink. The Cup is something that glues people together. You just can't believe how much a championship cements your relationship with the guys."

It would be difficult for Risebrough to say that he enjoyed one Stanley Cup experience more than another, although he will say that serving as an assistant coach for the Calgary Flames in their championship run in 1989 wasn't the same as winning the Cup as a player.

"I couldn't believe the satisfaction of being involved in a Cup as a member of the management of the team," Risebrough said. "There weren't many of us in Calgary who had the experience of winning before. We were trying to tell people what it was like to be a first-time winner. I can remember people saying to me that it was exactly as I had described

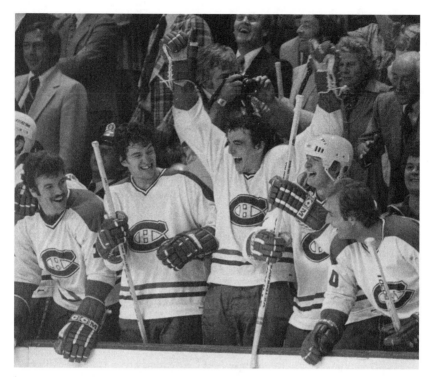

*Canadiens players (from left: Yvon Lambert, Doug Risebrough, Mario Tremblay, Pierre Mondou, and Guy Lafleur) celebrate on the bench as their team defeats the New York Rangers 4–1 to win the Stanley Cup in Montreal on May 22, 1979.*

it to them. As a player, you are thinking, *If I do my job, I will be fine.* But when you are in coaching, you are trying to work through people. You are trying to motivate people in tough times. You are hard on people in tough times. You are trying to instill confidence in some who don't have confidence. Like I say, I couldn't believe the satisfaction I got from that."

## John Ferguson
*Montreal Canadiens, 1965, 1966, 1968, 1969, and 1971*
John Ferguson enjoyed a sporting moment that only Jimmy Brown, Michael Jordan, and a few others can truly understand.

"I went out on top," Ferguson said.

Ferguson might be the only player in NHL history who retired literally minutes after winning the Stanley Cup championship. Amid all the hugs and backslapping in the visitor's dressing room after a dramatic Game 7 win in Chicago Stadium in 1971, he told teammates Yvon Cournoyer and Ralph Backstrom that he was becoming a civilian at age 32. He made it official by giving his skates and sweater to a good friend named Shakie Louie, a horseplayer who was also buddies with Montreal's Serge Savard.

Revered by many as the top tough guy in NHL history, Ferguson had tried retiring the season before because he was making more money as a businessman than he was making in hockey. But he was talked into playing again 20 games into the 1970–1971 season. Ferguson considered his fifth championship his sweetest, maybe because no one expected the Canadiens to win that season, or maybe because he knew when entering the playoffs that he planned to retire for good this time. He didn't score on his last shot à la Michael Jordan, but he did assist on a goal in Montreal's 4–3 victory in Game 6 of the series against the Blackhawks. He produced 10 points in 18 games in the 1971 playoffs—the highest postseason production he ever had.

With five Stanley Cup championships to his credit, Ferguson's celebration memories have been melded together over time. He remembers one year going to Bernie "Boom Boom" Geoffrion's restaurant for a celebration that lasted until daylight. "We also had a ritual of visiting Toe Blake's tavern on St. Catharine Street," Ferguson said. "It was always standard to spend the day after with Toe at the tavern."

"You got a few photographs with the Cup in the dressing room and then you didn't see it again until next year," Ferguson said. Ferguson's words speak to the confidence the Canadiens' players and management had in this era; they expected to see and win the Stanley Cup every year. Montreal players were Montreal's celebrity class. They moved about the city like they were royalty, particularly in the summers after winning the Cup. When the Stanley Cup ended up at city hall, there was no need to give players a key to the city, because the door of every business was always open to a Canadiens player.

"The best way to say it is that I can still walk down the streets of Montreal [almost 30 years after his last championship], and people know who I am," Ferguson said. "We were the toast of the town."

One of Ferguson's memories of the final Cup win in Chicago was the excitement level of rookie Bobby Sheehan. The Canadiens' roster didn't turn over much in those days, and most of the players were veterans of multiple championships. This was 20-year-old Sheehan's first and only NHL crown.

"I think Bobby Sheehan was so happy, he missed the plane back from Chicago to Montreal," Ferguson said. "He was very happy."

Ferguson died in 2007, and his funeral, in Windsor, Ontario, drew the who's who of the hockey world. He was one of the most well-liked men in the NHL.

## Derek Sanderson

*Boston Bruins, 1970 and 1972*

The late Harold Sanderson earned about $22 take-home pay per week in the late 1950s when his son, Derek, came in and asked for a pair of Tack skates that retailed for $116.

"They were state of the art at that time," Derek Sanderson recalled. "They had kangaroo leather back then. That was before it was banned. They were the best. If you wore Tacks, you were a player."

The Sanderson household wasn't flush with cash, but Harold Sanderson carefully pondered his son's request. He certainly knew his son was a top player. The Bruins had given the Sandersons $100 to put him on their protected list at age 11.

"I will give you the Tacks," Harold Sanderson told his son. "But you have to promise me that I get the ring when you win the Stanley Cup."

The promise was made and quickly forgotten until the Bruins were celebrating their Stanley Cup on the ice after finishing the sweep of the St. Louis Blues. The fans were on the ice. Bodies were everywhere. It was a joyous riot of emotions and craziness. Derek Sanderson had to bully his way through fans just to get back to the dressing room. Slipping and sliding to maintain his balance, Derek caught a glimpse of a fan coming at him and lifted his shoulder to protect himself. He caught the man squarely in the jaw and decked him.

"Remember the ring—the ring is mine," Harold Sanderson said, grinning as he looked up at his son.

Sanderson laughs at the memory. "He never brought up that ring one time until the night we won the championship," Sanderson said.

When Sanderson remembers the 1970 and 1972 Stanley Cup championships, he focuses on the team's cohesiveness, bolstered by how much fun the Bruins had off the ice. He thinks the team would have had a long run of success had the Bruins not allowed coach Harry Sinden to walk away over $1,500. After coaching the Bruins to a championship in 1970, Sinden wanted a raise and didn't get it. He left to sell prefabricated housing.

"The day Harry retired, I said in the newspaper that it just cost us the Stanley Cup," Sanderson said.

The Bruins did not win in 1971 without Sinden. "Harry was the best coach I ever had," Sanderson said. "He just knew how to handle 20 very odd characters. He brought the best out of all of us. He handled the egos well. You got to remember in that day you had no assistants. You had one coach and a trainer. Harry did it all. He thought about the game around the clock, and he got us thinking the same way. He was a master at controlling the players, but Bobby Orr controlled the room."

According to Sanderson, Orr's ability to inspire others to a higher performance has been overshadowed by his greatness as a player.

"If you weren't playing well, he would just stare at you," Sanderson said. "And you would think, *Uh-oh*. If you didn't know how you were playing, you would look at Bobby. If he was looking at you, you were dead."

Sanderson views Orr as a man who puts loyalty at the top of his lists of desirable attributes in a friend.

"If you have done something that isn't classy or something that wasn't the right thing to do, or you have embarrassed a friend of his, he does not forget," Sanderson said. "He is extremely loyal and he expects others to be just as loyal."

Sanderson viewed Esposito "as a big happy bear."

"He loved life and he took a big bite out of it every day," Sanderson said. "He was extremely talented and a lot better defensively than anyone ever gave him credit for."

Sanderson's highlight of the 1970 Cup run was setting up Orr for the game-winner. "It was Bobby who led us to the championship," Sanderson said. "It was fitting that he scored the goal. No one ever resented Orr's success. I've seen superstars on other teams come and go, and I've seen people talk about them. Often teammates try to get in a little snipe or a little rip. But Bobby was a leader, and we never questioned it."

What Sanderson remembers about the play was that he was careful with the pass because if he missed Orr's stick "it would have been three-on-none going back the other way."

"There was no one behind Orr," Sanderson said. "It crossed my mind that Orr was taking a hell of a gamble. Bobby timed it and snapped it quickly. I saw it hit the mesh, and I was kind of mesmerized by the label of the puck spinning, and I thought, *Holy shit, we just won the Cup.*"

Hustling over to his close friend Orr, he found him with his arms open. Sanderson jumped on him. "We just laughed," Sanderson said.

Sanderson doesn't think much about the hijinks that followed the Bruins' championships. "Celebrations are all very anticlimactic," Sanderson said. "I used to look around at the Super Bowl and World Series, and the camera would always be on some jerk shaking up the champagne. The champagne part is all made up. It's sticky. It stings. It's a mess. Don't spray me with champagne. I don't want to hear about how you drank champagne. I always watched the guy in the background who is content, happy, and just smiling."

According to Sanderson, that's the face of a man who understands winning. "Winning is about delivering and not choking," Sanderson said. "When it's over, there's an empty feeling."

He pauses. "Really it is all about the ring," he said. "Athletes make enough money. You play for the ring. That's not made up. You want the ring because not many people have won. That's what you play for."

Harold Sanderson was quite proud of the Stanley Cup rings his son gave him, although Derek was flabbergasted one year when he found out where his father was keeping them. He discovered the secret hiding spot when he took his girlfriend back home to meet his family. He wanted to show her the rings, and he asked his father to get them.

Moving back the couch, Harold Sanderson started playing with the hem of the living room curtains until he extracted the rings from a small pouch within that hem.

"What the hell are they doing there?" Derek asked his father.

*Derek Sanderson of the Boston Bruins fondly recalls the times spent off the ice with teammates during the Bruins' championship runs in the early 1970s.* Photo courtesy of Getty Images

"Well, I can't wear them because I didn't earn them," Harold said. "That would be a little pretentious. And I don't want anyone to steal them."

Harold Sanderson has since passed away, and Derek gave his sons, Michael and Ryan, his two rings. It was a highly meaningful gift to his children because Sanderson treasures those rings.

When he reviews his career, Sanderson thinks it was a godsend that he gave his father those championship rings. Otherwise they might not have survived his party years. This was the 1970s, and Sanderson was a symbol of the excesses of the decade. He stayed out too late, lived too hard, and found himself in situations that weren't in his best interest.

He will be the first to admit that today. He went broke, even though he signed a big contract to jump to the World Hockey Association. (The Bruins' hope of a dynasty was killed by five key players defecting to the WHA, including Sanderson and Cheevers.) At the wildest point in his life, Sanderson owned a farm and had to use a Rolls Royce to transport hay because he was forced to sell his truck to pay bills. He lived on the edge in those days.

"If I had those rings during my crazier period," he said, "I might have sold them. I'm thankful I still have them."

## Terry Crisp

*Philadelphia Flyers, 1974 and 1975*
*Coach, Calgary Flames, 1989*

As bedlam engulfed the Spectrum after the Philadelphia Flyers defeated the Boston Bruins 1–0 to win the Stanley Cup, player Terry Crisp remembers that he had focus amid chaos. "I went behind the net and picked up the puck, and I still have it," Crisp said. "And even in the midst of that pandemonium I wanted to make eye contact with my mom and dad [Nibs and Toots Crisp] and my wife, Sheila. Just to say it was all worth it."

Crisp, then 31, probably appreciated the sweetness of the Cup as much as, if not more than, anyone in a Flyers uniform that afternoon. He was a journeyman player with his fourth organization; he was a role player, a checker, and a penalty killer who never lost sight of what he needed to do to stay in the game. He never scored more than 13 goals in one season, and the 10 he scored that season for the Flyers was the second-highest total of his career. He scored two goals that post-season; but one had been in Game 3 of the Finals. The game was tied 1–1 when Crisp netted the go-ahead and eventual winning goal in a 4–1 win.

"When you are a fringe player and never know whether you are ever going to play in the NHL, and then to reach the pinnacle, I was ecstatic," Crisp said. "If nothing else ever happens good for you, you know you still have this."

What Crisp didn't know was that he would win another Cup as a member of the Philadelphia Flyers the following year and then come back in 1989 to win the Cup as coach of the Calgary Flames. He joined a select number of men such as Cy Denneny, Al Arbour, Art Ross, and Toe Blake, who won hockey's grand prize as both player and coach.

As a player, what Crisp remembers was the pure joy that was present in Philadelphia when the Flyers won the Cup. He remembers with great delight the fans pouring onto the ice and the mass of humanity that stood between him and the dressing room. It may have been as difficult to navigate through the crowd in the postgame celebration as it was for the Flyers to pick their way through the Bruins' strong defense. "There was no such thing as security when it was over," Crisp remembered.

Crisp's memories of his first Stanley Cup center on the length of the celebration. "Hell, we didn't go to bed for three days," he said, laughing. "I told my wife to put out some clean shirts and clothes, and I will be in and out frequently. For the next three days, whenever you would get a call to go somewhere for a party, off you would go."

Fourteen years later, winning the Stanley Cup was far different because he was the coach, instead of a player. "When you are the coach, you worry and fret over 23 guys," Crisp said. "It's the mother hen versus the little hen in the parade. The mother hen has to worry about them all, and the little hen just worries, *Am I in the right line to get food?*"

The Flames won their Stanley Cup victory on the road in Montreal, and the plane ride home stands out in Crisp's mind. "I think the Cup was flying the plane for a while," Crisp recalled, chuckling. "The pilot and copilot got their picture with the Cup. It might have been the first time that Lord Stanley was at the helm of a plane. Imagine them calling in and saying, 'This is Lord Stanley coming in for a landing.'"

His regret is that the NHL didn't allow players to take the Stanley Cup to their hometowns like they do today. "I'm still a little bitter about that," Crisp said.

Crisp, now a television analyst for the Nashville Predators, would have liked just 24 hours more to savor his triumphs with his friends and family. "Everything happens so fast, so quick when you win," Crisp said. "You have these intense meetings and games, and then you win 1–0 against Boston [in 1974]. You have the Cup, and suddenly, poof, it's all over. It's a blur. All that fun blends together. When you win, it's almost as if you say, 'Now what?'"

One of the most famous quotes in NHL history was the late Flyers coach Fred Shero telling his team, "If we win tonight, we will walk together forever," before the Stanley Cup clinching game on May 19, 1974.

But Crisp recalls another sliver of Shero wisdom after the 1–0 win against Boston that now rings prophetic to him. When Shero addressed his champions after they clinched the first Stanley Cup in franchise history, he told them, "You will not realize what you have done until 10 years down the road."

"You know what, he was dead on right," Crisp said. "That night we thought utopia would last forever. We won again in 1975, but then you take it for granted. It is 10 years later before you realize what you've done. I'll tell you when the memories come flooding back: when you are sitting in your living room watching Buffalo and Dallas play for the Cup, and you are thinking, *I reached that point once*. Fred Shero had it dead on."

## Bill Clement
*Philadelphia Flyers, 1974 and 1975*
In the spring of 1974 the city of Philadelphia seemed like an infertile sports landscape where championship-caliber teams simply wouldn't take root.

The Philadelphia Eagles were 5–8–1 in 1973, which actually had been an improvement from the 2–11–1 mark they posted the season before. No one in the National Football League was fearful of an encounter in Philadelphia. In baseball, Philadelphia pitcher Steve Carlton intimidated opponents, but no one took the franchise all that seriously. Carlton had posted 27 of the team's 59 victories in 1972, and in 1973 the Phillies were 20 games under .500. The Philadelphia 76ers, meanwhile, were an NBA doormat. "The city was so ripe for an injection of B-12 into the self-esteem vein," said Bill Clement, who played for Philadelphia from 1971 to 1975.

That may explain why Philly fans went several degrees beyond letting their hair down when the Philadelphia Flyers won back-to-back Stanley Cup crowns in 1974 and 1975. The intensity of the two years of celebrations certainly is among player Bill Clement's vivid memories of his two championships.

The second Cup was captured in Buffalo, and the Flyers chartered back to Philadelphia. Although it was after 1:00 AM when they landed, players immediately headed to the Ovations club in the Spectrum to join the fan celebration.

"When we first got there, we got greeted with, 'Hey, way to go, you won another Cup, but did you hear that Mary Jones got laid on table No. 6?'" Clement says. "That was the buzz when we came in."

Legend has it that a woman known to many Ovations patrons, Mary Jones (not her real name), and an unknown man became so carried away during the Flyers' celebration that they commingled in a carnal way right there in full sight of other celebrating fans. Whether the story is true or not, it certainly provides a glimpse of how fans may have released some pent-up emotion during the Flyers' championship run.

"I understand the impact it had on the city now more than I did then," Clement said. "I still live in the area, people are always coming up to me and saying, 'I skipped school to be at the parade,' and their parents faking being mad at them because they really understood why the kids needed to go. I've heard that some classes had four students in them and that teachers didn't show up. Companies locked their doors. It was as if the war had just ended."

He remembers that the parade down Broad Street was dotted with craziness, including women taking off their shirts and streakers. In that era it was a fad to run nude through a big event.

When the parade finally arrived at JFK Stadium, Clement remembers being in awe of how many fans were jammed into the stadium when the two floats carrying the Flyers' players entered.

"Then this guy runs bare-ass naked from goal post to goal post," Clement said. "All I can say is that it was like a cross between a rock concert and the celebration that would accompany the end of a war."

Each of the Flyers' championships has its own unique flavor in Clement's mind. He has plenty of pride about the first title because he played through the Finals with the excruciating pain of a partially torn medial collateral ligament in his left knee. He suffered the injury in the semifinals against the New York Rangers and sat out the first two games of the Stanley Cup Finals against Boston before asking doctors to take him out of the cast 10 days earlier than expected. He was dismayed that he was still limping and felt he couldn't skate well enough to play in Game 3.

He remembers sitting in the whirlpool before Game 4, angered about his injury, when team captain Bobby Clarke approached him. According to Clement, their conversation went something like this:

Clarke: "How are you feeling?"

Clement: "Awful."

Clarke: "We have guys called up from the minors who can't do what you can do. If you could just kill penalties, it would help us."

Clement: "I'll be out there."

Clement retells that tale often when he gives motivational speeches because he believes it shows why Clarke was a great leader and why people should never underestimate the value of positive reinforcement in the workplace.

He played Games 4, 5, and 6, even scoring a goal in Game 5. "I really wouldn't have been in uniform if Clarke hadn't made me feel as if the team couldn't win without me," Clement said. "I think that many things can be accomplished when you make someone feel as if he or she is vital to the outcome. My head was spinning after Clarke talked to me. I wondered, *Can I really do this?* But when I look back at the videos, I played okay. I'm happy with the way I played. Today I must look at Bob Clarke objectively with the work he does as a general manager, but when he played, I would stack him up with some of the greatest leaders of all time."

On the night of May 19, 1974, Clement kept his jersey on for four hours after the game in a dressing room overflowing with well-wishers. Clement was glad that he opted not to strip off his jersey because many of those who did found out after the room was clear that their clothes had been pilfered.

Eccentric Flyers coach Fred Shero often said and did things that simply couldn't be forgotten. When Clement tries to sum up the late Shero's relationship with players during the championship celebration, he is drawn to a scene that played out earlier in the playoffs. This was the 1970s, when many people, including star athletes, ignored the surgeon general's warning about the evils of cigarette smoking. Clement recalled that about half the team smoked, including himself. Even Shero could be seen regularly puffing on Lucky Strike cigarettes. But as common as it was, smoking during a game was taboo to the point that players felt obliged to sneak into the bathroom to catch their puffs between periods. During one playoff game intermission, Shero came in and started sniffing at the air as if he were trying to determine the odor.

"Don't think you are fooling me," Shero said. "I know you are going into the bathroom to smoke." Shero kept pacing back and fourth. "I don't like that very much," he continued.

The players prepared themselves for a tongue-lashing. Then Shero said simply, "You are going to ruin your skates in there. For God's sake, go sit on the couch and be comfortable."

The players all started to laugh. "He was a master at keeping us poised," Clement remembered.

The Flyers team was as close as any group of men could be. "It was a foxhole mentality," said Clement. "You almost cannot describe the bond we had."

After the first Cup triumph, Clement remembers he only slept from 6:00 to 8:00 AM. "I got up and had to go to my neighbors to borrow a six-pack because I was all out," Clement said, laughing.

The second Flyers Cup was captured on the road in Buffalo. Not even the wives came along because the Flyers were preparing themselves for the possibility of a Game 7. After defeating the Sabres 2–0, the Flyers discovered that this would at least start out as a different kind of celebration. "It was almost as if we had quiet time together as champions before we opened the doors to the rest of the world," Clement said. "We flew home together and spent time together."

One of Clement's fondest memories was the parade after the first Cup win in 1974. One million fans turned out to salute their warriors, many of whom were primed with celebratory alcohol and suffering from sleep deprivation.

Players were divided between two floats, with Clement in the back float. As the parade crept along Broad Street, Clement recalls he had a pressing need to find a urinal to pay the price for too much beverage intake. Spying a service station up the road, Clement climbed down the side of the float and commenced his journey. After working his way through the horde of onlookers trying to shake his hand or pat him on the back, he finally arrived at the service station's bathroom only to find it was locked. By the time he received the key and relieved himself, he realized he had a more daunting task in front of him. The parade had not stopped to accommodate Bill Clement's bladder. About 4,000 people were between Clement and his float, which was now a block up the road.

"When I came out of the bathroom, two cops were waiting for me," Clement said. "They told me I was never going to make it back. But they put their billy clubs in the shape of a V, and they began to barge through the crowd. They told me to grab the back of their belts and hang on."

Much to even the police officers' surprise, they were able to get Clement back to the float. They both grabbed an end of a billy club to give him a ladder to climb back onto the float. He had just climbed back on the float and was in the midst of accepting his teammates' congratulations for surviving his journey when the parade came to a halt.

"The little staircase rolls down off the float, and Bernie Parent steps out, and the crowd parts like it's the Red Sea," Clement remembered. "Bernie has to piss. He walks to a typical row house where a little lady is standing there—obviously honored that Bernie is going to whiz in her commode."

The crowd kept the path clear for Parent, who exited the house still fussing with the belt on his pants.

"The stairs come out, Bernie goes up. The stairs are rolled up, and off we go," Clement said, laughing. "I'm sitting back there going, 'Yeah, right. You got to be kidding.' The parade stops so Bernie can whiz after I had to fight my way through 4,000 people."

Clement laughs about the old story that the lady had the toilet seat bronzed.

"I tell people jokingly that I have this recurring nightmare that I'm stranded outside the service station with the owner not believing who I am and not wanting to give me the key," Clement said. "In the back of my mind, I see people throwing coins into this shrine which is the commode that has been bronzed and put on Broad Street and called the Bernie Parent Shrine."

Actually, Clement wasn't the least bit upset that Parent, the team's star player, got the red carpet treatment during his potty stop.

"I didn't begrudge him his piss, because I knew that I wouldn't have had the opportunity to piss in that situation had Bernie not been Bernie," Clement said. "My kidneys wouldn't have been backed up if Bernie wasn't in our net."

Clement has two championship rings and both of his jerseys from those championship teams, but he doesn't treasure the tangible evidence of his success as much as his memories. "I wouldn't trade the memories for anything," Clement said.

## Dave Schultz

*Philadelphia Flyers, 1974 and 1975*

A war of words doesn't traditionally decide the outcome of a Stanley Cup championship, but one ill-timed bellow by a Boston Bruins fan may have been the catalyst for one of the most memorable moments in Philadelphia Flyers' winger Dave Schultz's career.

It was about 11-plus minutes into overtime of Game 2 of the Finals in Boston when an anonymous fan yelled at the Flyers' bench, "Hey, put Schultz out there so we can score a goal!" Coach Fred Shero then almost instantly shouted, "Schultz, Flett, and Clarke, get out there!"

Schultz recalls being mildly surprised because he hadn't played the final 10 minutes of regulation and hadn't seen any action in overtime. Schultz was one of the league's most intimidating fighters and had led the NHL in penalty minutes that season with 348. He had also netted 20 goals that season. But he wasn't really the first player that came to a coach's mind when the game was tight. Up until the moment the fan yelled, it didn't appear that Shero was thinking much about him at all.

But shortly thereafter, Schultz gained control of the puck near the boards and, with Terry O'Reilly coming after him, fed the puck back to the high slot. The late Bill "Cowboy" Flett then sent the puck toward the net, where Bobby Clarke knocked it home with his second swipe to win the game at 12:01.

"That was probably the biggest goal in Flyers' history," Schultz said. "If we hadn't won that game, I don't know if we would have won the series."

*Dave "the Hammer" Schultz, of the Philadelphia Flyers, is restrained by a linesman as he tries to continue a fight that had been halted. Schultz was the most penalized man in the NHL in 1975—mostly due to fighting.*

The Flyers had lost Game 1 by a 3–2 decision on Bobby Orr's timely tally with 22 seconds remaining in the third period. Another loss in Boston, particularly in overtime, would have been a broadside blast to the Flyers' psyche. Winning Game 2 seemed to give rise to the thought that the Flyers' were a team of destiny.

Who knows whether the late Shero put Schultz on the ice in response to the fan or whether it was simply time, in his estimation, to put fresh legs on the ice? Regardless, the move may have altered the course of Flyers history.

"Sometimes you get lucky," Schultz said. "I could say I saw the man and made a great pass. But I just went in the corner and threw it out to the deep slot."

That's the moment that has stayed with Schultz more than any other in the quarter-century since the play occurred. He scored an important goal in Game 4, but that memory doesn't seem as vivid as the assist in Game 2. What fans remember about Schultz in 1974 was the whipping he laid on New York Rangers' defenseman Dale Rolfe during a fight in Game 7 of the semifinals. The Flyers won that game 4–3, with some believing Schultz had set a tone with his triumph.

"People always talk about that fight. 'Why didn't some of the Rangers' jump in?' 'What happened?' I've heard it all," he said. "But I never thought it had any effect on the game. Actually, one of our assistants said, 'If you get a chance, hit Rolfe. He's playing well.' What happened was he was tussling with Orest Kindrachuk. And I came over. Remember, if you came over back then, a lot of guys would think, *Here comes Schultz, I guess I will have to fight.* He basically started it, or at least responded without much [prodding]."

In retrospect, Schultz has the common athlete's lament of wishing he spent more time soaking in the moment of the championship, particularly when the Flyers won their first Cup on home ice in 1974.

"What I remember was being upset because they had opened the doors and let everyone in the building after we won. People who weren't even at the game ended up on the ice," Schultz said. "Where were those people going? They were going to go on the ice. And they did. The glass wasn't as high as it is today. It was easy to get over. And then people who were at the game saw that, and they came on the ice. We couldn't skate around in our own building with the Cup because there were so many people on the ice."

But through the years he has come to understand why fans reacted the way they did. "My appreciation of what we accomplished is 100 times greater today than it was when we won," Schultz said. "The reaction of the fans in the Delaware Valley was unreal. People today can still tell you where they were when we won."

## Brian Engblom

*Montreal Canadiens, 1977, 1978, and 1979*

The Stanley Cup is the NHL's symbol of excellence, but when Engblom thinks about his three NHL championship experiences, he thinks about Toe Blake's fedora.

"I called it his Eliot Ness hat," Engblom said. "It was really right out of *The Untouchables* television series."

For Engblom the visits to Blake's tavern after a Stanley Cup triumph was a treasured highlight of his three championship memories. But Engblom was younger than most of the Canadiens, and the impact Blake's aura had on his experience seems even more pronounced. He can describe in rich detail Blake's long, narrow office and Blake sitting at his desk at the end of the table as if he were a CEO at a meeting with major stockholders. In actuality, Blake was the CEO of the Canadiens' mystique. He certainly had helped create it with eight Stanley Cup titles as a coach and three more as a player (1935 with the Montreal Maroons and 1944 and 1946 with the Canadiens).

A multitude of classic old photos adorned the walls from the 1930s, '40s, '50s, and '60s, a virtual history of the Canadiens, most of which Blake was in. "There was the odd color photo," Engblom said. "But it was the black-and-white ones that caught your eye."

Blake was like an aging chief to the Canadiens' tribe; he seemed to feel as if it were his duty to pass along the Canadiens' history and traditions.

"Just to be in that room when he spoke was an honor," Engblom remembered. "He had a gravelly, raspy, deep voice, but not much volume to it. So whenever he would talk, everyone would just shut up, whether it was Kenny Dryden, or [Serge] Savard, or one of the young guys. We all listened."

He would regale the Montreal players with vivid stories from the years when he played or coached. Players listened as if Blake were giving them secrets to immortality. Perhaps in a way he was; the idea of "once a Canadien, always a Canadien" certainly was propagated by Blake's presence and stories.

"Another thing about Toe was that he also loved to sit back and listen," Engblom said. "He wasn't one to command everyone to listen to him. He wasn't there to put on a show. He loved to hear the other stories."

Blake had no official capacity with the Canadiens back then, but he was viewed with so much respect that no one thought it strange that Blake would travel with the team in the playoffs. "You have to remember how [coach] Scotty Bowman felt about Toe," Engblom said. "I'm sure Scotty loved having him around, and I'm sure he put his two cents in now and then."

He had a stately presence that no one mocked, although Savard once pushed the outside edge of propriety when he cut V-shaped gouges into the brim of Blake's famed hat. "That really pissed off Toe," Engblom said. "Serge thought it was hilarious, but you could see that Toe wasn't happy."

A younger player would never have dreamed of doing anything that brazen, even though Engblom earned the respect of his teammates with a noteworthy NHL debut. During the 1976–1977 season, he played in Nova Scotia, not believing he had any shot to make the parent team, not when it had seven talented defensemen. But flu went through the team during the playoffs, and injuries hit hard. With only four healthy defensemen available, Engblom was first to make his NHL debut in a playoff game against the St. Louis Blues.

He played in the second and third rounds, but everyone had regained their health for the Finals, and he watched from the stands. It never occurred to him until later that he wouldn't get his name on the Cup because he didn't play in the Finals or didn't have the requisite 40 games played in the regular season. Fortunately for Engblom, he was playing for a team that expected to win more championships, and it did.

One regret about that first Cup was that he didn't step back and soak up even more of the atmosphere. To Engblom, the first Cup celebration was played at fast-forward speed. "It's all a flood in your mind," Engblom said. "It all blends together. The clock ticks down. Everyone piles on the ice. People are everywhere. One minute you are next to the Cup, and the next minute it's on the other side of the ice. Everyone piles on again, and there's more pandemonium."

Other memories of his Cups include sitting next to Bowman at one of the Stanley Cup championship banquets. He felt like a child being forced to sit next to the teacher.

"Scotty doesn't make small talk during the season," Engblom said. "You didn't have a conversation with him that wasn't about hockey. When he said something to you, it was short, sweet, and to the point. Then you went on your way."

When Bowman started making casual conversation with Engblom, he almost wanted to make sure he was really talking to him. "He asked me what I was going to do in the summer, and I was so surprised I almost didn't know what to say," Engblom said.

Engblom owns only one photo of himself with the Cup. He remembers seeking out fellow Winnipegger Cam Connor in 1979 to make sure they had their picture together. Connor didn't play in the Finals that year, but he was a Canadien, and Engblom treasures the photo. Engblom went home to Manitoba after the first Cup, but after the next Stanley Cup he stayed in Montreal to soak in the atmosphere and afterglow that go with the championship. He wanted to be able to walk down the street and have people congratulate him for the championship.

Beyond his memories of the moments with Blake, what Engblom recalls is the feeling of camaraderie that was present in the dressing room. He says he feels fortunate to have played with players like Guy Lafleur, Larry Robinson, and Bob Gainey, among others, whose legends weren't even fully developed at that point. "Nine guys I played with are in the Hall of Fame," Engblom said.

He believed in the Canadiens' mystique—and still does in some respects. All the plaques listing the members of the championship teams that hang in the dressing room, along with the faces of great Canadiens heroes like Rocket Richard, Jean Beliveau, and others, were a daily reminder of the hallowed nature of being a Canadiens player.

"All of those faces on the wall," Engblom said. "It really does affect you. People can say it's corny. But it's not when you are in there. You look at the faces, and it's all part of being a Montreal Canadien. There is a rich history in winning. Any organization or business is smart to use their history. Why would you ignore it? Remember, we had Rocket Richard, Toe Blake, and Jacques Laperriere coming around all the time. It made a difference."

Engblom believes that the mystique weighed on everyone's minds.

"A lot of it was the Forum," Engblom said. "Young kids get overwhelmed by it. I was. You grow up watching the Canadiens every Saturday on *Hockey Night in Canada*. You start thinking this place has been around forever, and all of these great players played here. You are in awe."

The Canadiens, particularly Scotty Bowman, worked to magnify the mystique. He always made sure that at the morning skate, when he knew the opposing team would be in the building watching, he would run a snappy, high tempo practice with plenty of high-speed passing. Lafleur would always be zipping around at top speed.

"There was a saying that we had about how some teams lost to us at the morning skate," Engblom said. "They would see us get on and off the ice in a hurry, and some teams were overwhelmed, and it was just 11:00 in the morning."

Every Canadien had a sense that he was carrying the torch for his teammates as well as those who had come before him. Even today, when championships are far more infrequent, the championship Canadiens of yesteryear are treated like megastars.

"Al Langlois played in the 1950s with Dick Moore and Jean Beliveau, but they can't walk down the street in Montreal without being recognized," Engblom said.

Engblom said his glory years with the Montreal dynasty have given him an identity—a special kind of fame that at least means his name will never die in Canadiens lore. That's what those meetings with Blake were all about, cementing the bond, unifying past and present.

"From what I've read and seen," Engblom said, "being a Canadien is like being a New York Yankee or a Boston Celtic. No matter what age you are, people keep track of you. You never lose your identity of being a Canadiens' player."

## Ron Caron
*Assistant General Manager, Montreal Canadiens, 1971*
Ron Caron enjoyed the ambience of the Montreal Canadiens' championship success a few years before he would play a significant role in creating more of it.

In 1964–1965 he was a scout for the Montreal Junior Canadiens and was being groomed for an expanded role within the organization. He was a member of the Canadiens' family, and when the Canadiens defeated Chicago 4–0 in Game 7 of the Stanley Cup Finals on Gump Worsley's shutout, Caron was among the first at the party at the Queen Elizabeth Hotel.

To appreciate the intensity of a Canadiens celebration, it is crucial to remember that the Canadiens approached the postseason as if embarking on a religious pilgrimage. In fact, during the playoffs, the Canadiens would sequester players miles outside of town. "They were like monks forming a family," Caron said.

Vows of silence weren't necessary to be a member of the Canadiens organization in the postseason, but a myopic focus on hockey was a minimum requirement. "Everyone knew that they had to continue on to win the Stanley Cup to call it a good year," Caron remembered.

When the Cup was finally won, the Canadiens management shared the experience with all of the franchise's employees—everyone from Jean Beliveau to the Zamboni driver was invited to the celebration party. The night after the glorious victory against Chicago, Caron remembered the official party went until about 3:00 AM, and then players and special guests headed to the Laval home of Henri Richard's cousin for an after-hours party. That started at about 4:15, and by 5:30 the champagne had run out. "So we switched to the champagne of the poor," Caron said.

The beer didn't run out, and Caron chuckles at the memory of Claude Larose asking Caron to borrow his car at 7:30 in the morning. "I told him, 'If you want to throw up, you are going to have to throw up in your own car,'" Caron remembered vividly.

He also remembered that a priest was among the all-night revelers. It was Father Aquin, known as the chaplain of the cab drivers. The Cup had been won on a Saturday night, and in the wee hours on Sunday, Father Aquin had a special message for the players, many of whom were Catholic.

"He said, 'I will give you the blessing, and you won't have to go to Mass,'" Caron said. Caron slept two hours that night and then got up to hit some golf balls with members of the organization. "Then it was time to get ready for another party, and that continued for six straight days," Caron recalled.

The seeds of Caron's ambition were sewn long before the Canadiens' 1965 title romp, but those special nights nurtured it through the addition of a heavy dose of inspiration. In that short period Caron had acquired a taste for success. That would serve him well as he worked his way up into the Canadiens' hierarchy. By 1968 he had become chief scout and one of general manager Sam Pollock's chief lieutenants.

The following season the Canadiens' aura had begun to lose its power. Montreal missed the playoffs, and when the 1970–1971 season started, it appeared the Canadiens' struggles might be long-term. By December, Canadiens boss David Molson had told Pollock that he had to replace Claude Ruel.

What Caron says no one ever knew was that he had been Pollock's first choice to replace Ruel as coach. Caron had been summoned to drive with Pollock to Quebec City on December 2, 1970.

"He told me, 'I have made up my mind that you will coach the Canadiens,'" Caron recalled. "I told him, 'Sam, you are under pressure. I would be honored, but I think that Al MacNeil should be given a chance to take over.'"

That suggestion seemed to satisfy Pollock, but he quickly decided that Caron would become the team's assistant general manager. Pollock didn't fly, and Caron was told that he would have to be at every game, home and away. "Sam didn't believe in listening to games on the radio," Caron said. "So it was my job to call him from the road. If we won, I would let Al call. If we lost, I would call. He knew as soon as he heard my voice that we lost."

Caron clearly views the 1970–1971 season as one of the highlights of his NHL career. There is considerable pride in his voice as he talks about convincing Pollock to make a trade to land Frank Mahovlich from the Detroit Red Wings. "Detroit was confused, and I thought we could get Frank. Sam said he didn't know whether Frank Mahovlich still wanted to play," Caron said. "I told him we can find out in a minute because his brother Peter was on the team. Peter was always jovial, and when I asked him how long Frank was going to play, he said, 'As long as there is money.'"

The Canadiens gave up Mickey Redmond, Billy Collins, and Guy Charron to get Mahovlich. The Canadiens were a better team with

Mahovlich, but they still finished third in the league—24 points behind the Bobby Orr–led Bruins. The Canadiens were always a confident organization, but Caron still looks at the team picture taken a few weeks before the start of the playoffs "and no one is smiling."

The Canadiens played a wild-card late in the season that seemed to change the game. Rookie goaltender Ken Dryden was 6–0 at the completion of the regular season.

The Bruins had won the 1970 Stanley Cup championship, and they had plenty of talent beyond Orr, including Gerry Cheevers in goal. No one was surprised Cheevers won Game 1, and everyone was stunned when Eddie Johnston was chosen to be the Bruins' goaltender in Game 2. Seven minutes into the game, Boston led 5–1, but Caron still felt they could come back against Johnston. They came back to win that game 7–5, and suddenly the Canadiens began to believe they could win the series. Caron remembers that the Canadiens had two small strategy moves that helped in the victory. Caron had suggested that Jacques Laperriere play the point on the power play, even though a hairline fracture prevented him from shooting. This move was made to combat the possibility that Orr might break up the ice short-handed. Caron believed that Laperriere was best suited to deal with Orr. Pollock also noted that Ferguson, a little older now, didn't seem to enjoy playing against Ken Hodge. He told MacNeil to keep Ferguson away from Hodge. Small factors? Absolutely, but it demonstrated how the Canadiens analyzed and re-analyzed every element in the playoffs. They finally beat the Bruins in seven games.

"Talking to him was like talking to my dad," Caron said. "I always gave him respect, but he gave me respect."

The Canadiens needed six games to dispose of the Minnesota North Stars, and the triumph didn't come without controversy. MacNeil had benched Henri Richard and John Ferguson during the third period of a loss, and Richard had called him the "worst coach" he had ever played for. Ferguson reportedly broke a door on his way out of the dressing room. Once that was smoothed over, the Canadiens defeated Minnesota to set up the Stanley Cup Finals meeting with the Chicago Blackhawks. This was a hotly contested series, with the Blackhawks winning the first two at home and the Canadiens winning the next two in Montreal.

Chicago won again at home to make it 3–2, and Peter Mahovlich scored the game-winner in the Canadiens' 4–3 win at Montreal in Game 6.

At all of the games in Chicago Stadium, Caron always sat next to Pollock and behind Mayor Richard J. Daley. Caron remembers Daley always had a religious person next to him, either a priest or a nun. Chicago Stadium was alive that day in 1971. "You have to be confident when you are a winner," Caron said. "You couldn't let the fear get to you. That was the Montreal way. But I can't tell you what goes on in your soul in a Game 7. It was unreal what I felt."

The Blackhawks claimed a 1–0 lead on a late first-period goal by Dennis Hull and then made it 2–0 at 7:33 of the second period on Danny O'Shea's tally. Caron remembers that Daley and he talked only about 10 seconds per period, but Daley felt obliged midway through the second period to do some crowing. "You are invited to taste the champagne after the game," Daley supposedly said.

Caron countered that it was a little early to be taking bows. "Ten seconds later I had the greatest moment of my life," Caron said.

Jacques Lemaire came over the red line and whistled a shot that Hall of Fame goaltender Tony Esposito inexplicably fumbled; the puck fell into the net to make it 2–1. About four minutes later Henri Richard scored to tie the game. "Lemaire is a very special person," Caron said. "He's brainy. He's timid in terms of ambition and achievement. But he knows the game big-time."

Early in the third period, Richard netted another goal to give Montreal a 3–2 lead. "Then God was on our side," Caron said. Bobby Hull hit two goal posts in the third period, and Jim Pappin rang a shot off the crossbar. Meanwhile, Ken Dryden played the third period as if he were invincible. As time wound down, Caron invited Mayor Daley to enjoy some of Montreal's champagne. When the game was over, Caron remembers bounding down eight steps, carrying the 200-pound Pollock with one arm.

"This is the feeling that you want to translate into this book," Caron said. "The joy and sense of achievement that comes when people believe you have no hope of doing it."

No one was happier to win the Cup than MacNeil. He had been forced to move his family out of his home after receiving a death threat presumably because he had benched Richard during the Minnesota series.

True to his history, Pollock didn't fly during the Canadiens' postseason. His chauffeur drove him to Boston, Minnesota, and Chicago during the championship run. He put 10,600 miles on the automobile. At some point after the championship was won, Pollock told Caron that the 1971 title had provided him with the most joy of any he had won.

As the players boisterously celebrated their victory in the Chicago Stadium visitors' dressing room, Caron remembers asking Pollock if he would be at the parade the following afternoon. "No, it's a 900-mile drive," Pollock said. "But I will be at the party tomorrow night."

## Ken Morrow

*New York Islanders, 1980–1983*

Defenseman Ken Morrow was one of the hardest-working warriors of the United States' Olympic gold medal triumph at the Lake Placid Winter Olympics in February 1980, and he thought he would never again know such an emotionally draining experience. He was wrong.

Three months later he was a regular on the New York Islanders blue line and playing an equally significant role in helping the Islanders win their first Stanley Cup in franchise history. He is the only player in hockey history to win an Olympic gold medal and a Stanley Cup championship in such a compressed period of time. Before joining the U.S. team, Morrow was at Bowling Green University in Ohio. He was considered a good prospect, and after watching him perform, particularly against the vaunted Soviets, the Islanders decided he was ready to play a vital role on their team.

"Winning the Stanley Cup was a completely different experience," Morrow said. "It's such a grueling, demanding grind. You win one series and you go right to the next. At the end it's almost a relief when you finally do win it. You're just physically and emotionally spent."

The Americans had to beat the Germans, Czechs, Soviets, and Finns to win the gold medal. The Islanders had to win 16 games to win the Stanley Cup. When the Americans won at Lake Placid, there was a sweetness and a thrill to their success. When the Islanders won the Cup, Morrow initially felt more like a survivor than a champion. Even though he had been a member of the team for only a couple of months, Morrow understood that this team felt pressure to win now.

"The Islanders had been trying to win for many years, and they had experienced such disappointment—losing to Toronto in the quarters [in 1978] and to the Rangers in the semis [in 1979]," Morrow said. "I think if they hadn't won that year [in 1980], they would have been broken up. That's why I think there was such a huge celebration when they finally won it."

When the United States won the gold medal, family and friends were brought into the locker room for a quiet celebration. Morrow remembers how touching those moments were.

"You couldn't do something like that immediately after winning the Stanley Cup," Morrow said.

When the Islanders won, it was like army buddies celebrating an armistice. The partying was nonstop on the island, but what Morrow remembers most was the 48 hours he had with the Cup in his possession. This was before the Hall of Fame demanded that the Cup be accompanied by one of its Cup babysitters. "There's an aura about it," Morrow said. "When you walked into the room with it, I loved the look on people's faces. They couldn't stop smiling. Their mouths fell agape, like kids looking inside a candy store window."

Having the Cup in one's possession is like having a pass key to every door in the city. "The Stanley Cup is a great way to set yourself up in the community," Morrow said. "You bring it to a restaurant and you eat for free. You bring it to a bar, you are drinking for free."

His Olympic and Stanley Cup experiences were so unique that Morrow says it's impossible to compare the two. But he allows himself one commingling of the two greatest accomplishments of his hockey career.

Said Morrow, "I did take some pictures of the Cup with the gold medal hanging around it."

# chapter 4

# Fab Four

## Maurice "Rocket" Richard

*Montreal Canadiens, 1944, 1946, 1953, 1956–1960*

When the late Maurice "Rocket" Richard played in the NHL, his expression always said: do not disturb. He owned a stare that could burn through titanium and a competitive fire that was molten.

"For 10 years I checked Rocket Richard, and he tried to kill me one night," former Detroit Red Wings player Marty Pavelich said, chuckling. "Other than that, it was a pretty good job."

When Richard died at age 78, on May 27, 2000, the NHL may have lost the most passionate champion in NHL history.

With a record 34 goals scored in Stanley Cup Finals games, Richard's career defines Stanley Cup excellence. No one pushed the outer edges of his limitations with greater ferocity than Richard. It was his obsession to be the best. To him, being the best meant winning the Stanley Cup every year.

Richard's life was celebrated in a poignant national funeral with services held at the Notre Dame Basilica in Montreal. The day before, he laid in state at the Molson Centre. Thousands paid their respects. Tears puddled in the eyes of older fans, many of whom viewed him as an icon of French Canadian pride. Perhaps some of the senior citizens remembered the days when Richard would gain control of the puck, and fans would rise in unison and say, "Envoye, Maurice!" The English slang translation would be, "Let's go, Maurice!"

Even in death, Maurice brought fans to their feet as they lined the road to pay their final respects to one of the true heroes of hockey.

As the years went along, Richard's personality seemed to mellow. But he never became verbose. The few times I spoke to him in the 1980s and 1990s he seemed gentlemanly and classy. But I would never have used the word *open* to describe him. He was not someone who was going to let you analyze his feelings. He was not the kind of person who would have submitted to a Barbara Walters–style interview concerning his innermost thoughts. He certainly wasn't going to go into great detail about why he broke down and cried after he scored a dramatic playoff goal against Boston in 1952. He probably wouldn't have explained—at least not in great detail—what his father had said to soothe him after that famous goal. That didn't seem to be Rocket Richard's style.

Perhaps others tell Richard's story better, anyway.

His playoff numbers scream about his legend. He netted 18 game-winning goals in just 82 playoff games. He boasts the NHL record of six overtime playoff goals. He once scored all five Montreal goals in a playoff game against Toronto—a performance that still places him in the record book with a handful of other great scorers. No one has ever netted six goals in a game.

Richard, who played from 1942 to 1960, played on the Punch Line with Elmer Lach and Toe Blake until Blake retired after suffering a broken leg in 1947. He played with Lach until Lach retired in 1954. Regardless of whom Richard played with, however, he would have been a star. He was a powerful skater who charged down the ice more like a skilled, fast fullback in the open field. He used his arms and strength to shield the puck from defenders, much like a running back might use a stiff arm to keep defenders away.

It was that heroic playoff goal in 1952 that will forever symbolize Rocket's competitiveness. Some call it his greatest goal. It came in Game 7 of the semifinals against the Boston Bruins at the Montreal Forum.

Earlier in the period he was bloodied and rendered unconscious by a gash he suffered over his left eyelid. How he was hurt seems have been forgotten over time. What was known was that Richard spent most of the game in the dressing room before coming out in the third period. Legend has it that Richard was so dazed he couldn't read the scoreboard and had to continually ask what the score was and how much time was left.

*Maurice "Rocket" Richard of the Montreal Canadiens poses with his hockey stick marked "600" and a puck after a game against the New York Rangers in New York City on November 26, 1958. Richard scored the 600ᵗʰ goal of his NHL career.*

With four minutes remaining, Richard summoned all of his bravado, leaped over the board, claimed the puck as his own, and crackled down the ice like he was lightning rippling across a low horizon. He slipped past Woody Dumart with two powerful strides and swung wide to avoid the Bruins' defense. According to reports of the game, Richard then whipped across the front of the net like he had been propelled by a slingshot. He whistled one of his sidewinders through Bruins keeper Sugar Jim Henry for the game-winner.

A famous photo of the bandaged and still-bleeding Richard meeting up with Henry, whose own eyes had been blackened, has frozen the Rocket's dramatic exploit in time. Wrote Elmer Ferguson in the next day's edition of the *Montreal Herald*: "That beautiful bastard scored semiconscious."

Richard had the ego that all great athletes should have—one that needs to be fed with heroics on an almost daily basis. In 1944–1945 Richard became the first player to score 50 goals in a season, and he did that in only 50 games. He was very proud of that record. When Gordie Howe reached 49 goals with one game to go in the 70-game 1952–1953 season, Richard was clearly glad that Howe would have to face Richard's Canadiens in the final regular-season game.

"The night of that game was the only time I was ever afraid to be a hockey player on the ice," Montreal coach Dick Irvin told *Sports Illustrated* in 1954. "I remember watching Rocket's eyes as we were going across the city in the cab. *I can't play him tonight*, I said to myself. *He'll kill somebody.*"

Irvin couldn't keep Richard away from Howe all night; first chance he got, he went after Howe. He took a charging penalty. As if fate appreciated Richard's pride, Howe was unable to tie Richard's record that night.

Pavelich can also bear witness to Richard's intensity. He accidently cut Richard one night when his stick came up during a body check.

"Rocket was madder then hell, and he wanted to clobber me," Pavelich recalled. "He was the one who got the penalty because he came after me."

When Richard's penalty was over, he went right after Pavelich again, and only a "look out" shout from Detroit defenseman Bob Goldham prevented a calamity for Pavelich. He ducked just in time to miss the full force of Richard coming at him head high. "He just scraped the top of my head with his stick, and I remember thinking, *Oh, my goodness gracious, this has to change*," Pavelich said.

He decided he would try to make friends with Richard, and it actually worked. "I would get him laughing," Pavelich said. "I would score a goal, and I would say, 'I'm hot tonight. You'd better check me.'"

They became friends to the point that Pavelich was spared some bruises. "I checked him hard, but sometimes he would have me lined up for a big hit and then just make a left turn and not hit me," Pavelich said.

That was a side of Richard that most competitors didn't see. Most competitors knew Richard as a ruthless warrior.

It seemed eerily ironic that Richard should die in late May, at the start of the 2000 Stanley Cup Finals, the venue where he often did his best work. All of the players competing for the New Jersey Devils and Dallas Stars knew Richard's legacy. Asking a hockey player about Richard is like asking a baseball player about Ted Williams or Joe DiMaggio. You need not be a history buff to know that Richard was one of the best there ever was.

Some of the former Canadiens and Quebec natives understood best of all. Claude Lemieux told the media that when he played in Montreal, he would always stick around if he heard that Richard was in the building, hoping he would get a chance to shake his hand. "Young French Canadiens view him as a god of hockey, and he will always be," said Lemieux, a four-time Stanley Cup champion and ex-Montreal player.

Top scorers have traditionally worn No. 9, but it was Richard who wore it first. He was proud that the Canadiens retired his number.

When the All-Star Game was played in Montreal, Canadiens' forward Kirk Muller was assigned to wear No. 9 for the Eastern Conference All-Stars. Richard took note of Muller wearing that number and made a point to speak to him.

"You're a Canadien, don't make a habit of wearing No. 9," Richard reportedly told Muller.

Muller remembers Richard's eyes lasering through him as he spoke his words. "He didn't joke or laugh," Muller said.

Howe says what he remembers most about Richard was the intensity in his eyes. "He could burn a hole through the back of your head with those eyes," Howe recalled.

Even though those eyes have closed for the last time, the legend of the Rocket will soar on through eternity.

## Gordie Howe

*Detroit Red Wings, 1950, 1952, 1954, and 1955*

After Gordie Howe's mother and father died, he told his sister repeatedly that he didn't want anything from the old Howe homestead in Saskatchewan.

"I said, 'Take anything you want,'" Howe said, smiling at the memory. "She came up to me with this old flower pot and said, 'You might want this.' I said, 'Read my lips: I don't want anything.'"

Howe's sister turned over the flower pot to show him the inscription. It read: "Stanley Cup Champion, 1951–52."

"I changed my mind," Howe remembered saying sheepishly. "I will take that."

To the best of Howe's recollections, that was the only keepsake "Mr. Hockey" received for winning any of his four Stanley Cup championships. He remembers giving it to his mother because a young bachelor didn't have much use for a flower pot, regardless of its inscription.

Winning the Cup in the 1950s was far different than it is today. The playoff intensity was similar. The passion was similar, the pride was similar. But the celebration time was shorter, says Howe. It lasted a night or two at best. When the Red Wings won in 1952, Howe was anxious to get out of town because in the summer he played semipro baseball in Saskatchewan. His baseball team paid him more per game than the Red Wings did. He played first and third base.

After Howe was married, he remembers packing up the car quickly and heading off to Florida. "Remember, we had to work in the summer," Howe said. "It cost us money to play for the Stanley Cup because we had to pay another month's rent."

Howe would attend the Red Wings' season-ending celebrations, although he confesses he didn't much like them for a couple of reasons. "When you were there, you realized that some of the guys wouldn't be around the following season," Howe said. "It was sad."

He was convinced that All-Star defenseman Bill Quackenbush was traded before the 1950 championship season because of something he said at the 1949 season-ending party. "You shouldn't mix management with the players like that," Howe said. "Players are drinking, having fun, and getting a little cocky. They say things they shouldn't."

Goaltender Terry Sawchuk, who won three Stanley Cups with Howe (1952, 1954, and 1955), was always a candidate to say something he shouldn't. Sometimes Sawchuk came across as not being happy to hang out with his teammates. But Howe said Sawchuk was often misunderstood. "He didn't like crowds, and this is a bad game to play if you don't like crowds," Howe said. "He would be at our gatherings, but he would be in the background."

Sawchuk had a temper, but Howe said he got along with him better than most people did. They had one confrontation away from the rink.

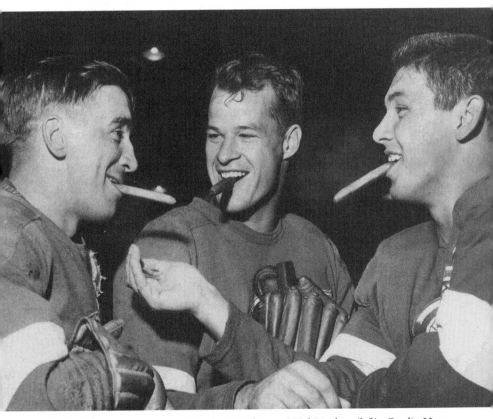

*When it came to stopping the Detroit Red Wings' Ted Lindsay (left), Gordie Howe (center), and Alex Delvecchio, it was no cigar. The trio ranked fifth, first, and second, respectively, on the team's all-time points list when this photo was taken. Howe finished his career, which spanned four decades and 2,421 games, with 1,071 goals and 21 All-Star appearances.*

"He got mad at me, and I told him to back off," Howe remembered. "I said, 'I will get 10 shots on you tomorrow in practice, and I can probably hit you between the eyes at least once.' He moved on to another table."

The next day in practice Howe sent his first shot whizzing over his head. Sawchuk came out with his own personal brand of apologies. "He said he had too much to drink," Howe remembered. "I told him, 'Then don't have so much to drink.'"

Sawchuk's moodiness could be heightened during the playoffs. He would treat autograph seekers with disdain, even children. Howe remembered that other Detroit players would go over and make some excuse to the fan. Howe remembers one story in particular that sums up how Sawchuk perceived the world. While the Red Wings were in an airport, Sawchuk saw singer Nat King Cole. "He said 'That's one of my favorite singers,'" Howe recalled. "I told him to go get his autograph, or he would be kicking himself if he didn't do it."

Cole dutifully put down his bag and signed his name. But he really just looked straight ahead and didn't acknowledge Sawchuk's presence. Sawchuk tore up the autograph and said, "If that's how you feel about it, I don't even want it."

Sawchuk's volatility was another reason why a championship celebration was also a cause for Howe to be on guard. Howe never gave too much thought to the fact that he wasn't showered with mementos when he won his Stanley Cup championships. But family members must have sensed that Howe regretted that he never received a championship ring. When son Mark was playing for the Philadelphia Flyers in the mid-1980s, he said frequently that if he won a Stanley Cup, he was going to order a ring for his father. The late Tommy Ivan, Gordie Howe's second NHL coach, saw Mark Howe being interviewed. When he mentioned the possibility of getting his father a ring, Ivan decided to take action. Ivan, then working for the Chicago Blackhawks, was quite close to Howe.

"He [Ivan] did things that were disturbing, like pulling me out of the game," Howe said.

Early in his career he remembers he got into a scrap on the ice, and when he came to the bench, Ivan quizzed him about the encounter.

"Don't you like that guy?" Ivan asked.

"I don't like anyone out there," Howe replied.

After his career ended, he asked Ivan whether he had appreciated that answer. "You played all the time, didn't you?" Ivan said.

Said Howe, "I think he thought I came of age then."

What Howe didn't know was that, after Ivan saw Max McNab's ring, he vowed to have one made for himself, and "one for the man who made me a lot of money."

That was Gordie Howe.

A box showed up at the Hartford Whalers' office where Howe was still working in the 1980s. Whalers' general manager Emile Francis brought it to Howe, and both were stunned by its magnificence.

Said Howe as he tried it on, "I think he likes me."

"No," said Francis. "He's in love."

Howe is proud of his accomplishments, but it was the accomplishments of another Howe that gave him the most joy. Mark Howe never won a Stanley Cup in 16 seasons as an NHL player. But he was a pro scout for the Detroit Red Wings when they won four Stanley Cup championships. "I was more excited to see Mark's name on the Cup than my own," Howe said.

## Bobby Orr

*Boston Bruins, 1970 and 1972*

Bobby Orr's best moment with the Stanley Cup probably came 20 years after he actually won Lord Stanley's prize for the first time.

In 1990 the Bruins gathered for their 20-year reunion, and former Bruins player Ted Green, then an assistant coach with the Stanley Cup–champion Edmonton Oilers, managed to convince the Oilers (and presumably the Hall of Fame) to allow him to bring Lord Stanley's chalice to the Bruins' party.

Most of the Bruins can barely remember having the Cup in 1970 because in that era it was whisked in and out of the city rather quickly. Most of the Bruins really never had an opportunity to inspect the Cup and stare at their names on it until that party.

To Orr, that reunion was special because it reminded him of how it took every last Bruins player to win that first championship.

*Boston Bruins star Bobby Orr flies through the air after driving the winning goal by St. Louis Blues goalie Glenn Hall in the sudden-death overtime period of their NHL Finals game in Boston Garden on May 10, 1970. Boston won 4–3 to win the series four straight and return the Stanley Cup to Boston for the first time in 29 years.*

"When you look at teams that win championships, it is the guys you don't hear much about that make a real difference," Orr said. "There are always MVPs that you don't expect. Every team has guys that you know what they are going to do. You could look at our team and expect certain performances out of guys like Esposito or [Gerry] Cheevers and, I guess, myself. But the other team always has their stars. You also know what to expect from them. That's why it's the guys you don't always read about that become the key guys. We had guys like Derek Sanderson, Eddie Westfall, Wayne Carleton, and Ace Bailey. And Dallas Smith and Don

Awrey played solid for us on defense. These guys all played the best hockey of their careers."

Orr doesn't remember much about the on- or off-ice celebration, particularly at the moment he was buried by teammates after netting the series-clinching goal. That tally now lives on in perpetuity thanks to the famous photo of Orr flying through the air, parallel to the ice, after scoring against Blues' netminder Glenn Hall. Orr had no understanding of how magnificent that goal was when he was in the midst of scoring it. This is how Orr described it: "The puck came off the board. I went in to try to cue it in. I knocked it back in the corner to Derek Sanderson. I went to the front of the net. He gave me a perfect pass. I was really just trying to get it on net. As I was moving across, and as I shot it towards the net and I was moving across, Glenn Hall, the goalie for St. Louis at that time, had to move with me. As he moved across, his legs opened. Now, I would like to say that I turned it up on its edge, I saw his legs open, and I shot it. That's not how it happened at all, guys. I put it on net and I was lucky. He opened his legs because he had to move across with me a little bit, and it went between his legs."

How did he become airborne? "I jumped, and Noel Picard, the St. Louis defenseman, helped a little bit with a stick under one of my legs, and he lifted me up out of frustration. But most of it was a jump for me, because I looked back over my shoulder and saw it going in."

Orr recalls his father, Doug, being there that night, along with the fathers of the other players. "The parents were more excited than the players, for God's sake," Orr said, laughing.

He added another element to the famous story of John McKenzie pouring the beer over Mayor Kevin White. "As I recall, the next time we won [in 1972] he poured one on Johnny," Orr said.

It is the fun-loving nature of the Bruins that Orr remembers. That's why the reunion was so special. Said Orr, laughing, "The guys hadn't changed much except they were a lot quieter."

## Wayne Gretzky
*Edmonton Oilers, 1984, 1985, 1987, and 1988*

About three hours after the Edmonton Oilers won their first Stanley Cup on May 17, 1984, a champagne-drenched Wayne Gretzky left the partying in the Oilers' dressing room to find general manager Glen Sather in his private office. "Hey, Glen," Gretzky said, "we're all about to leave. What do we do with the Stanley Cup?"

Sather grinned. "You won it. The Cup is yours to do what you want with."

Gretzky remembers that moment as if it happened last night. He remembers him and his father, Walter, walking out of the Northlands Coliseum with the Stanley Cup under his arm. "No one guarded it back then. The NHL president [John Zieger] handed it to you, and suddenly the Cup is yours," Gretzky said. "We put it in the car, drove a block and a half to the party, and took it in. That's what happened, and we just all had the Cup for the next five days."

Although it's difficult to prove or disprove (since the early records of Cup possession are little more than a collection of hand-me-down stories), it appears that the Edmonton Oilers were the first championship team that allowed players to take complete control of the Cup for an extended period without any supervision. In the 1950s and 1960s players recall seeing the Cup only on the night of the celebration, and in the 1970s Guy Lafleur had to steal the Stanley Cup to get private moments. Islanders captain Bryan Trottier says that players viewed GM Bill Torrey as being in charge of the Cup during the Islanders' four consecutive championships, although he didn't keep a very tight watch on it.

When the Oilers were dominating the NHL—winning five Cups in seven seasons from 1984 to 1990—veteran players like Gretzky, Mark Messier, and Kevin Lowe seemed to be in charge of making sure every player got his time with the Cup. Today, most Oilers say that they were quite democratic about making sure that every player had his moments with Lord Stanley's gift to hockey. "Players usually took it to their favorite restaurant or to their child's daycare, places like that," Gretzky recalled.

Edmonton was probably the first city to believe it owned the Stanley Cup. Gretzky said he never worried about anything untoward happening to the Cup because fans seemed to revere the town's connection to the trophy as much as the players did. "It was like a magnet," Gretzky said. "You would take the Stanley Cup down, and suddenly, wow, there would be people everywhere."

*"The Great One" Wayne Gretzky and the Edmonton Oilers carry off the Stanley Cup in Edmonton on May 19, 1984.*

The Oilers were almost too comfortable having the Cup. "We actually did lose the Cup when we won it the third time," Gretzky said. "You couldn't drive down the street with the Cup in the car so we would throw it in the trunk." He laughed. "Once we really did forget which trunk we had thrown it in. We couldn't figure out where it was one night. I don't remember whose trunk it was actually in, but I remember we couldn't find it."

Gretzky's former agent, Mike Barnett, recalled the incident quite well because the Cup was actually in his trunk. The Oilers had thrown it in there before a party, and only he remembered where it was the next day.

Gretzky insists he personally didn't do anything outlandish during his Cup celebrations, out of respect for the Cup's tradition. But he has fond memories of some of the more poignant moments with the trophy, such as the third Cup in 1987 when, after Ziegler presented him with the Cup, he gave it immediately to Oilers defenseman Steve Smith. Smith had been reduced to tears the year before when he accidentally shot the puck into his own net, eliminating the Oilers from the playoffs and allowing the Calgary Flames to reach the Stanley Cup Finals, where they lost to Montreal. Had the Oilers defeated the Flames in 1986, many believe they would have won five Stanley Cup championships in a row. The Montreal Canadiens (1956–1960) are the only NHL team to accomplish that feat.

Gretzky's gesture of allowing Smith to skate around with the Cup is one of the great moments in Stanley Cup lore. "It was something that the older players had talked about," Gretzky said about his decision to give Smith the special honor. "Mark and Kevin [Lowe] and I discussed it. No one in our dressing room had pointed the finger at Steve. But we knew he had taken public heat and mental abuse. He had battled through the year. He became a better player. One big reason why we ended up winning the championship was his play that year."

Gretzky said circumstances helped heighten that moment. "On the third Cup, the whole ceremony seemed to slow down," Gretzky remembered. "The first two seemed chaotic. The president walked on the ice and kind of threw the Cup at you. He didn't say anything. By [1987], they started to make it more of a presentation. It wasn't as chaotic, and I was able to give the Cup to Steve."

Gretzky's other memorable Cup moment came when he and his father had a private moment with the Cup in their possession. "I won't forget my dad saying, 'Who would have ever imagined that you would have won the Stanley Cup?'"

Actually, Walter Gretzky probably imagined that long before anyone else did.

# chapter 5

# Mario's Pool

## Phil Bourque
*Pittsburgh Penguins, 1991 and 1992*

By all accounts the Pittsburgh Penguins' Stanley Cup party at Mario Lemieux's Mt. Lebanon, Pennsylvania, house in 1992 was a tame affair until valuable role player Phil Bourque, attired only in his skivvies, climbed the waterfall sometime after 3:00 AM.

The Penguins had reason to let their hair down after winning their second consecutive Stanley Cup. For much of that season it looked as if the Penguins' Cup victories would be limited to one. After winning the Cup in 1991, the Penguins had only finished third in their division in 1991–1992, and they weren't even sure of making the playoffs until they got hot late in the season.

"There was a big meeting three-quarters of the way through the season in Calgary," Bourque remembered. "Craig Patrick came in and explained to us what Scotty Bowman is about. That really put us over the top."

The much-heralded Bowman had replaced the late Bob Johnson as head coach at the start of the 1991–1992 season after Johnson was diagnosed with brain cancer. The difference between the two coaching styles was pronounced: Johnson was a rah-rah coach who had optimism spilling out of every pore of his being. He was enthusiastic, chatty—a true people person. Bowman was more accomplished than Johnson in terms of NHL success. Before moving behind the Pittsburgh bench, he had already won five Stanley Cup championships with the Montreal Canadiens. But Bowman was far less communicative than Johnson; he was old-school in his approach about who played and who didn't. He didn't feel a need to explain his actions. Complicating the situation was the fact that the Penguins boasted many veteran players who were also set in their ways.

"We didn't know how to take Scotty's personality," Bourque remembered. "And he certainly didn't know how to adapt to our team. We had a lot of unique characters."

Patrick's talk helped immeasurably. "He let us understand how Scotty operates," Bourque said. "That was a major hurdle for us. He changed a bit, and we changed a bit. We started to play better. I really don't know if we would have even made the playoffs without that meeting."

Lemieux was clearly the most crucial player because he was simply a dominant offensive player. He could take over a hockey game like Michael Jordan could take over a basketball game or Tiger Woods can command a golf tournament. He inspired the Penguins through his on-ice dominance and his willingness to play through pain. It was difficult not to play with heart and purpose when you saw how much pain Lemieux had to endure just to get on the ice. But Lemieux was a reserved man in the dressing room. "He wouldn't say boo," Bourque remembered. "So when he did speak, and you were lacing up your skates or whatever you were doing, you stopped," Bourque said. "You directed your attention to him because, if he was speaking, you knew it was important."

In addition to Lemieux, Bourque recalls, there were also "three or four other guys who were the glue in the room."

He remembers Ulfie Samuelsson and Bob Errey keeping things light with their humor. He remembers Ron Francis as the team's composure monitor. "He had a calming effect on the team when things got scrambly or even if there was an issue with Scotty," Bourque said. "He didn't say a lot of words, but his choice of words was always on the money."

Next to Lemieux, the most important player on the team was probably Kevin Stevens. "He was the go-between for every guy on the team," Bourque said. "On every team you have your millionaires club and then you have the guys swimming in the bottom. Kevin was the guy in the middle keeping us all together."

*Phil Bourque of the Pittsburgh Penguins, shown here in action during a game against the Philadelphia Flyers in the early 1990s, forever etched himself in Stanley Cup lore when he heaved the Cup into Mario Lemieux's swimming pool.* Photo courtesy of Getty Images

Stevens was as close to the role players and the clubhouse attendants as he was to Mario. He was very democratic in spreading around his time and friendships. He made it his business to make sure that everyone felt comfortable. According to Bourque, the role players on the Penguins were afforded the same amount of respect as the stars. "That's what balanced our team," Bourque recalled. "The role players took pride in their contributions, and we all got along. There was no place for an ego on this team. It didn't matter whether you were Mario Lemieux or [tough guy] Jay Caufield, who wasn't playing. You didn't get away with anything in that room. It didn't matter how much money you had or how many goals you scored. If you weren't cutting the mustard, you were hearing about it from someone."

Bourque's job was primarily as a checker. He was supposed to use his speed to be an effective defensive player. But in the Finals against Chicago, he scored what seems now to have been an important goal. The Blackhawks had taken a 3–0 lead in Game 1; then Bourque scored to make it 3–1, and suddenly the Penguins believed they had a shot. They ended up winning that game 5–4 and swept the series.

In celebration, Lemieux invited everyone to his home for a team party. He had never before held a team function at his house, and when all of the coaches, teammates, and families arrived that night, the sense of accomplishment was heavy in the air.

Bourque recalls Lemieux's house as "a palace." One highlight was a regulation in-ground pool, with an adjacent four-layered waterfall that sloped down to the decking. Neon lights had been installed at each level, providing a festive background for the party. Goaltender Tom Barrasso was the first to take the Cup to the summit of the waterfall, leading to a picture-taking frenzy.

At about 3:00 AM, Bourque was sitting in the hot tub "enjoying a cocktail" and marveling at how awe-inspiring the Cup looked with the waterfall backdrop when he was moved to act in a manner that would forever make him a legend in Stanley Cup lore.

If ever a man was born to march to the beat of a different percussionist, it was Bourque. He was a proud American, a Chelmsford, Massachusetts, native, who went against New England tradition by electing to play Canadian junior hockey rather than college hockey. Not gifted enough to play alongside the elite players of the game, Bourque carved his own path to the NHL with a blue-collar work ethic and a Tasmanian devil playing style that always endeared him to fans and coaches. Pittsburghers loved Bourque. He may not have been a native, but he seemed to embody the city's spirit as much as Iron City beer and a lunch pail. In Pittsburgh, you must work for what you have; Bourque seemed like a poster boy for that kind of thinking. He once aspired to host his own hockey commentary television show, much like Don Cherry has in Canada. He's always had a flair for the unexpected. Once, much to the chagrin of Coach Johnson, Bourque found himself on a breakaway and decided to push the blade of his stick nose-down and pinned the puck to the ice. He carried the puck down the ice in that manner. He didn't score, but he made every highlight show in North America. That indeed had been his goal. Bourque was a spirited player on and off the ice. That is the simple explanation of why he did what he did.

"It hit me that this Cup needs to go in the water," Bourque remembered. "I hiked up there and grabbed the Cup."

As the underwear-clad Bourque stood up and held the Stanley Cup above his head, he struck a pose that was ever so close to King Kong standing on top of the Empire State Building.

It's unclear whether people really thought Bourque would throw the Cup, but when he heaved it over his head, it was as if the party started anew. The Cup filled with water and sank to the bottom. It took five or six players to dive in and pull it out. Some say it was more like seven or eight players. People were stunned at how heavy the Cup was after it had been filled with water.

Asked whether Lemieux was a member of the Cup rescue team, Bourque laughed. "I think Mario was just trying to hold down the fort. This was a multimillion-dollar mansion, and there was water all over and food everywhere. He had his hands full. And, truthfully, it is hard to picture him stripped down to his skivvies and jumping in the water."

Once the Cup had taken its first belly flop into the water, a new round of picture-taking began. The Cup stayed in the pool for the rest of the night. "As soon as the Cup made contact with the water, it got wild after that," Bourque said. "Before then, the party was going all right, but it wasn't really jumping. I remember thinking, *We've got to get a little crazy.*"

Originally the Penguins were guarded about the evening's events, thinking they would be submerged in trouble for their shenanigans. "We weren't being disrespectful," Bourque said. "We were just letting loose."

Only through the years did the Penguins come to understand that they weren't the first, nor would they be the last Stanley Cup winners to swim with the Stanley Cup. The Hall of Fame now expects the Stanley Cup to be baptized in chlorine on a yearly basis. The removal of the Cup's tarnish is a fall ritual at the Hall of Fame. Engravers know immediately how much pool time the Cup has received simply by the look of the Cup.

Instead of getting himself and the Penguins in trouble, Bourque made himself a Stanley Cup legend that starry night in Mt. Lebanon.

He would touch the Cup again before it was returned to the Hall of Fame. After the second consecutive championship, the Cup was passed among the players more than it was after the first title. Through a quirk in the informal scheduling, he picked up the Cup from team president Paul Martha on a Thursday. Today's formalized Cup sharing allows for each player to have it only for 24 hours, but when Bourque received it in 1992 he was told that the Cup's next appearance wasn't scheduled until Paul Coffey got it at a Toronto golf tournament. That meant Bourque had possession of it for four days.

He loaded the Cup in the back of his Ford Bronco and immediately headed off to see a friend at the Baltimore shore, where he set up shop in a bar. Plenty of friends and acquaintances drank out of Lord Stanley's mug that weekend.

"But what was really neat was going down the highway with the Cup bouncing around in the Bronco. "The look on everyone's faces as they looked inside," Bourque said, laughing, "they were trying to figure out if that was the real Cup."

But the legend of Bourque's Cup escapade doesn't end with the dunking in Mario's pool or the drive to Baltimore. When he returned home, he discovered a rattling in the Cup. A quick investigation showed him that the nonmetal base was held together only by four bolts. Although he confesses that he isn't mechanically inclined, he thought he might be able to take the Cup apart and determine the cause of the rattle. He put a pen light in his mouth, stuck his whole head in the Cup, and quickly determined that one nut holding on the bowl at the top had become loose. He quickly solved that problem. But while his noggin was up there, he saw that those who had repaired the Cup before him had engraved their names. There were three names and dates showing. An idea began brewing in Bourque's head.

He found a screwdriver and, near the names of the formal engravers, began chiseling in his own inscription. It took him three hours. When it was done it read: "Enjoy it...Phil 'Bubba' Bourque."

Proud of his work, Bourque presumed that he would forever be the only player to have his name engraved on both the front and inside of the Cup. Already a legend for his Cup toss, Bourque didn't feel obliged to share his secret engraver's life with the rest of the world. His only fear was that the Hall of Fame, during its annual summer cleaning of the Cup, might discover his handiwork. If someone did uncover his secret, he wondered whether his crude effort would be buffed out. But that thought certainly didn't consume the rest of his summer. Having earned a reputation as a strong role player and coming off a 20-goal season, he was able to get a good free-agent contract from the New York Rangers that following summer.

He actually forgot about his Cup caper until he was on the National Hockey League boat cruise in the summer of 1993. Fans pay to take a cruise with NHL players; Bourque signed on for the journey.

Defenseman J.J. Daigneault, a member of the Montreal Canadiens' 1993 championship team, was also on the NHL cruise. At one point on the trip, he came up to Bourque and started laughing before words finally emerged from his month, "I saw what you did!"

Bourque looked at him in a quizzical manner; he had no idea what Daigneault was talking about.

"I saw your name inside the Cup," Daigneault said. Bourque was stunned. "How did you see it?"

Daigneault just grinned. "Because I put my name there, too."

## Pierre McGuire
*Assistant Coach, Pittsburgh Penguins, 1991 and 1992*
As Pierre McGuire recalls, as soon as the Stanley Cup hit Mario Lemieux's pool, he and coach Scotty Bowman hit the road.

"We were sitting there having a good time," McGuire said, chuckling at the memory. "And we saw Bourque throw the Cup off the waterfall, and Scotty grabbed me and said, 'It's time to go.' He said, 'This is not a time for coaches to be here.'"

McGuire recalls seeing the Stanley Cup placed on the table the next morning "and it was rocking back and forth. The whole base of the Cup was dented."

But McGuire's memory of Pittsburgh's back-to-back championships have more to do with pain and determination than the celebration. "In year one, Mario Lemieux's back was so bad that he couldn't tie his own skates," McGuire said. "We had a locker room attendant who tied his skates. He could barely bend over."

In the second Cup run, McGuire said Lemieux was in even worse physical shape. "It was more of the same, plus he had a broken hand that happened in the second round when Adam Graves slashed him," McGuire said. "The Rangers thought they had us because Mario was done."

The Rangers won Games 2 and 3, and then the series turned in the Penguins' favor when Ron Francis beat goalie Mike Richter with a lengthy shot from outside the blue line. "Our whole team hung in there, but it was Ron Francis that steered the ship in year two," McGuire said.

Although Lemieux was limited to just 15 games in the 1992 play-offs, he scored 16 goals and added 18 assists to win his second consecutive Conn Smythe Trophy.

But the Penguins' team had a strong supporting cast. "Bryan Trottier taught everyone how to win, and Troy Loney and Bourque were spectacular penalty killers," McGuire said. "Bob Errey was very unsung."

In year two, defenseman Kjell Samuelsson was in Lemieux's league in terms of pain tolerance. "He played through unbelievable agony because of a severely broken hand," McGuire said. Samuelsson needed pain injections to stay in the lineup. "I used to go into the training room so he could grab my arm just to take the needle," McGuire said.

Bob Johnson was the coach in the first championship year, and Scotty Bowman took over in year two after Johnson was diagnosed with cancer. McGuire said the two coaching giants had different styles, and yet each had his own way of getting the most out of the Penguins.

"Bob was able to delegate with more ease," McGuire said. "There was an air of calmness around the group because Bob was like that."

Bowman had been out of coaching for several years before general manager Craig Patrick asked him to go back behind the bench. "With Scotty, everyone was always on edge," McGuire said. "He was coaching like the old days, very authoritative. But Scotty changed after a while."

McGuire understood Bowman's methods better than players because he discussed strategy with him on a daily basis. More important, he watched and learned. "What made Scotty successful?" McGuire asked. "It was his ability to change on the fly, to evaluate the strengths of his teams on a shift-to-shift basis and recognizing who was going great and the players that needed to be sat."

McGuire said Bowman's intellect helped him adapt to whatever happened with the rules, the players, or the game on the ice. "He could have been anything he wanted to be," McGuire said. " He could have been a doctor, lawyer, coach. His IQ is off the chart."

Bowman's competitiveness was Rocket Richard quality. "He really did coach every game like it was the Stanley Cup Finals," McGuire said.

During the 1991–1992 regular season, McGuire recalls Bowman and he were walking across the ice to take their positions behind the bench before a home game against the Chicago Blackhawks. The crowd was loud and boisterous. "I said to Scotty, 'This is a big game tonight,'" McGuire said. "Suddenly he grabbed my coat and said, 'Don't ever tell me tonight's game is a big game. They are all big games in this league.' I was so shocked by his reaction. But it's a lesson I've never forgotten."

## Troy Loney
*Pittsburgh Penguins, 1991 and 1992*

When tough guy Jay Caufield raised the Stanley Cup at a raucous Pittsburgh Penguins championship pep rally at Point State Park, the overflowing horde of fans had no idea that all of his teammates were overcome by a feeling of pending disaster. Phil Bourque's now-famous Stanley Cup splash in Mario Lemieux's pool had happened the night before and, by all accounts, the Cup was being held together only by the grace of a higher power.

"We kept telling each other to be careful when you pick it up because it was going to snap apart," Troy Loney recalled. "We all remembered when it was our turn to lift the Cup, except Caufield. And when he picked it up by the end, we all backed up, going, 'Whoa.' I could envision the top of the Cup falling off as he lifted it over his head."

Perhaps Lord Stanley's spirit was watching over the Penguins that day—because the Cup held together as Caufield hoisted it high in the air. That image isn't likely to ever be erased from Loney's memory.

Loney admits that the Penguins had quite a bit of difficulty raising the Cup from the bottom of Lemieux's pool. "It didn't come out unscathed," he said. His memory of who exactly rescued the Cup is hazy.

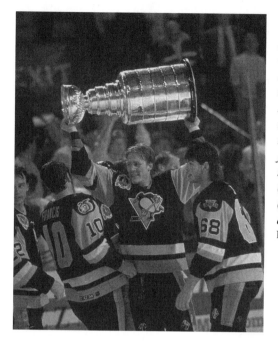

*Troy Loney of the Pittsburgh Penguins hoists the Stanley Cup over his head as he celebrates his team's 6–5 victory over the Chicago Blackhawks in Game 4 of the Stanley Cup Finals at the Chicago Stadium on June 1, 1992. Penguins teammates Ron Francis (No. 10) and Jaromir Jagr (No. 68) join in the celebration.*
Photo courtesy of Getty Images

He knows he made a few dives, but probably not as many as Bourque. "I think Phil felt pretty responsible," Loney said. "We had great reverence for the Cup. No one was trying to damage the Cup."

The Hall of Fame had anticipated that the trophy was due to break apart at some point. But the Penguins didn't know that, and were rather horrified about its condition when it emerged from its underwater journey. "We are hemming and hawing and looking at it, and we can see that underneath the old Cup it's hanging by a thread," Loney said. "And it certainly wasn't as shiny as it was going into the pool."

The Bourque episode is the signature event of the Penguins' glory years, but Loney has other Cup memories that he cherishes as much, if not more. When the Penguins won their first championship, no system had been established for granting players time with the Cup. Since not many Penguins lived in Pittsburgh during the summer, and most went home shortly after the postseason ended, those who did live in town were able to get the Cup for an extended period.

After the first Penguins victory, Loney had it for three days. On the first morning, he filled the bowl with Wheaties and ate his breakfast from the Stanley Cup. It made perfect sense, considering Wheaties is billed as "the Breakfast of Champions." And he won't forget that he took the Cup out to show a neighbor in Pittsburgh, a trip he thought would take only a few moments. "And four hours later I got off my lawn," Loney recalled.

Loney's opportunity to carry the Stanley Cup around the ice was indeed special to him. But what he remembers most was carrying the Cup across Alberta in a half-ton farm truck for three hours in 1992. "I'm with my dad [Roy] and brother [Todd], and we have the Cup crated in the back, and we are just giggling about what we are doing," Loney said. "I still remember the look on their faces. It was as if they just couldn't believe what we were doing. There was a giddiness that surrounded them."

Born in Bow Island, Alberta, Loney received permission to transport the Cup back to his hometown after the Pittsburgh Penguins' second triumph. Although at that time players were not officially given time with the Cup, it was starting to become more common for them to request private time.

Loney wanted to take the Cup back home to use as part of a fund-raising effort with his charity golf tournament. He auctioned off a bottle of champagne and a chance to drink from the Stanley Cup. The event fetched $1,200 for his charitable cause.

On another occasion, after a late-night party, he remembers escorting the Cup back home with some buddies—a four-block walk across the TransCanada highway—when a trucker spotted the Cup being carried. "It was 2:00 in the morning, and he is laying on the air horn," Loney recalled.

He also remembered the awe that his father had for the Cup and how good it felt to take the Cup to the house of a neighbor, Pat Knibbs, who had been his hockey mentor. Knibbs' son, Darrell, had been drafted by an NHL team, but hadn't reached the show. "He didn't know what to do or say," Loney said. "It was very emotional."

What has stuck with Loney through the years about the Penguins' championship run was that they were not a particularly close team off the ice. "But on the ice we were very close," Loney recalled. "You can have a coach tell you what your role is, but what was key on our team was that everyone accepted their role. We understood in order to succeed we all had to do what we had to do. Everyone recognized the importance of those who scored the goals and the importance of those who stopped the goals from being scored."

Loney said it was impossible for him to pinpoint an unsung hero from that team. Everyone understood even then that every player is indispensable at some point. "What made that team amazing is that everyone did contribute," Loney said. "Randy Gilhen scored a big goal. Bob Errey had some big goals. Phil Bourque had big goals. Gordie Roberts played well on defense. Everyone stepped up at his time."

Although he didn't mention it, Loney himself was one of the role players who had his moments in the spotlight. He was a physical player who wasn't known as a goal-scorer; still, he had six playoff goals in 1991 and 1992 and was always known as a man who efficiently did his job. "When we went through the first time, I didn't experience everything," Loney said, "because I was just focused on doing my job. I just didn't want to be the guy to make the mistake."

Loney hopes that the passage of time won't erase the importance of another man from the first Penguins championship. "The guy who did the greatest job of keeping us all together was [coach] Bob Johnson," Loney said. "He defined our roles. We had guys screaming that they wanted more ice time, and he just said no."

Johnson just had a knack for being firm without causing insurrection among his troops. He was fatherly in that he was tough when he had to be and yet always treated players as if they were members of his family. He was always positive and seemed to know how to deal with both stars and role players.

The Penguins were devastated when Johnson was diagnosed with cancer during the summer after their first championship. He died in November of 1991. All of the Penguins attended the funeral in Colorado. "It was one of the saddest moments of my life," Loney recalled.

At the end of the service at the burial site, Loney thinks it was Bourque, a Johnson favorite, who went up first and tapped his championship ring on Johnson's casket. One by one, each Penguins player did the same in a final salute to the man who had guided them on their journey to become champions.

# chapter 6

# Keepers of the Cup

## Phil Pritchard
*Hockey Hall of Fame Director of Information and Acquisitions*
Phil Pritchard didn't play for the 1974 Stanley Cup champion Philadelphia Flyers, but 20 years later he took bows as if he had.

Serving in his role as one of the Stanley Cup guardians in 1994, Pritchard was pressed into service as a Flyers' stand-in during a parade to honor the 20th anniversary of Philadelphia's first NHL championship. Short on players to ride on a float, ex-Flyers player Joe Watson drafted Pritchard to play a role.

"Joe said, 'Just get on the float and wave and pretend you are Gary Dornhoefer,'" Pritchard recalled. "There I was with Bernie Parent, Bob Kelly, and Watson going down the street, waving at everyone."

No fan asked him who he was. Did he feel like a Flyer? "No," he said, chuckling. "I felt like an idiot."

Whether Pritchard enjoyed that particular day or not, his Stanley Cup duty has put him in a variety of roles that most fans can only dream of. He has sat in a sauna with Dallas Stars winger Jere Lehtinen in Finland as part of a Stanley Cup celebration. He went fishing with then–Colorado Avalanche winger Chris Simon and golfing with Patrick Roy in a pro tournament.

Aside from NHL players, no one is more intimate with the Cup's aura and mystique than Pritchard. No matter who wins the championship series, Pritchard is there when the Cup is presented. Other employees now serve as bodyguard/babysitter for the Cup on visits to players' hometowns, but for big events Pritchard is the one wearing the white gloves necessary to handle the world's most famous sports trophy.

It's part of Pritchard's job to assure that the Cup is treated with the respect and dignity befitting its history and tradition. He finds that is the easiest aspect of his job. Despite the public perception that the Stanley Cup is often treated like a giant beer stein, it has been Pritchard's observation that many players treat the Cup like a religious artifact. Players do have fun with the Cup, but that doesn't mean they abuse its symbolism.

"What I've always found is that the players respect it so much," Pritchard said. "The other thing is that the players that you think would have the wildest celebrations are the ones that usually have the quiet celebrations with family."

One of the most memorable moments of Pritchard's Cup tour was being with Lehtinen when he invited all of his childhood hockey buddies to the Stanley Cup sauna party at his cottage on an island off the coast of Finland. Pritchard traveled in an army boat to reach the location.

"But he wouldn't bring the Stanley Cup inside the sauna and close the doors, because he thought the heat might wreck the Cup," Pritchard said. "He just put it right at the entrance. But it was a traditional Finnish scene."

He went fishing with Simon and the Stanley Cup on a lake in the small northern Ontario hamlet of Wawa. Nary a walleye or perch landed in their bucket, and yet it was the best day of fishing Simon and Pritchard can ever remember experiencing.

"Chris put his arm around me at the end of the day and said, 'A lot of people never fulfill their dream. Today I fulfilled two. I had the Cup in my hometown and I went fishing.' He was so emotional," said Pritchard.

Pritchard was struck by Roy's generosity as he played in a pro-am tournament with the Cup in Lake Tahoe, Nevada. "He was playing the course, but every hole that he finished he came back to meet the people and have photos taken with fans and the Cup," Pritchard said. "It made me proud to be associated with hockey because the other athletes weren't doing this. Only Patrick was. To be in a nontraditional hockey place like Nevada with people lining up to see the Cup, it was amazing. And

Patrick was so good with the fans. He was like a god in this non-hockey environment."

According to Pritchard, players police themselves, particularly with regard to the unwritten rule about non-winning players lifting the Cup.

The Stanley Cup's unwritten rules were lost in translation on a night in 1998 when some Japanese hockey fans tried to convince then–Vancouver Canucks player Trevor Linden to pose with the Cup in Tokyo.

Attending a party at the Canadian Embassy during the season-opening Anaheim-Vancouver series at the start of the 1998–1999 season, Linden struggled to overcome the language barrier and find a polite way to explain why he couldn't touch the Stanley Cup.

"The friendly Japanese people kept telling him to come closer and look at it, and he wouldn't," Pritchard said. "He stayed five feet away and looked at some of the names, and he wouldn't go closer. When he left, I tried to explain to them that he wouldn't come closer because he has never won the Cup."

No rule exists that bars a player from hoisting the Cup before he has won it. Yet current and even former players act as if they might face criminal charges if they touch the Cup without having actually won it. That tradition has grown stronger in recent years, with the Cup travelling around the globe. Today, even European players know the NHL's tradition. But that wasn't always the case. "When we took the Cup over to Finland, some Finnish players got their pictures taken with the Cup," Pritchard recalled. "Today you wouldn't see Saku Koivu getting his picture with the Cup if it was in Finland."

Hall of Fame officials have noted that Darryl Sittler, who played 15 seasons without winning the Cup, won't have his picture taken with it. "He will stand near it, but he won't have his picture taken with it," Pritchard said.

Although the Hall of Fame has never tried to hide it, most fans don't realize that there are actually two Cups. In 1993 the Hall of Fame had a duplicate Stanley Cup produced at a cost of $75,000. The engraving was copied exactly, although legend now has it that some of the misspelled names of the past were corrected on the duplicate. The only real

*Curators from the Hockey Hall of Fame, Craig Campbell and Phil Pritchard, carry the Stanley Cup onto the ice after Game 6 of the 2008 NHL Stanley Cup Finals at Mellon Arena on June 4, 2008, in Pittsburgh.* Photo courtesy of Getty Images

difference is supposed to be the Hall of Fame seal on the bottom of the true Stanley Cup.

Most fans presume incorrectly that the duplicate Stanley Cup is the one that travels to the players' hometowns. "That's the most popular question that we get at the Hall of Fame," Pritchard said. "Which Cup goes out to the players?"

When the duplicate Cup was created, NHL commissioner and then–Hall of Fame director Scotty Morrison conducted a meeting at which the issue was discussed at length. It was unanimously agreed upon that NHL players should always have the true Cup at their personal celebrations.

"It's felt that players work so hard to earn this Cup that they deserve nothing but the real one," Pritchard said. "You wouldn't want a guy who works for 35 years to win the Cup to get the fake one."

Pritchard said he has never had to step in and say no to a player's idea of what to do with the Stanley Cup. "[Dallas Stars winger] Blake Sloan said he was going to take it sky diving, but I think he was kidding," Pritchard said.

When it comes to the Stanley Cup, you really can't be too sure.

## Walt Neubrand

*Keeper of the Cup*

As a keeper of the Stanley Cup, Walt Neubrand feels as if his relationship with players should be treated as if it included a lawyer-client privilege.

"Some guys have asked me if I would ever write a book," Neubrand said. "And I tell them I would never write a book because people don't want to hear that a player takes the Cup to a hospital. They want dirt, and I'm never going to blow the whistle on all of these players who have been really nice to me, and frankly it's none of my business how they choose to celebrate."

Neubrand says "99 percent" of the players don't do anything that isn't an accepted practice on their day with the Stanley Cup. "If you took away alcohol, our job would be much easier," Neubrand said. "If the Stanley Cup didn't have a bowl on top, our job would be easier."

Neubrand's job as one of the Stanley Cup keepers has afforded him as many special Cup moments as the players who have won it. He's witnessed two wedding proposals, seen a monkey sitting in the Cup, been "screeched in" as part of a Newfoundland celebration, stood next to the Hollywood sign in Southern California, and, most important, met his wife while on Stanley Cup duty.

Although Neubrand did once have to remove the Stanley Cup from Dominik Hasek's party in the Czech Republic, he finds that his Cup keeper duties are more rewarding than risky. "Players' personalities dictate what they do with the Cup," Neubrand said. "Nick Lidstrom isn't going to do the same thing that Chris Chelios would do."

Neubrand said the general rule is that the more times a player has won the Stanley Cup the less wild his celebration will be. "Honestly, players are always scared at first when they get it because they know that if something bad happens, it will come back to them," Neubrand said. "The problem we often have is that a player's friends believe they have the same rights as the player, and we have to tell them it doesn't work like that."

Neubrand said he almost feels bad for the first-time Cup winners because most don't realize how draining the day will be. "You almost want to go up to them and warn them, 'Are you ready for this?'" Neubrand said. "They usually have a long itinerary, and they don't realize they will have tons of people in their face and tons of requests. Their mom and dad will have people they want to see it, and their grandparents will have people. They won't have much time by themselves."

According to the general Stanley Cup guidelines, Lord Stanley's Cup should not make any appearances in casinos or strip clubs, and Cup keepers will prevent it from entering swimming pools because of the damage it causes. But everything else is really up to the keeper's discretion. He has to make a judgment call about whether it is appropriate behavior.

"There isn't anything in stone, but I'm sure someday there is going to be," Neubrand said. It's generally held that only someone who has won a Stanley Cup is allowed to hold it over his head. However, Neubrand said the policing of that rule differs depending upon which keeper is with the Cup.

"As Cup guys, we interpret the rules," Neubrand said. "Some guys don't want it to be picked up by anyone who hasn't won. But I will allow someone pick it up as long as it is being given to a player."

The big argument Cup keepers have comes when a player allows a friend to raise the Cup. "If Lidstrom gives the Cup to his buddy, and he raises it, I'm not going to say anything," Neubrand said. "I've had arguments with other guys over that. To me, that's a player's prerogative. And why not? He has earned the right to have the Cup, and if he wants to share it someone, who am I to say it is wrong?"

That's how he felt when Carolina equipment manager Skip Cunningham took the Stanley Cup to a Boston Red Sox game and a request was made to allow a monkey to sit in it for special photos.

"I said, 'Why not? Just put a towel down,'" Neubrand recalled.

He said not even all keepers agree on what should be allowed and what shouldn't. There's an ongoing debate.

On his watch, Neubrand has seen Sergei Zubov and Brad Richard both place lobsters in the Stanley Cup. "Cereal, popcorn, ice cream—those are all boring now," he said, laughing.

Neubrand teaches elementary school as his full-time job and started his Stanley Cup career in 1997. "Everyone thinks we take training for weeks and weeks and that we go to some kind of school to handle the Cup," Neubrand said. "Phil Pritchard asked me on a Wednesday if I wanted to be one of the guys to take the Cup, and I said okay, and on Saturday I took the Stanley Cup to Scotty Bowman."

Coincidentally, Neubrand brought the Stanley Cup back to Bowman in 2008. "The funny thing was that he did almost exactly the same thing with the Cup that he did the first time I went," Neubrand said.

Neubrand spends about 30 to 40 nights on the road with the Stanley Cup, and most of his days are very long because player parties are similar to wedding receptions. Some party-goers stay beyond 2:00 AM. "I've gotten a lot smarter on how to do it in terms of getting sleep," Neubrand said. "When I first started, I was gung-ho and I didn't want to miss anything. I worked on very little sleep. Now I try to get sleep when I can…. But if I get five hours per night, I'm lucky."

In the summer of 2004 he handled the Cup for Tampa Bay players Andre Roy, Martin St. Louis, and Eric Perrin, and ended up going 42 hours without sleep at one stretch. Neubrand was in the helicopter when Roy proposed to his girlfriend, using the Stanley Cup to hold the ring. "She was totally floored," Neubrand said.

Neubrand was also a witness in a New York City nightclub when Ryan Shannon, then with Anaheim, proposed during a Stanley Cup celebration.

He said it's difficult to say what Cup experiences he liked best, but among his most memorable was Luc Robitaille's Stanley Cup photo session at the Hollywood sign. "We went to all of the Los Angeles landmarks, and he got a special permit to go up to the Hollywood sign," Neubrand said. "I never realized how big those letters were. They are like 35 feet high."

Although there were no players involved, Neubrand enjoyed a trip to Arctic Canada for a Native American Tournament in Nunavut. "It was in February, and it was minus-65 [centigrade, or minus-85 fahrenheit]," Neubrand said. "You could only be outside two minutes or you would freeze. I brought the biggest, heaviest jacket I owned, and they all laughed at me. 'What is that?' They were all wearing deer hide or caribou."

As an outdoorsman, Neubrand also enjoyed his trip to Dawson City in the Yukon Territory. The Cup was brought in to help commemorate the 100th anniversary of the Dawson City Nuggets' month-long trip to Ottawa to play the Silver Seven for the Stanley Cup in 1904. "They had a ritual of drinking some kind of liquor with a frostbitten toe in it," Neubrand said. "I didn't do it, but Phil Pritchard did."

Neubrand did "screech in" when he accompanied the Stanley Cup to Newfoundland in the summer of 2008 for Dan Cleary's memorable day with the Stanley Cup, which will be detailed later in the book. Visitors to Newfoundland are asked to participate in an initiation ritual. "The screeching-in was great," Cleary said. "We had a professional guy, like a comedian, come by and get some of the Cup keepers and some of the family members from abroad. It was great. You have to kiss a cod, eat bologna and the hard bread, singing the 'Newfie Jig'—there's a few different things that come along with it."

Participants are also asked to down a shot of a rum-like liquor called "screech." "Every time we screwed up something, they added more to it, and by the time we were done, I had a half a glass of screech," Neubrand said. "But it was all in good fun."

Neubrand's top life-altering Cup experience came when he accompanied the Stanley Cup to Tampa for the 1999 All-Star Game. While standing by the Cup and answering questions, Neubrand started chatting with a volunteer named Laura Fowler.

When the event was over, they exchanged emails and then started to date. Four years later they married. As they were planning their nuptials, they realized they didn't know anyone who could perform the ceremony. Then Neubrand, who knew the Ilitch family from handling Detroit Red Wings Cup celebrations, remembered that Red Wings owner Mike

Ilitch's daughter, Lisa, had told him she was an ordained minister. She ended up performing their marriage ceremony.

Although Neubrand allows players their private moments with the Stanley Cup, he also doesn't mind sharing the story of the Dallas Stars' crazy night with the Cup because the bad behavior didn't come from the Stars. "That was the wildest night ever," Neubrand said.

According to Neubrand, it was Derian Hatcher and Craig Ludwig who asked him at a team party at the Apple Grill whether he would bring the Stanley Cup to a party hosted by the heavy metal group Pantera. "I had never heard of them, but I found out who they were that night," Neubrand said. "You know how you go to someone's house and you see *Time* or *Newsweek* or *National Geographic* on the coffee table? Here in this house, there were *Shaved* and *Hustler* magazines. And I remember thinking, *Uh-oh, what kind of night am I in for?*"

Vinnie Paul was the drummer, and his house had a pool that was shaped like a Crown Royal whiskey bottle. "Because that's all he drank," Neubrand said. "The label was at the bottom, and the cap of the pool was a hot tub.... I never saw it, but some of the players told me the house had a wall straight out of a James Bond movie. It revolved and went back into a secret bedroom."

Neubrand only tells this story because he wants to again exonerate Guy Carbonneau of the charge that he tossed the Cup in the pool from the balcony.

"I can tell you that the Cup never got thrown from the balcony," Neubrand said. "I'm not positive, but I think Joe Nieuwendyk got pushed in with the Cup."

It was Vinnie Paul who said Carbonneau threw it. "I never understood that made-up rumor," Neubrand said. "If you make up a rumor, why would you pick Guy Carbonneau? He's a respectful guy. When they did that, Guy was livid. He was furious. I saw him later, and he wanted to sue them."

After the Cup went into the pool, Neubrand asked the players to get it out, and they did. "Then I went to get something to drink, and it was in the hot tub," Neubrand said. At 5:00 AM Neubrand said he went to Joe Nieuwendyk and suggested that it would be a good idea for the

Stanley Cup to be taken back to the hotel and cleaned up so it could be ready for the parade.

"Two days later," Neubrand said, "I'm at the gate at the airport, and I'm looking at a TV, and there's Vinnie Paul saying, 'Yeah, Mr. Hockey himself Guy Carbonneau threw the cup in from the balcony. Why would he do that?'"

Neubrand's good experiences far outweigh the bad ones. The reason the Cup was removed from Hasek's backyard in the Czech Republic is that Hasek took the Cup into his pool after he was told that it was against the rules. When Neubrand's fellow Cup keeper attempted to rescue the Cup, he was pulled into the water. That's when Neubrand decided the Cup was leaving the party.

That story had a happy ending because 2002 Cup winner Jiri Slegr was at the party, and he approached the Cup keepers and negotiated a compromise. "He said, 'I'm really sorry what happened, and I under-stand how you feel,'" Neubrand said. "'But we have 25,000 fans waiting at the town square to see the Cup. And they have been there since 5:00 in the morning.'"

As part of the plea agreement, Slegr agreed to help safeguard the Cup at the event. Neubrand didn't want to disappoint the fans, and he agreed. True to his word, Slegr made sure there were no more incidents.

It wasn't easy for Neubrand to strip Hasek of the Cup, because his own rule is that he tries not to interfere with player plans. "I consider myself the background," Neubrand said. "I'm there because I have to be, and I feel sometimes like I'm imposing...but sometimes because I've been to so many of these gatherings I can offer tips to make their days more memorable or easier."

Neubrand said his other rule is, "I like to share the Cup with people.... I'm not going to pull a guy off the street and say, 'Hey, come and touch the Cup,' But if I see a volunteer working for the Red Wings all day, I'm going to let her hold the Cup. That doesn't mean she is going to raise it over her head."

# chapter 7

# The Detroit Red Wings

## Nicklas Lidstrom

*Detroit Red Wings, 1997, 1998, 2002, and 2008*

When NHL Commissioner Gary Bettman called Detroit Red Wings captain Nicklas Lidstrom to claim the championship trophy in 2008, it would have been appropriate for Lidstrom to raise his passport with the Stanley Cup.

Lidstrom tore down another league barrier by becoming the first European captain to win the Stanley Cup. "I'm proud to be the first," Lidstrom said. "People said you can't win with Europeans, and we proved that wrong. As long as you can skate well, as long as you can be tough to play against, you can still play."

Starting with former general manager Jim Devellano, the Red Wings have long embraced European talent. The Red Wings won four Stanley Cup championships from 1997 to 2008, and European players played significant roles in each of those championships.

Lidstrom was one of seven Swedes—Henrik Zetterberg, Tomas Holmstrom, Johan Franzen, Mikael Samuelsson, Niklas Kronwall, and Andreas Lilja were the others—on the Red Wings' 2008 championship team. Detroit's United Nations–style roster also included two Czechs (Jiri Hudler and Dominik Hasek), a Slovakian (Tomas Kopecky), a Russian (Pavel Datsyuk), and the first Finnish player (Valtteri Filppula) in team history.

Having replaced retired Steve Yzerman in October 2006, Lidstrom had only been captain 20 months when he led the Red Wings to a Stanley Cup title. "There was never a doubt in my mind that Nick would replace Yzerman as captain," said Devellano, who still works for the Red Wings as a senior vice president.

Red Wings coach Mike Babcock said Lidstrom was the right choice because "no one does the right thing every day more than Nick."

It was a near-impossible mission to succeed Yzerman, who is generally regarded as one of the most respected captains in NHL history. But Lidstrom's credentials as one of the top defensemen in NHL history made it seem as if one legend was simply following another.

Yzerman was never a speechmaker, and Lidstrom's quiet, composed style made it seem like nothing had changed. "I looked at it as another challenge for me late in my career to be captain of a great team with a lot of history and a great tradition," Lidstrom said.

Knowing he might someday receive an opportunity to lead, Lidstrom had studied Yzerman's leadership style. "What I learned," he said, "is that you can't just say all the things in the locker room. You have to show up and prove it on the ice."

In 2002 Lidstrom had become the first European to win the Conn Smythe Trophy as the NHL's postseason MVP. He has now won the Norris Trophy six times as the league's top defenseman.

"If you see him play one game he won't wow you, but when you see him play night after night, you realize he makes every little play," Holland said. "He's playing as well as he ever has. He hasn't slipped."

Although there is still work to be done, it's possible that when Lidstrom retires he will have enough credentials to be considered the second-best defenseman in NHL history. He's already in the top five. "He's a great defender because of his stick skills and his intelligence," Holland said. "He still has passion."

Not all that long ago, it was unthinkable for a team to consider naming a European captain because it was often said that Europeans didn't appreciate the Stanley Cup as much as they admired an Olympic gold medal or a World Championship.

Don't tell that to Lidstrom, who has traditionally played his best hockey in the playoffs, sometimes playing 30 minutes per game.

In 2007–2008, the NHL seemed more open to the idea of European captains, because at one point 13 of the 30 NHL teams had one. However, it was appropriate that the Red Wings be the first because the

*Detroit Red Wings captain Nicklas Lidstrom, of Sweden, holds the Stanley Cup during the team's championship-banner raising prior to their NHL hockey season opener against the Toronto Maple Leafs in Detroit on October 9, 2008.*

Red Wings had blazed the trail for European acceptance. "I've been here through the Russian Five and now the Swedish Seven," said Detroit center Kris Draper. "I've played with a lot of Europeans. Nationality is just not an issue [in Detroit]."

Lidstrom has been in Detroit since 1991, meaning he has spent almost as many years in the United States as he has in Sweden. "[Zetterberg] said, 'He's not a Swede. He's an American [because] he's been here so long,'" Babcock said.

When Lidstrom raised the Stanley Cup on Pittsburgh ice, he made it official that no one cared what passport NHL captains carry.

# Jim Nill

*Assistant GM, Detroit Red Wings, 1997, 1998, 2002, 2008*

Jim Nill recalls that when Steve Yzerman won his first Stanley Cup with the Detroit Red Wings in 1997 he didn't have enough energy remaining to accept congratulations. "I went to hug him, and he couldn't," Nill recalled. "He said, 'I just want to get this equipment off. I'm worn out.' I don't think people understand the mental and physical fatigue that players have when they win the Stanley Cup."

Nill perhaps owns a more extensive understanding of Stanley Cup success because of his own failed quest to win it as a player and the critical management role he played in helping the Red Wings win four championships in a span of 11 years.

In 1982 Nill reached the Stanley Cup Finals in just his second NHL season, but his upstart Vancouver Canucks lost to the New York Islanders. Nill didn't retire until 1992, but he never again got close to winning the Cup as a player.

"You always think you going to get back," Nill said. "But when I was in Winnipeg, we had Calgary or Edmonton to play in the first round, and they were two of the top teams in the league."

Moving into management in Detroit, Nill quickly became one of the NHL's most respected talent evaluators. Today, he is known as general manager Ken Holland's chief of staff, and he has a major voice in decision-making.

Now he understands the process of winning more than he did as a player. "It's just so hard to win a Cup," Nill said. "There are so many things that have to take place. First, you have to stay healthy, and then you have to have the right matchups and the right travel, and you have to get lucky."

The difference, Nill says, between failure and success in the NHL playoffs can come down to one play or one bounce. "The story I like to tell is that the Montreal Canadiens won 10 consecutive overtime games to win the Stanley Cup in 1993," Nill said. "If they lose four of those, they might get knocked out in the second round, and people would be saying to break up the team."

Even when the Red Wings won in 2008, Nill found that there was a narrow margin between championship and heartache. "I thought we were in control of the [championship] series against Pittsburgh, but we lose Game 5 on home ice, which we should have won," Nill said. "Then in Game 6, in Pittsburgh, I thought we played a great game and still with five seconds to go [Marian Hossa] has a shot to tie. If that shot goes in, the game goes into overtime, and history could have changed."

Nill had a hand in the drafting of players such as Pavel Datsyuk, Henrik Zetterberg, Tomas Holmstrom, and many others. His role is vital, but Nill says there is a significant difference between winning a Stanley Cup as a player and as a member of management.

"As a player, you are giving every ounce of energy that your body will give you," Nill said. "And when it's over, you are done and spent. Only a player can understand that. I don't think that anyone in management or a coach can understand that unless they have gone through it."

Nill says winning as a coach is closest to winning as a player "because you are on the ice every day and living and dying with each game—you feel the emotion." Members of management, because of their job description, must have detachment from the emotion. "In management, you hire the guys that [supply] the emotion," Nill said. "You have to keep a calmness to you because you have to make short- and long-term decisions. When you lose, you have to sit back and analyze; sometimes those decisions are not easy. Every time we lost, there was talk that we should blow the thing up. Every time we lost, people said it was because we weren't big enough or physical enough. So we have to be in control of our emotions."

The euphoria of winning doesn't last as long for management. "When you win, players are running around celebrating with the Stanley Cup, as they should, because they paid the price," Nill said. "But in management, you win it and then a week later you have the draft coming up and guys to sign, and you have free agency to deal with. You really don't have much time to enjoy it."

## Joe Kocur

*New York Rangers, 1994 • Detroit Red Wings, 1997 and 1998*
Having hung out with the Stanley Cup on three separate occasions, Joe Kocur looks at the Cup almost like a very close friend. Kocur has been tubing with Stanley. He has partied with Stanley. He has sung with

Stanley. He has fished with Stanley. He and Stanley took a ride on a waverunner. Like any good friend, Kocur even put Stanley back together after it fell apart after too many days of revelry.

In 1994, when the New York Rangers won the Cup, the NHL was still one year away from enacting the official plan to allow players to have possession of the Stanley Cup for 24 hours. The Rangers had worked out their own travel itinerary for the Cup. Many members of the Rangers' organization were given their opportunity to have Stanley as a house-guest, and somewhere in the process Stanley had literally come unglued. When Kocur received the trophy, the bowl was separated from the main trophy.

That unfortunate event paved the way for Kocur to become one of the legendary figures in Stanley Cup folklore. He was the first player who actually tried to repair the Cup himself. Knowing he and his friends were going to want to lift Stanley and drink from the bowl, Kocur took it to a machine shop and had it soldered back together. Respectful of the Cup's time-honored tradition, he instructed the worker to use sterling silver solder and to tack it only in five places around the rim.

"I was not trying to put a weld on it," Kocur said. "I was just trying to tack it, to hold it in place. From what I understand, it held together for another month or two. The tacks were small enough that you couldn't tell."

Kocur has long believed that the Cup should be shared with fans, and he has endeavored to allow as many fans as possible to enjoy the three-year ride he's had with the Cup.

On one of Stanley's visits to Kocur's lakefront home out near Milford, Michigan, Kocur put a ski jacket on Stanley and secured it in an inner tube. (He tested the Cup's ski jacket–aided floating potential in four feet of water before starting his perhaps questionable journey.) He jumped into another inner tube and had his wife pull Stanley around the lake with him. Stanley needed no introduction to the lake dwellers. As soon as they spotted the trophy, the honking and hollering began.

During his Red Wings tour, Kocur had several Cup highlights, including an almost all-night bonfire where Stanley's Hall of Fame escort Paul Oke played the guitar and sang into the night. After partying with Stanley nearly all night, Kocur got up before dawn, and he and Stanley went fishing with friends. "We put some lake water in it, and that was our live well," Kocur said. "We put the fish right in there."

Kocur was always happy to be part of the tamer team celebrations, but no player ever enjoyed his private moments with Stanley more than Kocur. When one Red Wings team function broke up at 2:00 AM, Kocur noted that "the Cup had nowhere to go." He called a friend at Lutteman's tavern in Highland, Michigan, and he kept the bar open all night to accommodate Kocur and Stanley's thirst for some after-hours celebrating.

"We kept it open all night, and every time you looked up, someone new would come in with their hair all messed up," Kocur remembered. "Everyone there was calling someone. It was 4:00 in the morning, but people were getting up to come in and get their picture taken with the Cup."

Kocur was disappointed once to read that some people complained when his former New York Rangers teammate Ed Olczyk fed a Kentucky Derby horse out of the Cup. Kocur felt that the complainants didn't understand what the Cup is about. To Kocur, the Cup is about hockey and its fans.

"Letting a horse eat out of it...well, he was a champion, too," Kocur said. "When the players get the Cup, they should share it with the fans."

It's impossible for Kocur to understate his feelings about winning a Stanley Cup as a member of the New York Rangers. When the Rangers won in 1994, it ended the organization's 54-year Cup drought. New York was infatuated with the Rangers when they won the Cup.

But Kocur doesn't need much coaxing to admit that winning the Cup in Detroit might have been more special for a variety of reasons. First, he had started his career in Detroit in 1984 and lived in Michigan during the off-season, regardless of where he played. Second, his career seemed over when the Red Wings called him out of retirement in late December 1996. Finally, Kocur was a member of the Grind Line and a far more crucial contributor to the Red Wings' success than he had been with the Rangers.

Kocur was 32 and playing in an over-30 "beer league" when captain Steve Yzerman, among others, lobbied the Red Wings to bring him back. Playing on a line with Kirk Maltby and Kris Draper, Kocur was a key checking-line performer in both 1997 and 1998. In the 1998 playoffs he had four goals in 18 games. He had managed six goals in 97 postseason games before that great season.

"To win it in New York was incredible," Kocur said. "But I was a bigger part of the team in Detroit. That is my home, and I could walk with my head higher after winning it there."

To go from the beer league to having his name inscribed once again on the Stanley Cup in a span of about five months was significant enough that the Hall of Fame asked for both his beer league jersey and his Stanley Cup Red Wings jersey.

That should tell you that the Hall of Fame wasn't really all that upset that Kocur had tried to repair the Cup without consulting them. Privately, Hall of Fame representatives knew it was just a matter of time before the Cup broke.

Kocur confessed to having the Cup fixed and said that the Cup had been broken when it had been given to him. To this day Kocur won't say what member of the Rangers' organization had the Cup before him. He just says it wasn't a player.

## Aaron Ward

*Detroit Red Wings, 1997 and 1998 • Carolina Hurricanes, 2006*
The euphoria that comes with a Stanley Cup celebration started for defenseman Aaron Ward a few hours before the Red Wings actually finished their four-game sweep of the Philadelphia Flyers in 1997.

Driving down Brush Street near Joe Louis Arena at 4:00 PM, he could feel the buzz in the air. Banners hung from the buildings, and people were hanging out windows. Talk of the Red Wings filled the radio airwaves. Cars were honking. Traffic moved slowly. "It started to hit me that we can win this thing tonight," Ward said. "I really started to absorb what was happening. Then I remember counting down on the ice and throwing stuff in the air, and everything seemed to slow down."

Ward said that day was the longest and most exciting of his life. After finishing off the Flyers and partying in the dressing room for what seemed like an eternity, the Red Wings headed off to Big Daddy's restaurant in West Bloomfield. "You completely lose track of time," Ward recalled. "I never saw a party like that, not even in college. People were just so happy seeing each other. Everyone had something in common to celebrate. It was unbelievable."

Leaving the party at 6:00 AM, Ward remembers listening to radio personality Art Regner on WDFN, who had stayed on the air all night to talk about the Detroit Red Wings' first Stanley Cup championship since 1955. He was hoarse from his marathon radio session and yet had never lost his enthusiasm. "I remember guys under the influence of alcohol calling up Art at 6:00 AM," Ward said. "I can remember Marty Lapointe calling him at 6:30, mocking him, but still excited about winning."

The whole party sequence was a blur to Ward, who had difficulty believing the Red Wings had won. "I grew up a Toronto Maple Leafs fan, and I never saw them win," Ward said. "Just having the wish and hope that my favorite team would win was a dream, let alone me winning the Cup."

When he had his 24 hours with the Stanley Cup, Ward rented a limousine to transport it to various locales. Included on his itinerary was a stop at a children's hospital. "We quickly got an understanding of what kids know and don't know," Ward said. "To some kids, the Stanley Cup was just a big, giant, robot-looking thing that scared the living daylights out of them. To others, they absorbed it. I think it was a bigger deal for the employees."

As part of his celebration, Ward rented a wedding hall and held a party for 400 people. Later he had a private party at his house for some of his closest friends. There really wasn't a need for the Hall of Fame to have a keeper of the Cup in attendance because Ward remembers one of his pals, Brian Niemy, standing guard over the Cup for the better part of eight hours. When people wanted to snap pictures, he would move away, but when they were done Niemy would resume hugging the trophy. "We joke how that was the closest he ever came to getting married," Ward said.

Another Ward memory is of how sore his arms were at the end of the day from everyone asking him to raise the Cup over his head for pictures. "It weighs 35 pounds—you are so sore you just want to say, 'No, you lift it up, and I'll take the picture,'" Ward recalled, laughing.

Ward said the highlight of his celebrations was being able to share his championship with his parents, Keith and Wendy, and his wife, Kelly.

"Your wife endures a lot for you to win the Stanley Cup," Ward said. "Maybe you aren't quarantined, but you are put away at a hotel even at home. She doesn't see much of you. Your life is put on hold. She must do everything. As hard as you have worked to achieve this, she has been the backbone in support."

Upon winning, he thought of his parents getting up at 4:00 AM to make sure he was transported 45 minutes away to Russell, Ontario, to get to practice on time. "Being Canadian, my parents had so much

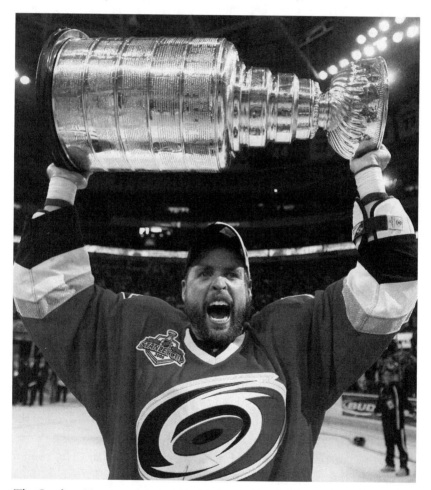

*The Carolina Hurricanes' Aaron Ward hoists the Stanley Cup in Raleigh, North Carolina, on June 19, 2006.*

respect for the Cup. They know how hard you have to work to get it," Ward said. "My dad wouldn't come near it. Finally, I said, 'Go ahead and touch it. You have to go near it to get our picture taken with it.'"

When Ward won his third Stanley Cup title in 2006 with Carolina, he was punked by Hurricanes teammate Matt Cullen during the summer's celebrations. Cullen's day with the Stanley Cup was the day before Ward was to receive it for an event that he was planning at his home in the Detroit area. Late in Cullen's day, he dialed up Ward and informed him that the revelry at his house had raged out of control, and the Cup had been dropped and severely damaged. Cullen said he regretted to inform Ward that the Stanley Cup was heading to Montreal to be repaired, and not heading to Michigan for Ward's gathering.

At first Ward didn't believe his buddy Cully, but Cullen convinced him that it was true, and then Ward said he had to go because he needed to notify his wife that all of their elaborate plans were now on hold. Only then did Cullen admit, amid howls of laughter, that he had just pulled off the best prank of his hockey career. The highly amused Ward promised Cullen that he would someday pay a price for his hijinks.

But all of that was forgotten the next day when Ward took the Cup to Mott's Children's Hospital, and then slept with it, just like he did when he won it in Detroit.

## Darren McCarty

*Detroit Red Wings, 1997, 1998, 2002, and 2008*
Players often save mementos from their Stanley Cup championships. Jerseys autographed by every member of the team are a favorite, along with signed sticks and the replica Stanley Cups given to them by the NHL.

McCarty's favorite memento is a photograph of him scoring the Stanley Cup–clinching goal against the Flyers in 1997. The fact that a fan in the first row snapped the picture makes it even more special.

"It's right where I scored on [Ron] Hextall," McCarty said. "It's awesome. It's right where I cut around him. It's got [Philadelphia defenseman Janne] Niinimaa diving and Hextall. You see me blowing snow and you see people in the background getting ready to jump. That's great personal memorabilia."

He had the picture blown up to 16" x 20", and it's framed on a wall in his basement.

Like any avid collector, McCarty had to wheel and deal to obtain another one of his favorite collectibles from the Stanley Cup championship. He kept the stick that delivered that winning goal, but he had to trade for the puck.

"[Referee] Bill McCreary originally had the puck," McCarty said. "He got the puck for his kid. He asked me if I'd like to have it. I gave his son a jersey. It's cool because it goes with the stick."

McCarty's other treasured memento from his two Stanley Cups is his collection of videotapes from each game. "It still gives me chills to watch them," McCarty said.

## Kris Draper
*Detroit Red Wings, 1997, 1998, 2002, and 2008*
Many of the players on Stanley Cup–winning teams can recite the order of hoisting the Cup as if it were the batting order of a World Series championship team.

Detroit's Kris Draper, the speedy, feisty center on Detroit's key checking line on back-to-back champion teams, remembers that he followed Joe Kocur as the Cup was passed from player to player during the postgame, on-ice revelry at Joe Louis Arena in 1997.

"Joey Kocur skated up to me and said, 'Take her for a spin around the rink,'" Draper remembered.

His other favorite Stanley Cup memory occurred when he had his 24 hours with the Cup in his hometown of Toronto. For a Detroit player to take a Cup to championship-starved Toronto is akin to waving red in a bull's face. Draper relished being able to showcase the Cup on a ride down Danforth Avenue in Toronto.

"There was this guy in a Wendel Clark jersey who yelled, 'Wings suck!' as we drove by," Draper said, smiling at the memory.

## Vladimir Konstantinov
*Detroit Red Wings, 1997*
When the Detroit Red Wings gathered for a post–Stanley Cup golf outing in the summer of 1997, they thought they were acting in an

*Former defenseman Vladimir Konstantinov is surrounded by his Detroit Red Wings teammates after their 4–1 Stanley Cup victory over the Washington Capitals on June 16, 1998, at MCI Center in Washington. Konstantinov was badly injured in a car crash on June 13, 1997. Martin Lapointe is at left, and Sergei Fedorov is at right.*

intelligent and cautious manner by hiring limousines to transport players back to their homes after a day of revelry.

To this day, it still haunts the Red Wings that star defenseman Vladimir Konstantinov and popular team masseur Sergei Mnatsakanov suffered permanent, career-ending, and life-changing injuries at one of the happiest times of their lives. The limousine driver, who served jail time because of the accident, allegedly fell asleep at the wheel. Both Konstantinov and Mnatsakanov suffered brain injuries in the ensuing accident. Mnatsakanov is now confined to a wheelchair, and Konstantinov struggles with his short-term memory to this day. He will never play hockey again.

"It just makes no sense," says Detroit vice president Jim Devellano. "This didn't happen on some dark highway late at night. He was in a limousine on Woodward Avenue at 9:15 in the evening. It just should not have happened."

What gnaws at their former teammates is that the two were hurt while acting responsibly. "It's just so senseless that it happened," says Red Wings left wing Darren McCarty. "The toughest thing is that you think you do everything right—you think, you plan, and then this happens."

He adds, "Sometimes pro athletes and those in the entertainment field are put on a pedestal. They are considered untouchable. But the only difference between us and everyone else is what we do for a living. We are just as susceptible to fate as everyone else. Stuff like this happens all the time, and when it happens to John Doe, it isn't any less significant to his family than it is for us because it's Vladie."

Konstantinov had become a Norris Trophy finalist that season and was generally considered one of the NHL's top defensemen. Devellano remembers the first time he met Konstantinov, the then 22-year-old captain of the Central Red Army hockey team, in Detroit for an exhibition game in 1992. Devellano arranged for Konstantinov to sneak out of his hotel room and meet him at 1:00 AM at Joe Louis Arena. Armed with an appealing five-year contract, Devellano tried to persuade Konstantinov to defect, as Sergei Fedorov had the summer before. "But he told me he had a wife and family back in Russia, and he would worry about them if he joined the Red Wings," Devellano said.

It was impressive family dedication for a player so young, Devellano thought to himself. "If he was single, I would have pressured him to sign," Devellano said. "But when he told me he had a family, I backed off."

Konstantinov always played hockey like a commando soldier on an assault mission. Some say he was a dirty player, but others argue he played the game with the same razor-sharp edge as Mark Messier, Doug Gilmour, or Chris Chelios, all of whom are exalted for their playing style.

Off the ice, Konstantinov was a very different character: quiet, soft-spoken, quick to smile, appreciative of a funny line. He was nicknamed "the Vladinator" by fans; at each game, the scoreboard showed a collection of his greatest hits, followed by Konstantinov, wearing sunglasses and saying, "Hasta la vista, baby."

Devellano said that Konstantinov ranked only behind Denis Potvin in terms of the most-talented defensemen who played on his teams. "Vladie probably would have played another seven or eight years, and I think he probably would have made the Hall of Fame," Devellano said.

In the limousine that night with Konstantinov and Mnatsakanov was Slava Fetisov. He suffered a lung injury, but was able to recover quickly. Three years later he still feels sadness about the events and the fact that Konstantinov was unable to make the trip to Russia after their Cup.

The night the Red Wings won the Stanley Cup in 1997 Konstantinov reveled in the victory, calling it the "best night of my career." Konstantinov hadn't been back to Russia since he left and, before the accident, he had bubbled about the proposed Stanley Cup trip to his homeland.

"All I can remember is how excited he was," Fetisov said. "There was sadness to be over there without him."

The following year, the Red Wings dedicated their season to Konstantinov, and when they captured their second consecutive Stanley Cup, captain Steve Yzerman elected not to take the traditional lap around the Washington arena.

Instead, Konstantinov was brought onto the ice in his wheelchair, and Yzerman handed him the Stanley Cup. Even in an opponent's arena, there weren't many dry eyes in the house.

## Dan Cleary
*Detroit Red Wings, 2002 and 2008*
When Detroit Red Wings forward Dan Cleary hoisted the Stanley Cup over his head in Pittsburgh on June 5, 2008, he became the most accomplished NHL player from the Canadian island of Newfoundland.

Cleary, raised in Harbour Grace, was only the second player from Newfoundland to make the Finals, and the first to win.

The only other player from Newfoundland to advance to the NHL's championship series was Alex Faulkner, who played for the Red Wings in 1962–1963 when they lost in the Stanley Cup Finals to Toronto.

"Being a Newfoundlander is something I'm proud of," Cleary said. "And being able to take the Cup back home was special for me." Newfoundland has a population of just over 500,000, and the primary sources of income there are mining, logging, and fishing. Newfoundland is part of the Canadian province of Newfoundland and Labrador.

The area is also hockey-crazed, evident during the Finals when Cleary received a banner signed by 30,000 fans in Newfoundland who were rooting for him, even though Newfoundland is primarily home to Toronto Maple Leafs fans.

Only about 3,100 people live in Harbour Grace, but there were an estimated 30,000 or more people in town on July 1, 2008, when Cleary brought the Cup home for a parade. It was considered such a major Canadian event for a Newfoundlander to win the Cup that 104 credentialed journalists were on hand to chronicle the celebration.

"My favorite part was coming into the field and seeing 30,000 people there to celebrate the Cup with you—that was pretty cool," Cleary said.

According to news accounts, Newfoundland and Labrador premier Danny Williams was on hand, and concluded his speech, with a chorus of "Danny Boy," sung to Cleary.

Cleary also paid tribute to his youth coach Dick Powers for turning him into an NHL talent, and he saluted 72-year-old Faulkner "for paving the way."

For a small town, Harbour Grace has had its share of major moments. Famed female aviator Amelia Earhart lifted off from Harbour Grace on May 20, 1932, when she braved 15 hours of fog, winds, rain, and mechanical issues to become the first female to fly solo across the Atlantic Ocean. In 2006 in Turin, Italy, Harbour Grace's Jamie Korab earned an Olympic gold medal as a member of Canada's top curling team.

Newfoundland had been excessively proud of Faulkner just for reaching the Stanley Cup Finals in 1963. Faulkner had scored the game-winning goal in the only game the Red Wings won in that series. When he returned home that summer, then-premier Joey Smallwood declared it "Alex Faulkner Day," and a parade was held in his honor.

Only 26 players born in Newfoundland have played in the NHL. Among the more prominent besides Faulkner and Cleary are Ryane Clowe, who now plays for the San Jose Sharks; Michael Ryder, who plays for the Boston Bruins; and defenseman Keith Brown, who played 16 NHL seasons.

It was not an easy climb to success for Cleary, who didn't distinguish himself in his first NHL stops in Chicago, Edmonton, and Phoenix. Chicago traded him, Edmonton bought out his contract, and Phoenix didn't offer Cleary a qualifying offer, making him an unrestricted free agent.

The Red Wings offered him a tryout, and Cleary took his game to a higher level, developing into a 20-goal scorer who was comfortable playing as a role player or in the top six forwards. In 2008 the Red Wings rewarded him with a five-year deal worth $14 million.

While Cleary claims Harbour Grace as his hometown, he actually grew up in the River Head section. He says about 300 people live there. Said Cleary, "If a little kid from Riverhead can win the Stanley Cup, you can do anything."

## Dallas Drake

*Detroit Red Wings, 2008*

When the Detroit Red Wings signed Dallas Drake in the summer of 2007, the fan reaction was as if the team had acquired a toothless lion.

At one point, Drake had been one of the beasts of the NHL jungle. In his prime, Drake was considered among the league's most dangerous open-ice hitters in the welterweight division. He wasn't a big guy, weighing only 180 pounds, but he could plow the road in front of him to get to the net. He bulldozed bigger opponents.

"I remember being stunned by the negative reaction," recalled his agent, Tom Laidlaw. "I read a story that speculated that Dallas would

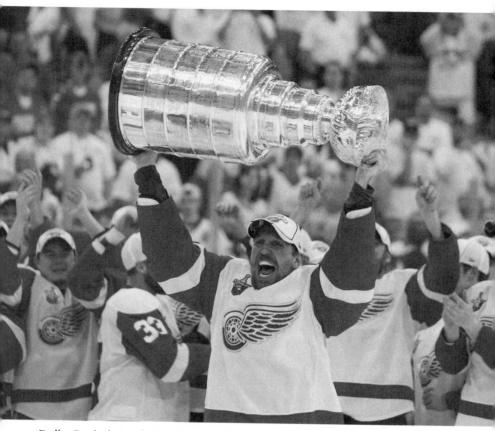

*Dallas Drake hoists the Stanley Cup after the Detroit Red Wings defeated the Pittsburgh Penguins 3–2 in Game 6 of the NHL Stanley Cup Finals on June 4, 2008, in Pittsburgh.*

simply be an extra player who could end playing with Detroit's minor-league affiliate in Grand Rapids."

Drake, from Trail, British Columbia, had actually started his NHL career with Detroit in 1992, after leaving Northern Michigan University, where he had essentially been a goal-per-game scorer his senior year.

"What I remember is when he came into the NHL, he was thought to be too small, but he always played like he weighed 250 pounds," Laidlaw said.

Detroit coach Scotty Bowman once remarked that Drake probably hit too hard, suggesting when Drake was traded to the Winnipeg Jets in

1994 that he felt Drake often inspired opponents to play at a higher level because he had riled them up.

He never changed, and his work ethic, character, and grit were appreciated in his NHL tour stops, which also included Phoenix and St. Louis. The Blues named Drake captain in 2006. However, the years of physical play had treated his body like a crash dummy. After the 2007 season, Laidlaw recalls Drake telling him that he didn't know whether his body could take one more season of abuse. According to Laidlaw, the Blues' lack of competitiveness probably made Drake's body aches and pains more pronounced.

Then the Blues surprised Drake by telling him that they were buying out his $1 million contract. "That got him fired up because he felt like he had a chance to perhaps get with the Red Wings and have a chance to win a Stanley Cup," Laidlaw recalled. "He really wanted to win." Drake had played 14 seasons without even reaching the Stanley Cup Finals.

Drake's wife, Amy, was from Traverse City, Michigan, and that's where Drake lived in the summer and planned to settle after retirement. The Red Wings were a perfect fit, especially since they seemed to be looking for a gritty role player. "I remember, he told me, 'Don't screw this up by asking for too much money,'" Laidlaw said. "I thought he was just joking around, but he was serious."

The San Jose Sharks were interested, as well, and Laidlaw said there were other inquiries. But Drake only had eyes for the Red Wings. The Red Wings were only offering $550,000. "But the money didn't matter to him," Laidlaw said.

The deal was announced July 9, and Detroit fans were underwhelmed. All they knew was that Drake was a worn-down warrior who had scored just eight goals in his last 122 games in a St. Louis sweater. Essentially, Holland said he signed Drake because he knew Drake would be a team guy, someone who would do whatever was asked in the name of winning.

"The physical pounding that Dallas laid on the other teams' defenses is something we didn't have in the last couple of years," Holland said. Holland said the team signed Drake as a "perfect third-line, fourth-line player," as the Wings looked to improve on their loss in the Western Conference Finals to the Anaheim Ducks in 2007.

Drake only played about 10 minutes per game in the regular season, and it took a while for fans to appreciate what Drake added to the team. The Red Wings weren't an overly physical team, and Drake's willingness to throw heavy checks did stand out.

Once the playoffs began, his contributions became increasingly more noticeable. "He took his game to another level in the playoffs," said Detroit assistant general manager Jim Nill. He laughs at the memory of coaches worrying about what Drake might do in Game 6 of the conference finals against Dallas. "They were a little bit scared because he was like a rocket coming out of the gate, and you didn't know where it was going," Nill said. "He wanted to be on the ice and set the tone." Nill recalled that Drake made a big hit in that game on his first shift, and he did give the Red Wings a lift.

The Red Wings' 21st-century approach to building a hockey team doesn't mean that they don't have room for a player who has a 1950s approach to shot-blocking. Multi-scarred Drake blocked several key shots in the postseason with no regard for potential damage to his body. His fearlessness became the talk of the 2008 playoffs.

"He [was] a perfect example of an older player who plays for the team and will do whatever it takes to win," said NBC analyst Pierre McGuire. "Championship teams need players like him."

Most players go low, force their pads in front of them, and get as close to the shooter as possible to reduce the chance of serious injury. But a few times in the 2008 postseason, Drake, 39, simply dropped to his knees and let the shot hit him in the torso. It was as if fans were watching NHL great Bob Goldham blocking a shot in the 1950s.

"You have to want to do that," Laidlaw said. "You want to get as close to the shooter as you can, no more than five to 10 feet. But he's blocking them from 20 feet away. The puck's coming from the blue line, and he's at the faceoff dot. It didn't matter to him where it hit him."

When the Red Wings were playing the Pittsburgh Penguins in the Finals, goalie Chris Osgood even mentioned that the team had extra incentive because they wanted to win the Cup for Drake, who was down to his last chance.

It took the Red Wings six games to dispatch the Penguins, and no one was happier in the postgame revelry than Drake. Captain Nick

Lidstrom raised the Stanley Cup first and then gave it to Drake. "I was shaky," Drake said. "I was just trying to keep it over my head."

Lidstrom said he had actually decided in the first round that, if the Red Wings won, Drake would lift the Cup after him. "I didn't tell anyone else," Lidstrom said. "I thought Dally would be a great choice, having played so many years in the league and never being to the Finals before and finally getting a chance to touch the Cup. He really deserved that."

Drake was touched by the respect Lidstrom showed him. "It meant an awful lot to me that the guys let me go grab it next," Drake said after the victory. "It was a great feeling. I didn't think it was going to happen. I didn't think I was ever going to get a chance to lift it up. The dream came true tonight."

It was agonizing for Drake to deal with the final two minutes of the clinching game as the Penguins came close to tying. "That clock wasn't moving at times," Drake said. "I tried to stay as calm as I could. I kept staring at my skates, thinking time would go by faster. But it didn't."

Drake had played 1,009 regular-season games. He had played 84 playoff games, and only seven others had played more without reaching the Finals. The Detroit players, especially those who had already won a Cup before, seemed to be happier for Drake than they were for themselves. "That was what they said in Colorado about Ray Bourque," Laidlaw said. "I'm not putting Dallas in his category, but he is always popular with his teammates, and they respect him. That was the way it was in St. Louis, too. I got an email from [Blues player] Ryan Johnson, and he said he had tears in his eyes watching Dallas with the Cup."

Red Wings general manager Ken Holland said Drake was "a big part of us winning the Stanley Cup this year."

His body battered, Drake retired the following month. That meant that his last official day as an NHL player ended with his hoisting the Stanley Cup. Said Laidlaw, "He got more out of his talent level than most people in this league."

# chapter 8

# Championship Stories, 1984–Present

## Jacques Demers
*Coach, Montreal Canadiens, 1993*

Coach Jacques Demers truly understood the aura of the Stanley Cup the night it helped him gain safe passage through a frenzied mob on the streets of Montreal, June 10, 1993.

The moment came after midnight, a couple of hours after Demers' Montreal Canadiens had defeated the Los Angeles Kings 4–1 to win the 24th NHL championship in the Canadiens' storied history. Unlike most of the previous championships, this crown had been unexpected. The Canadiens owned the NHL's sixth-best record and, going into the play-offs, most pundits presumed the Mario Lemieux–charged Pittsburgh Penguins were the team to beat. No one could have foreseen the Canadiens winning 10 consecutive playoff games in overtime and posting a 16–4 playoff mark. The unexpected joy of the occasion is the only explanation for why Montreal was engulfed in a celebratory riot into the wee hours of morning.

Members of the Canadiens organization were told to stay at the Montreal Forum until the celebration lost some of its steam. But when Demers and his family left a couple of hours later with the hope of going to an Italian restaurant, the streets were still a sea of celebrating fans.

Demers was in his brother-in-law's car, a 10-year-old Mercury Cougar, and as the car inched its way through the mob near the corner of Stanley and St. Catherine's Streets, the revelers began shaking the car. Demers was worried that they were going to tip over the automobile. "My daughter [Mylene] started crying, and it was very scary," Demers said.

Against his brother-in-law's pleading, Demers exited the car, and the crowd immediately recognized him. The crowd acted as if Demers were a deity who had suddenly appeared.

"It was like the parting of the Red Sea," Demers said. "How powerful can one man be for one night? I wasn't afraid to get out of the car. I told my brother-in-law, 'They aren't going to hurt me.' As soon as I got out of the car, everyone started yelling, 'Let the coach go through! Let him through!' and it just opened up. It wasn't me they were letting through; it was the coach of the Stanley Cup champions. Whoever it would have been, they would have let him through."

He remembers going against his wife Debbie's suggestion to leave the phone off the hook when they went to bed that night. He received his first congratulatory call at 6:00 AM, and the phone never stopped ringing.

Demers is an outgoing, friendly man who likes to talk to everyone. But he remembers that the week after he won the Cup he was uncharacteristically quiet. "People kept asking me if I was all right," Demers recalled.

He remembers he was emotionally tired from the two-month battle to win the Cup, but perhaps his mood also reflected the reverence he felt for having climbed the mountain. He was a native Montreal citizen who understood the importance of the Cup to Canadian culture.

"It was like a big dream," Demers said. "I never played pro hockey. I never even played junior hockey. All of a sudden I win the Cup in Montreal. Remember, I had seen Yvon Cournoyer and Serge Savard raise the Cup. Henri Richard. Now I'm doing it. It was like a dream. I would write a book, but no one would believe it. I came from nowhere—fired by Detroit, went into radio for a couple of years. I think my career could be over, and then Serge Savard gives me a call. I was on a high for the whole summer. This is like winning the Cup in your own backyard."

Emotionally, he was overextended that summer. "When I started training camp in September, I was tired," he remembered.

*Former NHL head coach Jacques Demers poses in his living room in Hudson, Quebec, in December 2005. The winner of consecutive NHL Coach of the Year Awards in 1987 and 1988 with the Detroit Red Wings, Demers lived out a dream in 1993 when he guided his hometown Montreal Canadiens to their most recent Stanley Cup.*

His other fond memory of the experience was seeing his name on the Stanley Cup the following season when he visited the Hall of Fame. "I had lifted the Stanley Cup and taken it to my golf tournament," Demers said. "But until you see your name on the Cup, you really don't believe you won it."

## Scott Niedermayer
*New Jersey Devils, 1995, 2000, 2003 • Anaheim Ducks, 2007*

## Rob Niedermayer
*Anaheim Ducks, 2007*

When four-time NHL champion Scott Niedermayer had to decide the Cup-raising order after the Anaheim Ducks won the Stanley Cup in 2007, he concluded that family ties were more important than seniority.

Teemu Selanne had played 1,041 regular-season games and 86 playoff games before his championship moment; Chris Pronger had played 868 regular-season games and 128 in the postseason. But after Niedermayer kissed the Cup and raised it once, he immediately handed it to his younger brother, Rob, who was winning his first.

Twice, with the Florida Panthers in 1996 and the Ducks in 2003, Rob had been to the Finals, and finally he had his Cup. "To be able to hand it to my brother—that was definitely the highlight of my career," Scott said.

The Niedermayers were the 15th set of brothers to win the Cup as teammates, and the first since since Brent and Duane Sutter captured their second title together with the New York Islanders in 1983.

Since 1968, Frank and Peter Mahovlich (Montreal, 1971 and 1973) and Jimmy and Joe Watson (Philadelphia Flyers, 1974 and 1975) were the only other brothers to win the Stanley Cup while playing on the same team. The most celebrated brother act to win a Stanley Cup was the Maurice and Henri Richard connection from the Montreal Canadiens' dynasty.

Although Selanne would have been the more traditional choice to carry the Cup second because he had labored for 16 seasons before winning, the Niedermayers were too close to let protocol interfere with their maximum enjoyment.

The Niedermayers are best friends as well as brothers, and one of the major reasons that Scott signed with Anaheim was to have a chance to win a Cup with his brother. Three times Scott had won a Stanley Cup and brought it back to his mother Carol's home in mountainous Cranbrook, British Columbia. Each time, younger brother Rob played the role of the dutiful brother, showing up to honor his brother's success. He celebrated with his brother, posed for pictures, shook the hands of many well-wishers, and he made it clear how proud he was of his older brother by 16 months.

"But of course I never touched the Cup," Rob admitted. "You don't want to touch it until you've won it."

He had come close twice: in 1996, when he scored 26 goals to help the Florida Panthers reach the Stanley Cup Finals only to lose to the Colorado Avalanche, and in 2003 when his Anaheim Ducks fell to Scott's New Jersey Devils. The encounter was the first brother-versus-brother meeting in the NHL Finals since 1946, when Montreal's Ken Reardon and Boston's Terry Reardon faced off.

Carol Niedermayer spiced the proceedings by confessing that she was openly rooting for Rob because "Scott already has won two Cups, and Rob hasn't won one. Scott understands."

There was good-natured family ribbing going on because Carol sat in the stands with Scott's wife, Lisa, and her family. In their younger days, their competitiveness sometimes collided with the idea of brotherly

*Anaheim Ducks captain Scott Niedermayer (right) and his brother, Rob Niedermayer, hold the Stanley Cup after the Ducks won the Finals with a 6–2 victory over the Ottawa Senators in Anaheim, California, on June 6, 2007.*

love. "They had the usual brotherly squabbles," Carol said. "When there was only one object and both wanted it, there was no negotiation."

Devils teammates kidded Scott about his mom rooting against him, and Carol received Donald Duck cards from family members who wanted to join in the gentle teasing. Scott and Rob share many of the same friends, and they have grown closer as they have grown older. Their nicknames are "Cliff" and "Norm," like the buddies from the TV show *Cheers*.

But all of the teasing stopped when the Devils finished off the Ducks. Scott owned his third Stanley Cup championship, and Rob still had none. There was another celebration in Cranbook, and another day of mixed feelings for Carol, who was saddened that her younger son hadn't been to the top of the mountain (literally) as Scott had.

To commemorate his NHL championship in 2000, Scott chartered a helicopter to transport him and the Stanley Cup to Cranbrook's Fisher's Peak, elevation 9,335 feet, to create a spectacular backdrop for photographs.

Seven years later, in the summer of 2007, a helicopter flew both Niedermayer boys to a glacier atop Bull Mountain. Each player was carefully lowered to where a photographer captured the majesty of their accomplishment with a gorgeous mountain backdrop.

Probably no one enjoys those photos more than Carol, who was overjoyed that both of her sons have now finally climbed to the top of their world.

## Andre Roy

*Tampa Bay Lightning, 2004*

Andre Roy has earned his keep for 12 NHL seasons on the strength of his fists. Reporter Erik Erlendsson of the *Tampa Tribune* ranked Roy as the fourth-best enforcer in the Tampa Bay Lightning's history.

Roy fought 42 times as a Lightning player, and he proved himself to be one of the roughest men in the NHL. "Everyone thinks I'm a badass, but I do have a romantic side to me," Roy said, laughing.

He proved that when he received his day with the Cup, choosing that occasion to propose to Karine Labelle, who had been his girlfriend for three and a half years. It's believed that it is the only use of the Stanley Cup as part of a marriage proposal.

The proposal plan was hatched after Roy's friend, the late Quebec television personality Paul Buisson, told him that he could secure a helicopter that could transport Roy and his girlfriend from Roy's home in Saint-Therese to Saint-Jerome, where he was raised. Buisson hosted a popular show called *Hors-Jen*, which took a lighthearted look at some of the top French Canadian hockey players. Roy had appeared on one of the funniest episodes, and they had forged a friendship, glued solidly by a shared enjoyment of laughing at themselves.

What Roy didn't know was that Buisson had cooked up his own surprise to make Roy's celebration more memorable. When Roy walked up to the helicopter, he was stunned to see his childhood idol, Guy Lafleur, waiting for him.

"What are you doing here ?" Roy said.

"I'm the pilot," Lafleur said.

By now, Buisson was laughing. Roy had no idea that Lafleur was a licensed helicopter pilot, nor did he know that Buisson wanted to surprise him with Lafleur's presence because he had grown up as a Montreal Canadiens' fan.

"Oh, my God, it was awesome," Roy recalled. "To have my idol fly me with the Stanley Cup to my hometown was unbelievable."

At that point, Roy's girlfriend had no idea that she would be next to be surprised. During the 20-minute flight, while Karine was looking out the window, Roy slipped a wrapped box into the bowl of the Stanley Cup that was standing up between the couple.

"Hey, do you want your surprise?" Roy asked his girlfriend.

"What are you talking about?" she asked.

"Look in the Cup," Roy said.

Roy said his girlfriend told him she never expected the proposal, and didn't instantly think "ring" when she saw the box. "She said she first thought maybe earrings. Yeah, right," Roy said, laughing. Roy then asked her directly whether she would marry him, and she said yes.

Later in the day Roy took the Stanley Cup to a spa, and then that night he rented a bar for an all-night gathering of 200 friends and family at Mont Tremblant. "We finished at 3:00 in the morning—that's not too bad," Roy said. "I could tell the Cup keeper, Walter, was pretty tired because he had done Vinny Lecavalier and Martin St. Louis before. I told him he could go with the Cup because he had to do Eric Perrin the next day."

As memorable as Roy's celebration was, it was just a continuation of the best few months of Roy's hockey career. Although known primarily as a tough guy, Roy was able to enjoy a long career because he could contribute beyond his ability to fight. He played 21 playoff games for the Lightning during their march to the NHL championship, and he contributed an important goal and several bits of humor that kept his team relaxed when the pressure was greatest.

In the first game of the playoffs, against the New York Islanders, the Lightning were struggling to ignite their offense. Only Nikolai Khabibulin's strong play had kept the game scoreless into the second.

Roy had only played one 41-second shift earlier in the second period when his name was called again. Coming off the bench, Roy swiped the puck from New York defenseman Eric Cairns, went in on a breakaway, and beat goalie Rick DiPietro with a high shot.

"It was the first goal of the playoffs," Roy said. "I roofed it, and then I raised the roof, and the crowd got into it. We started to get more momentum, and we went on to win the series. It was a great moment."

Former Tampa Bay general manager Jay Feaster recalls that "Roy's goal against the Islanders was huge, as was his contributions to our success." Feaster recalls Roy was part of a "tic-tac-toe" passing combination that resulted in an important goal against Philadelphia in the playoffs. "Andre contributed also as a physical presence," Feaster said. "He hit and forechecked extremely well."

It added to his enjoyment that the Lightning had to defeat his boyhood favorite Canadiens en route to the championship. His family and friends were in Montreal to see him play, and he remembers those games with fondness.

"It was the loudest building I've ever been in, in my career," Roy said. "The refs would have to blow the whistle three or four times so we could hear." According to Feaster, Roy's other major contribution was his ability to keep his team loose. His comedic touch was crucial in the championship series against Calgary, especially after the Lightning lost Game 5 in Tampa.

That meant the Flames would have champagne on ice during Game 6 in Calgary. Everyone knew that as they climbed aboard the team charter for the flight to Alberta.

On the flight, Roy went to work to get his teammates' minds off the pressure. "Andre stripped out of his pants and underwear, donned a pair of cowboy chaps, and proceeded to walk up and down the aisle in the player's area of the plane wearing those chaps with his butt hanging out," Feaster said. "He's carrying a silver serving tray, asking in a high-pitched female voice if he can get the boys anything…coffee, drinks, et cetera. The boys were howling, and it took their minds off the monumental task at hand. That's what he was so good at…keeping everyone loose."

Feaster said when Roy was lost to free agency, "we lost our personality." He added, "We had the most quiet hockey team I'd ever seen, and it didn't change until I got him back by claiming him off reentry waivers from Pittsburgh."

## Craig Simpson

*Edmonton Oilers, 1988 and 1990*

In the mid-1980s, the doorway into the Edmonton Oilers' dressing room seemed like a magic portal to a better world for those who were stuck on the outside looking in.

Around the NHL, players viewed the Oilers' room with respect, even reverence. It was as if the mysteries and secrets of hockey were revealed to all those who entered. Oilers players like Wayne Gretzky, Mark Messier, Kevin Lowe, and others were viewed as hockey's high priests, capable of helping others find their way to a wondrous level of performance. As rich as the Oilers were in talent, they also possessed another talent: they knew how to convert others to their beliefs. Ordinary players might go into that room, but champions came out. That's why players viewed a trade to the Oilers as if they had received a higher calling.

"From the minute you walked down the corridor—for me it was November 25, 1987—you honestly felt like you were part of a winner," remembered Craig Simpson. "From the minute you walked into the room, you weren't an outsider. They were going to help you. You were embraced. Success was a collective. It was a 'we' success. The reason why people went to the wall for Gretzky and Messier is because they were willing to share the credit." What was unsaid but immediately understood, Simpson recalled, was that "you had to be the best player you could be to help win a championship."

Simpson had come from the Pittsburgh Penguins, a team with no history of success at that time. "Oilers practices were a lot better than our games in Pittsburgh," Simpson said. "You had to bring up your level. It was hard work, but it was fun. The players made it fun."

Walking through the portal seemed to have a special effect on Simpson, who turned out to be a postseason point-scoring machine. In his NHL career, he averaged better than one point per game (36 goals and 32 assists for 68 points in 67 postseason games). During the Cup triumphs in 1988 and 1990, Simpson had 50 points in 41 games. He led all postseason scorers in 1990 with 16 goals and 15 assists in 22 games.

"What's so special is you don't think of yourself when you win a Stanley Cup," Simpson said. "You think of your parents, teammates, your family. That's what team sports are about—the connection with teammates. It's a huge bond. It's about sharing emotions."

Tales of all-night parties and strip-club escapades often captured the headlines, but there was another side of the Oilers' Stanley Cup revelry that went underreported. "Everyone felt a responsibility to have the Cup make a difference in someone's life," Simpson remembered. "Everyone took it to a school, or to a hospital…the healing power of the Cup is special. Everyone on that team knew that the Cup had to be shared with fans. And there was nothing quite like walking into a children's ward in a hospital with the Stanley Cup."

What made Simpson proud was that the Oilers made the Cup "accessible." He remembers all the players gathering at Barry T's, an Edmonton nightspot, setting the Cup on a table, and letting everyone in the bar take a turn holding it. The Oilers essentially ignored the Cup and let fans have their time with it.

At the time, Simpson lived in an Edmonton cul-de-sac that contained about 18 other homes. He really didn't know his neighbors all that well, but he printed up invitations and invited all of them to his home at 3:00 one afternoon. He told them they could bring their family and friends. He ended up with more than 100 people in his backyard. "And, honestly, I didn't know a lot of them," Simpson said. But a decade later he still has people come up to him and tell him that they were at his house that day and how much it meant to them.

Simpson also remembers that his second Stanley Cup was more special for a variety of reasons, not the least of which was that he was able to share it with his wife, Christine, who at the time was his girlfriend. "Her grandfather, Glenn Kirkland, was an intriguing, fun-loving guy," Simpson said. "He was an old train conductor. He had lost half his leg, but he was a feisty character. He was such a hockey fan that it was a joy to bring the Cup to his house and share it with him. He died in 1993."

The victory was also sweeter the second time around because he knew from his first experience that the incredible feeling would pass far too quickly. He purposely savored the second Cup, creating a mental scrapbook of his feelings and images. "The second time," he said, "you now realize how difficult it is to get back there."

In the days after the 1990 victory, friends kept telling him that they never spotted him on television in the euphoric Oilers' dressing room. That's because Simpson stood back and played the role of observer. He wanted a lasting picture to take with him.

In sweat-drenched underwear, he sat back in his cubicle in the cramped Boston Garden's visitors' dressing room and watched as the best team in the world celebrated its championship. Tina Turner's song "Simply the Best" was blaring loudly. Simpson sat swigging from his champagne bottle and thinking that professional sports couldn't get better than this.

"That was crystallized in my mind," Simpson said. "All of my real close friends—Mess, Andy, Kevin Lowe, Craig MacTavish, Steve Smith, Charlie Huddy—were all dancing around, hugging each other. They were enjoying the moment. I was exhilarated, exhausted, and spent. My body was telling me that I had been through a war. But I remember thinking, *This is why I spent my life playing the game of hockey.* That moment defined why I wanted to play hockey. To be in that room, as exhausted, battered, and bruised as I was, was worth it all."

His other memory of the Oilers' 1990 Cup triumph was sharing a private moment with the incomparable Gordie Howe, who Simpson had gotten to know at charity events. Long after the arena had emptied and the media was busy chronicling the Oilers' championship, Simpson sat in the stands with Howe and listened as Howe regaled him with tales of winning four Stanley Cup championships in the 1950s.

"That was a special moment," Simpson said. "What makes the Stanley Cup the greatest trophy in professional sports is that I was holding the same Cup that Gordie Howe held 35 years before."

Simpson works in television today as a reporter and analyst, and it's been his observation that the childlike pleasures of hockey are slipping away. He hopes he's wrong.

"Guys seem more serious, more focused, more concerned about everything," Simpson said. "Guys have to be focused, because you have to be ready. But part of why the Oilers would go through a wall for each other is that we all had fun together. We were all part of the practical jokes and going out together."

The Oilers were serious only on the ice. They were loose and relaxed in the dressing room. They didn't sweat the media or fan pressure, and certainly paid no attention to outside distractions. They seemed to approach the game like a bunch of close friends who believed that when they took to the ice together they were simply the best.

"After practice today, players go home and get on the Internet or they play video games," Simpson said. "It's almost like your kids today: you want them to go out and play, and they want to play video games. And it's a little like that for the teams, as well. You have to have a bit of a kid in you to be great and to be able to go to the wall like we did."

## Ed Olczyk
*New York Rangers, 1994*
Pictures are purported not to lie, but one of the most memorable photos in Stanley Cup folklore has an element of exaggerated legend.

Not long after the New York Rangers won the Stanley Cup in 1994, Rangers player and horse enthusiast Ed Olczyk took the trophy to the Meadowlands Race Track and then to Belmont Park. At Belmont, Olczyk was pictured feeding 1994 Kentucky Derby winner Go For Gin out of the Stanley Cup. The photo was picked up by the wire service, and some folks were offended by the shot, even though most people in the hockey world laughed at the thought that another layer of goofy history had been added to Stanley's legacy.

"Actually, I never fed him out of it," Olczyk now maintains. "Everyone just assumed there was food in the Cup. But the photo was just set up to make him look like he was drinking out of the Cup. It was just to be a photo of a Kentucky Derby winner and a Stanley Cup winner."

Olczyk is a one-time 42-goal scorer, but he wasn't a crucial performer on the Rangers' championship team. He played just one playoff game that season, but he remembers Rangers captain Mark Messier making every member of the organization feel like a part of the success.

"You don't realize how difficult it is to win it until you actually succeed," Olczyk said. "It just seems like yesterday. Even though my part in it was minimal, I still feel as if I was part of it. The bottom line was chemistry. We had it on that team. Mess treated everyone the same, from himself to the 28th guy. He kept everyone in line and he made everyone feel important. He knew the foot soldiers were important."

Olczyk grew up in Chicago as a Blackhawks fan, hoping that the franchise could break its long championship drought. There was a tinge of justice that Olczyk could be a part of the end of the Rangers' 54-year drought. Rangers' fans let loose in the summer of 1994.

Shortly after the Rangers disposed of the Vancouver Canucks in a dramatic Game 7, Messier and eight or nine Rangers went out for dinner in Manhattan. In characteristic fashion, Messier showed up in a limousine with the Cup in tow. Upon exiting, Olczyk remembers Messier parking Stanley on top of the luxury car's roof. An alien starship landing in Time's Square couldn't have created more commotion than the trophy did on that hot summer's evening.

"It stopped traffic," Olczyk said. "Taxicabs blocked off the intersection. People came out running. The attention the Cup got was surreal. It was like a magnet. People came from everywhere to check it out."

Most of the players in the group just stood and watched in amazement as people flocked to the Cup. "People kept coming up and saying thanks," Olczyk said. "In fact people still thank me for that championship."

*Mark Messier celebrates his second-period goal against the Vancouver Canucks in Game 7 of the Stanley Cup Finals at New York's Madison Square Garden on June 14, 1994. The Rangers went on to win 3–2 to take the Stanley Cup for the first time in 54 years.*

## Joe Murphy
*Edmonton Oilers, 1990*

Joe Murphy was the oldest member of the Edmonton Oilers' celebrated Kid Line when they defeated the Boston Bruins for the 1990 Stanley Cup championship. He was 22 years and nine months old. Adam Graves had just turned 22, and Martin Gelinas was the baby at 19.

Yet despite Murphy's youthfulness and the whirlwind nature of the Oilers' run toward a fifth Cup, he came away with a veteran's understanding of what it takes to become an NHL champion.

"I equate it to one of the most grueling things in sports," Murphy said. "It's an ego challenge. There's just so much to it. Every player is key. Every play is so important. It's a different array of events coming together. When we won it, I could see it in everyone's face. We had really accomplished something here."

The play of the Kid Line had been essential to the Oilers' success. Murphy had four points in the final, only one less than Messier. "We were really enthusiastic and we stuck up for each other," Murphy said. "We really did our job, and it was a great feeling."

Murphy can pinpoint the moment when he realized the magnitude of their accomplishment. When the team returned to Edmonton, captain Mark Messier invited all the Oilers players to his house for a night of shooting pool and camaraderie.

"He had miniature Stanley Cups, Canada Cup [memorabilia], his Conn Smythe Trophy on display," Murphy said. "When you see that in his house, you realize how great a thing it is to be a part of it all. That fueled my engine."

## Dave Lewis
*Associate Coach, Detroit Red Wings, 1997, 1998, 2002*

In early March 1980, New York Islanders defenseman Dave Lewis could have been forgiven for thinking that a date with the Stanley Cup was in his future. He was a vital contributor to an Islanders team that appeared to be primed for a strong run at multiple NHL championships.

What Lewis didn't know at the time was that he would get his name on the Cup, but it would be 16 years later than he had anticipated. What he also didn't know at the time was that he would help the Islanders win that Cup by being one of two players general manager Bill Torrey would ship to the Los Angeles Kings for Butch Goring. As it turned out, Goring was the final live wire in the Islanders' championship schematic. The Islanders won four consecutive championships, while Lewis was serving as a fixture on the Kings' blue line.

That scenario sheds some insight into the satisfaction Lewis felt when he was one of coach Scotty Bowman's associate coaches during the Red Wings' Stanley Cup triumphs in 1997 and 1998.

"I don't know if I can say that I got more satisfaction out of winning [because he had missed out on the Islanders' runs], but I got tremendous satisfaction out of winning it," Lewis said. "It was something that I really wanted."

Had he felt cheated out of the Cup until that point? "Yeah, I did miss out," Lewis admitted. "It had been very close. We were a very close team, and everyone pulled for one another on that team. Unfortunately, Billy Harris and I were plucked out of there. But they got Butch Goring, and he was the difference. He was the center to play behind Bryan Trottier."

Lewis got close to the Cup again in 1995 when he was an assistant coach on the Detroit Red Wings team that reached the Stanley Cup Finals. But the New Jersey Devils ruined the opportunity, sweeping the Red Wings.

When the Red Wings finally won in 1997 and Lewis was given his day with the Cup, he and his son, Ryan, went tooling down Detroit area highways and byways in a Dodge Viper with Ryan holding Stanley out of the sun roof.

"People followed us and yelled, 'Is that the real Stanley Cup?!'" Lewis said, chuckling. "We kept saying, 'No, we are just carrying a fake around in a Dodge Viper.'"

He then took the Cup for a reception at a local stable where the Lewis family horse, McLain, is kept. With 70 or 80 people gathered about, Lewis filled the Cup's bowl with cereal and allowed McLain to enjoy his lunch out of one of professional sports' most storied trophies.

"I don't think the horse realized the importance of the Stanley Cup," Lewis said. "But everyone else around there did."

The importance of winning was known to Lewis as he watched the Islanders win the four Cups almost two decades before. He had played 62 games for the Islanders that season to help them get in position for their title march.

"I was very excited for them when they won the Cup," Lewis said. "I was at home and I got a call from the locker room right after they won. Bob Bourne, Clark Gillies, Lorne Henning, and some of the other guys talked to me. It made me feel good."

Did he get a share of the championship money? Lewis laughed. "No, that's what I have to remember to ask those guys. Where is my money?"

## Scott Young
*Pittsburgh Penguins, 1991 • Colorado Avalanche, 1996*

When it comes to living life to the fullest, Scott Young knows how to have a blast, and not just because he once worked as a demolition assistant. In his younger days, he worked with explosives at construction sites. He would lug dynamite to the blasting area, place the cap in the hole, fill it with a pea stone, stand back, and let someone else rig it to explode.

"They didn't let me do the wires," Young said.

But with that kind of background, it shouldn't be surprising that the former U.S. Olympian would know how to push himself aggressively enough to become a two-time champion.

His favorite Stanley Cup celebration destination was taking the Cup to eat breakfast at 2:00 AM at Roger's Kitchen in Clinton, Massachusetts. It's a local diner. It's Young's local diner. "I loved watching the people in my hometown bending over, reading all the names, looking at all the old Bruins teams," Young said.

Young was just 23 when he won the Stanley Cup for the first time, and he recalls that the Cup was injured in the Pittsburgh Penguins' celebration. "The Cup was severed," Young said. "We were nervous. You couldn't hold it the way you usually did."

Although older and wiser when he won in 1996, Young still was involved in a Stanley Cup injury, although it was all rather innocent. Young remembers being out late with the Cup and then tip-toeing up the stairs of his home in the wee hours of the morning, hoping not to disturb his sleeping wife. Despite his desire to be careful, he tripped, and the Cup crashed roughly on the stairs. He was mortified to discover a large dent in it.

The keeper of the Cup was sleeping in Young's guest bedroom. Young was embarrassed to go and tell him that the Cup now had an indentation where one shouldn't be. After confessing, he was stunned when the keeper said, "No problem," then took out a hammer and banged the trophy back into shape.

The Cup isn't a finesse player. It can go in the corners, take a banging, and be ready to play the next day. Lord Stanley's Cup isn't soft. It's durable. It's made out of silver, but it's an iron-man performer.

That memory of the Cup spill is vivid in Young's mind, but another recollection seems more important to him. When the Avalanche finished off a sweep of Florida in Miami in 1996, the first guy he saw coming off the ice was his father, who was holding the gate for players. They hugged the way champions hug. "I don't know how he got there," said Young, clearly pleased with the memory.

## Brett Hull

*Dallas Stars, 1999 • Detroit Red Wings, 2002*

To appreciate how Brett Hull felt when he scored the dramatic triple-overtime goal against Buffalo to give the Dallas Stars the Stanley Cup championship, it must be remembered that Hull wakes up every day "scared to death" that he won't score another goal.

It wasn't satisfaction he felt, as much as it was an overwhelming sense of relief. "I can't say winning the Cup changed my life, but it added a piece to my career that everyone else seemed to think was missing," he said with the usual Hull candor. "It was punctuation."

Winning the Cup was also more like validation for a player who has looked for validation each morning he plays the game. Throughout his career he has been plagued by self-doubt, a bizarre, unfounded fear that he is going to be discovered as a fraud, a player who really isn't quite as dominant as he has always appeared to be. Never mind that he is one of the top scorers in NHL history and that the quickness of his shot release intimidates even Hall of Fame–bound goalkeepers.

It's difficult to know whether Hull's fear of failure is real or just his subconscious using psychological chicanery to give him added motivation. Whatever the basis for Hull's self doubt, it seems to have given him the push he needed to seize the moment in big games. Hull fought through a gruesome collection of medical woes to add another chapter to his legend with the controversial goal in Buffalo.

After playing with a torn groin muscle and a blown collateral knee ligament without a whimper, Brett Hull could be excused for grimacing over a few words of praise.

After Stars coach Ken Hitchcock compared Hull's performance in Game 6 to Bobby Baun scoring a 1964 Finals overtime goal on a broken leg, Hull scrunched up his face. "I'm no Bobby Baun—that's for sure," he said.

Hitchcock was less sure of that after watching Hull use his hobbled skating style to get to the front of the net to score the game-winner in the second-longest game in Finals history.

"When the dust settles, Brett Hull is going to be an incredible story," Hitchcock said. "What this man did to go on the ice and what we had to do to him between periods to get him back on the ice was incredible."

Hull hurt his knee on an open-ice hit by Buffalo defenseman Alexei Zhitnik earlier in the series. The Stars revealed only Hull's groin injury. "I was kind of numb on half of one leg, and the other one was all buggered up," he said. "You just go out and do the best you can."

His injuries were retaped between every period, and heat was applied. To make matters worse, he aggravated the groin injury with 17 seconds left in the first overtime.

"He limped around the ice," Hitchcock remembered. "The goal he scored, if you watch the shift, he limped into the corner, he limped in front of the net." Limping or not, he battled for position and swatted the puck past goalie Dominik Hasek for the controversial goal. Replays showed that Hull was in the crease, and yet for some reason the video replay judge did not overturn the goal. That fact caused a firestorm of protest in Buffalo. Somehow it was fitting that Hull had played a role in the controversy because his outspokenness had always put him in harm's way when it came to controversy.

*Dallas Stars hero Brett Hull hoists the Stanley Cup after the Stars defeated the Buffalo Sabres 2–1 in triple overtime in Game 6 of the Stanley Cup Finals in Buffalo, New York, early Sunday morning on June 20, 1999. Hull scored the game-winning goal.*

No player understood living on the edge of a deep fryer more than Hull. He always seemed to be just one topple away from getting scalded by all the heat directed toward him. His entertaining mouth always got him in trouble. It's also a heavy burden to have your team counting on you to score big goals in every big game. When he came to Dallas, he was viewed as the final piece in the Stars' puzzle.

"Do you know how much pressure that is?" Hull said.

That was why he felt such relief after he had delivered a championship to the Stars. "It is the most unbelievable feeling just to shut up all the naysayers," Hull said.

Despite producing Hall of Fame numbers in St. Louis, he left without a championship. "I don't have to answer to anyone anymore," Hull said. "And neither does Eddie [Belfour], Joe [Nieuwendyk], or Mike Modano.

Joe has a cadaver ligament in his knee. That's fabulous. Mike Modano. He's the biggest competitor I've seen."

He had added incentive to make sure the Stars won in six. "I don't think I could have played a Game 7," Hull said. "I really don't think I could have."

His only regret about 1999 is that the championship feeling came and went before he could actually savor the moment. That summer he took the Stanley Cup to Duluth, Minnesota, where he had first been discovered as a college standout. That's where he makes his summer home today. "You are just too emotionally spent to absorb the experience," Hull said.

But he had one epiphany regarding winning his Stanley Cup. "If I hadn't won," he said, "I don't think I would have gone to my grave thinking something was missing."

Hull won again with the Red Wings in 2002.

## Craig Ludwig
*Montreal Canadiens, 1986 • Dallas Stars, 1999*

Defenseman Craig Ludwig would have had no reason to feel like a fossil in his final NHL season if not for the fact that his dressing room stall became a museum. A teammate or member of the media was always stopping by to view the shin pads that had protected Ludwig's legs since the 1970s. He got them from trainer Dave Cameron when he was a college freshman at North Dakota and wore them through his final NHL campaign in 1998–1999. Ludwig was never sure how old the pads were, but in his last year he was sure the pads were older than 21-year-old teammate Jon Sim. "They were old when I got them," Ludwig said. "When you are a rookie like I was, you don't get the new stuff."

In the male tradition, Ludwig has kept the pads in working order with improvised repairs and a healthy dose of duct tape. "I just don't like new equipment," he said with a shrug. "I see guys now that go through five pairs of skates in one season."

He used the same pair of skates through his final three seasons in Dallas. He estimated he had about "two weeks left in them" in 1999 when the Stars wrapped up their first Stanley Cup championship in franchise history.

*Craig Ludwig rides a Harley-Davidson motorcycle with the Stanley Cup on his back seat during the 1999 Dallas Stars Stanley Cup Reunion at the American Airlines Center on January 22, 2007, in Dallas, Texas.* Photo courtesy of Getty Images

Having won his only other Cup in 1986, Ludwig established a new league mark of 13 seasons between Stanley Cup titles. The previous mark of 12 had been held by Terry Sawchuk, who captured the Stanley Cup in 1952, 1954, 1955, and not again until he and Johnny Bower shared goaltending duties with the Maple Leafs in 1967.

When given his time with the Cup, he opted to hold a party in his hometown of Elk River, Wisconsin, over the Fourth of July weekend. After picking up the Cup and its escort at the airport, Ludwig had to struggle to return to his house because so many cars were lining his street. More than 300 folks were at his house, including three Pee Wee hockey teams that just happened to be in town for a tournament.

"They came because they just figured they might not ever get a chance to see the Cup again," Ludwig said. "But I swear there were a ton of people there that I had never seen in my life."

At approximately 2:00 AM, the police showed up at the door asking for "Mr. Ludwig." Ludwig figured people had complained about the party, but much to his surprise he was asked if he would be willing to bring the Cup down to the police and fire stations so the officers and firemen on the night shift could get a look at Lord Stanley's prize. "It was surreal," Ludwig told members of the Dallas media. "Me, the cops, and the Stanley Cup at 3:00 AM."

Ludwig also put the Cup on display in the local Fourth of July parade. "It's like traveling with Elvis," Ludwig said. "The Cup is really a celebrity, and you don't know what people are going to do when they meet it."

Having won a second Cup at age 38, Ludwig felt no need to continue his career, particularly when it became clear that the Stars had decided not to bring him back. He was content to move more aggressively into his other passion—big-time, national-caliber softball.

In the end, his equipment was probably more tired than he was. While many hockey players are superstitious, that played no role in Ludwig's love of vintage equipment.

"It is a comfort thing," he said.

What's even more remarkable about the ragged nature of Ludwig's pads is that he was one of the league's premier shot-blockers. That means he was constantly trying to throw those pads toward shots coming at him at 85 miles per hour or more. His well-being relied on the duct tape holding up.

His shin pads are so legendary in the sport that the Hockey Hall of Fame has requested he donate them for display after his career is over. "I got two letters saying they wanted to put them in the Hall," Ludwig said. "I said, 'No thanks. If you take them, you have to take me,' and I never got a letter again."

Ludwig's plan was to display the pads in his bar in Wausau, Wisconsin. Presumably, if they are there on the wall, they are attached by duct tape.

## Claude Lemieux

*Montreal Canadiens, 1986* • *New Jersey Devils, 1995 and 2000*
*Colorado Avalanche, 1996*

Opponents have always sworn at Claude Lemieux's playing style. But teams trying to win the Stanley Cup have sworn by his playing style.

His nails-down-the-chalkboard on-ice behavior has forever made him public enemy No. 1 around the NHL. Detroit Red Wings winger Darren McCarty still won't shake hands with Lemieux because of his hit against Kris Draper in 1996. He is irritating, like a barking hound dog or a wasp at a company picnic. He is lippy, chippy, and not averse to applying lumber to the back of your leg. He's also one of the most proven winners in NHL history. He is one of only nine players to win a Stanley Cup with three different teams, joining Frank Foyston, Jack Walker, and Hap Holmes (who each played for Cup winners in Toronto, Seattle, and Victoria before 1925), plus Mike Keane (Montreal, Colorado, and Dallas), Larry Hillman (Detroit, Toronto, and Montreal), Al Arbour (Chicago, Detroit, and Toronto as a player, and New York Islanders as a coach), Gordon Pettinger (New York Rangers, Boston, and Detroit), and Joe Nieuwendyk (Calgary, Dallas, and New Jersey). Jack Marshall is the only player to earn a Stanley Cup championship with four different teams (1901 Winnipeg Vics, the 1902 Montreal AAA, 1910 Montreal Wanderers, and 1914 Toronto Blueshirts).

Lemieux and Nieuwendyk are the only players on that list to have won the Conn Smythe Trophy as playoff MVP. Lemieux did that in 1995 when he netted 13 goals in 20 games to help the New Jersey Devils win the first Stanley Cup in that franchise's history. "It's just incredible that my name is on that," Lemieux commented. "To be the most hated man in hockey and have your name on the Conn Smythe is really special."

Lemieux's fierce championship pride was nurtured in Montreal, where winning was intertwined with the dressing room culture. He was a 20-year-old rookie in 1986 when he netted 10 postseason goals to help the Canadiens win the 23rd Stanley Cup in franchise history. He says the experience he earned on the ice wasn't quite as valuable as what he learned in the dressing room. The Montreal organization was a like a village in which the secrets of winning were passed down from generation to generation.

"When I was 20 years old and in my first year, I looked up to Larry Robinson and Bob Gainey, and looked up to all the guys to see how they reacted," Lemieux said. "I remember how Gainey hardly showed any emotion or excitement until the moment, until it was done. He was never too high or too low. You learn from these guys. Then you pass it along. It isn't something you invent. It's something that is handed down to you. It's taught to you. You have to pass it down."

Lemieux believes that former Montreal players take their winning tradition wherever they go. "The fans in Montreal don't just expect you to play," Lemieux said. "They expect you to win."

That's why Lemieux played the way he did—on the border between shameless violence and championship caliber grit. By 2009 his résumé showed 19 game-winning playoff goals, tying him for third place on the NHL all-time list, only five away from co-leaders Wayne Gretzky and Brett Hull, who had 24 apiece.

The only way Lemieux knows how to play is with fixed bayonet. "You can call it old-school," Lemieux said. "But I think it's the only way to play the game. It's the way it was played 20 or 30 years ago. The game really hasn't changed. Look at the success of [coach] Scotty Bowman. That's the Montreal way of playing the game. The players have changed. You may call the drills by a different name, or the forechecking may be called a different kind of system. But it's still the same game."

Lemieux insists that each Cup victory has a unique identity of its own that is difficult to describe. "But the first one is probably the one you remember most, especially with me having grown up in Montreal," Lemieux said. "You have to put that one in first place."

In Lemieux's view, very few professional championship scenarios could match the grandeur associated with a Montreal fan growing up to become a member of a Canadiens' championship team.

"I would compare it to maybe growing up a baseball fan and a Yankee fan, playing the game from the time you are five or six," Lemieux said. "Then you are 20, and all of a sudden you are with the Yankees and you win the World Series. You are involved, chipping in, making a contribution. That is what it was like for me as a Montreal player. It was the ultimate. It doesn't get any better than that."

In 1986 the league wasn't involved in making sure each player got the Cup. But Lemieux was given his time with it, and he took it home. He remembers a parade and picture-taking but, to be truthful, he says, it was mostly a blur. But he does believe that possessing the Cup without a chaperone for a day or two back then meant more to him than his next possessions, when the Cup came with its babysitter.

"Back then you were just trusted to go get the Cup and then bring it back," Lemieux said, smiling. "I guess they had some adventures back then, and now they take better care of it. They make sure it's supervised. But back then we could do whatever we wanted to do."

Lemieux's favorite moments with the Stanley Cup came on the ice and in the dressing room, not in the subsequent victory celebrations around town. "When you win the first one, you don't remember much," Lemieux insists. "You win. It's over. When you have won the Cup before, you savor the moment more the second time. You watch the other guys a lot more. You understand what it means to all the young players who have never won before. Afterward, the Cup is for the fans, your family, and your kids. Afterward, it's about picture-taking."

His satisfaction came on the ice. "When you have the Cup and you are carrying it around, that's the best feeling in the world," Lemieux said. "It means the most when you are lifting it above your head on the ice."

However, winning his fourth Cup in 2000 was important to him for family reasons. "I have four kids, and one lacked a Stanley Cup victory," Lemieux said. "So the fourth [was] for my little girl. They are all blessed now."

Lemieux is proud of his reputation of being a player that coaches want around when the march for the Stanley Cup begins. "You can never get tired of winning," says Lemieux. "Once you get a taste of it, you want to do it every year."

He has never been able to kick his addiction to pursuing the Stanley Cup. It seemed as if his NHL career was over in 2003, although Lemieux did play briefly in Switzerland in 2003–2004. But he said he started thinking about a comeback "on the day I retired."

At age 43, Lemieux did come back, signing with the San Jose Sharks for the second half of the 2008–2009 season.

"He has always been the type of player you didn't want to see on the other team, but you loved to have in your dressing room," Sharks general manager Doug Wilson said. He was playing in the American League when the Sharks recalled him, and even had played briefly in China's league as part of his comeback process. "Someone asked why I would bring a player like this in, and my question would be why you wouldn't bring in a player like this when you are trying to get to where we are trying to get to," Wilson said. "Claude went into Worchester and made that team a better team."

## Guy Carbonneau
*Montreal Canadiens, 1986 and 1993 • Dallas Stars, 1999*
Guy Carbonneau believes he was framed with regard to the "Cup Caper" of 1999. Evidence suggests that he was.

Drummer Vinnie Paul fingered Carbonneau as the culprit in the denting of the Stanley Cup during a wild celebration at Paul's home. Carbonneau was charged with an errant throw of the Stanley Cup into a pool. Eyewitnesses say that never actually happened. Upon further review of replays, Hall of Fame Cup guru Phil Pritchard says that the Cup was probably dented in the celebration in the dressing room in Buffalo. He says that video shows that there was already a dent in the Cup when goaltender Ed Belfour showed off the Cup to fans when the Stars landed at the Dallas airport the day after the Cup-clinching.

The *Wall Street Journal* "broke" the story with Paul's allegations, and several newspapers actually pursued it as if a crime had been committed. The truth is that the Stanley Cup dents quite easily, and the Hall of Fame, although it would never admit it publicly, expects the Cup to come back dented. Precautions are taken to keep damage to a minimum, but the denting of the Cup is as inevitable as old age. It's going to happen. It's just a question of when.

Theories abounded in Dallas that summer on how the Cup actually became dented. One story had the Cup bouncing out of the back of a pickup truck as the Stars were caravanning to the Big Apple Café, a favorite Stars' watering hole. Although the truth is hardly important at this juncture, it probably did get dinged up in the visitor's dressing room in Buffalo. It got passed around quite a bit that night, and champagne-influenced reflexes probably weren't what they should be.

Whatever happened to the Cup, Carbonneau shouldn't have been treated like a perp. This is a guy who learned Stanley Cup reverence in Montreal. That's like studying Catholicism in the Vatican. Carbonneau believed in the Canadiens' mystique, and he took a piece of that with him.

"Everyone talks about the pressure of playing in Montreal," Carbonneau said. "I always say that, even though players in the 1990s don't like it, it does make them better players."

Carbonneau's comments came at the 2000 Stanley Cup Finals where the Dallas Stars, with ex-Canadiens star Bob Gainey as general manager, faced the New Jersey Devils, with ex-Canadiens star Larry Robinson as coach. Former Canadiens captains Carbonneau, Mike Keane, and Kirk Muller played on one Dallas line. Former Cup hero Claude Lemieux played for New Jersey. That's no coincidence, says Carbonneau.

"When you are a Canadien, it makes you perform every game," he insisted. "It makes you understand what it is to be a winning team. Everybody who left Montreal brought that with him."

In the misguided exposure of the Cup Caper, what Carbonneau really did with the Cup was nationally overlooked. His father died during the playoffs, and Carbonneau took the Cup to his grave. "It was very emotional," he said.

## Joe Nieuwendyk

*Calgary Flames, 1989 • Dallas Stars, 1999 • New Jersey Devils, 2003*
In 1989, when Lanny McDonald and Joe Mullen were preaching about what it means to win the Cup late in your career, Joe Nieuwendyk was listening. He wasn't really hearing, but he was definitely listening. It wasn't until a decade later that he understood completely. During the 1999 Stanley Cup Finals against Buffalo, Nieuwendyk talked about wanting to savor every moment of being there. He sounded almost as if it were the first time, even though he had won the Stanley Cup with McDonald, Mullen, and the Calgary Flames in 1989. In that series the

Flames won the Stanley Cup, and Nieuwendyk garnered the Conn Smythe Trophy with 11 goals and 21 points in 23 games.

Nieuwendyk seemed like a man on a mission in 1999. He boasted six game-winners in the Stars' 16 wins. He was 22 when he won his first Cup and 32 when he won his second. "I was a little naïve the first time I won the Cup," Nieuwendyk said. "I thought we had such a great team that we would be back. It took me 10 years to get back. That's when you realize what a battle it is to get to the Final. Then you have to win it. All the adversity, all of the injuries—it's just one battle after another."

The time interlude between Cups allowed Nieuwendyk to develop a greater sense of enjoyment about winning. When it came time for the Cup to be brought to a site of his choosing, Nieuwendyk talked the powers that be into letting him have the Cup in two different sites, squeezing an extra half-day into his celebration. He wanted to take it to his hometown of Whitby, Ontario, and his summer home in Ithaca, New York. In Whitby he took it to his local hockey arena. He also hosted a private party for 275 guests.

"To me it's the people's Cup," Nieuwendyk said. "I just get pleasure out of watching everyone's reaction to the Cup. I just enjoyed having a good time with it…my brother, Gill, and Rick in the back of the Chevy Tahoe going to downtown Whitby, hanging out of the back of the Tahoe with the Cup."

In Ithaca, his favorite Cup moment was less flamboyant and more poignant. While at Cornell, his favorite professor was Dan Sisler, who is blind. "I had a lot of respect for him," Nieuwendyk said. "I had a reception for some people at Cornell, and he was there. It was a neat feeling to see him scan the Cup with his hands. Everyone stopped what they were doing to see him going over the Cup. It was awesome."

During the 2000 Stanley Cup playoffs, Nieuwendyk was featured on ESPN in a comical commercial picturing him using the Stanley Cup as a Jell-O mold at a family gathering. Of course, that never happened. But Nieuwendyk reportedly did use the Stanley Cup as a serving bowl for the Canadian specialty of gravy and french fries.

Growing up in Whitby, Nieuwendyk always enjoyed his dining experiences, not to mention the hamburgers and fries at North End Burgers. If he won again, he said, he would take the Cup there. True to his word, Nieuwendyk showed up there with the Cup in the summer of 1999. A bowl of gravy was set inside the Cup, and Nieuwendyk and his friends began dipping their fries. Maybe the name should be changed to Lord Stanley's Gravy Bowl.

## Ed Belfour
*Dallas Stars, 1999*

The fact that Belfour needed a Learjet to accommodate his Stanley Cup party itinerary wasn't all that shocking to those who know him. This is a guy who rented Maple Leaf Gardens a couple of years ago so he could play an after-hours pick-up hockey game with friends from Michigan, Chicago, North Dakota, and Manitoba. It was Eddie the Eagle's way of saying good-bye to one of hockey's great arenas. Belfour played forward, not goaltender, and by all accounts had a grand time.

One story that made the rumor circuit was that Belfour dented the Cup as he brought it off the plane. But it didn't take much investigation to uncover that Belfour put only miles on the Cup, not dents.

In a span of 48 hours, he transported the Cup to his hometown of Carman, Manitoba, population 2,500, where he was greeted like a conquering hero. In North Dakota, he brought the Cup to accent the groundbreaking of an ice arena. Belfour played his college hockey at North Dakota. Then it was off to Chicago, where he hosted a gathering at the Palmer House Hilton. Belfour, a man of few words, said only that it was all that he had dreamed it would be.

## Dave Reid
*Dallas Stars, 1999 • Colorado Avalanche, 2001*

Dave Reid was 35 when he won his Stanley Cup in 1999 and figures that saved plenty of wear and tear on the Cup's bodyguard. "They like guys who are married," Reid joked. "Some of the single guys get in a little trouble with it. But the guy who brought it to my house got a lot of sleep."

Of all the stops he made, one highlight was simply taking the Cup around to his father's business associates in downtown Toronto. With parking a major headache, Reid found it easier just to walk up and down Yonge and Bloor Streets with the Cup on his shoulder.

*The Dallas Stars' Ed Belfour lifts the Stanley Cup while teammates (from right) Guy Carbonneau, Joe Nieuwendyk, and Mike Keane acknowledge the crowd during a victory parade in downtown Dallas in June 1999.*

"We were moving at a pretty good clip, so it wasn't like people were coming out of the buildings to see it," Reid said. "But people would pass you and say, 'Hey, is that the Stanley Cup?'"

The funny part was that some people didn't believe Reid when he told them that it was indeed the Cup. "They would say, 'That's not the Cup,'" Reid recalled.

What he remembers most about his Cup possession was spending the whole day taking pictures. "I always had one arm around the Cup and the other around whoever was next to the Cup."

One treasure for Reid was his championship ring. But that had to go on hiatus during the playoffs. After the Cup, Reid moved over to the Colorado Avalanche; he didn't feel right about wearing a Stars' ring in that dressing room, especially given that they played them in the Western Conference championship round.

## Pat Verbeek

*Dallas Stars, 1999*

The Stanley Cup has always been called hockey's Holy Grail, but that description took on a new meaning the day Pat Verbeek received the Cup in 1999.

Through the years, Stanley has seen its fair share of debauchery. Too many lost nights to accurately count. Way too much alcohol poured into its bowl. Stanley has seen the inside of strip joints and countless taverns and gin mills. So it seemed only right that Verbeek should introduce Stanley to his church and religion.

On July 3, 1999, Verbeek brought Stanley to the 5:30 PM Saturday Mass at Christ the King Catholic Church. The congregation broke out in sustained applause when Verbeek entered the church with Cup in hand. Verbeek, his wife, Dianne, and their five children had belonged to the parish since Verbeek joined the Dallas Stars in 1996. Verbeek's youngest child had been baptized there.

One reason why Verbeek brought the Cup to church is that he wanted his pastor, Monsignor Donald Zimmerman, to bless it. The parish arranged for a photographer to be present while the Cup was in the church, and after mass Verbeek obliged those who wanted to pose with him for pictures. In his homily, Pastor Zimmerman talked about hockey and jokingly offered his own prayer that the Stars' future Cup-clinchings would last only one overtime instead of three.

Verbeek, raised on a farm in Petrolia, Ontario, has always had a deep Catholic faith. He has always mixed his faith with his hockey. He has had a lasting friendship with Sister Eileen Marie Hunter, a nun who taught him at St. Patrick's High School in Sarnia, Ontario. Throughout Verbeek's career, he has made a habit of leaving Sister Eileen tickets when he plays in Detroit. It has been even easier for Sister Eileen to attend the games since she accepted a new assignment as coordinator for the Sisters of Saint Joseph Holy Rosary Convent in Windsor, Ontario, right across the river from the Red Wings' Joe Louis Arena. On one of the Stars' visits in 1998–1999, Sister Eileen pointed out that she had never seen Verbeek beat the Red Wings. He told her not to worry because he wasn't superstitious, even though the Stars had won only once in 20 games at Joe Louis Arena.

Verbeek jokingly suggested he should bring in Sister Eileen to perform "an exorcism" to remove the demons who haunted the Stars on their trips to Joe Louis Arena. Sister Eileen joked back that she would "leave the exorcisms to the priests." But she told Verbeek that before every game she prayed that he wouldn't be hurt, nor would any of his teammates or his opponents. For this game, she said, she was going to add an extra prayer for the Stars. The Stars ended up defeating the Red Wings 5–1.

Having once had his thumb reattached after a farming accident early in his NHL career, Verbeek has always been thankful to God for the longevity of his career. That's why he felt strongly about bringing the Stanley Cup to Mass after the Stars won the championship in 1999.

"My parents instilled the Catholic faith in me, and I've held onto it," Verbeek said. "God has always been a guide in my decisions in life. I thought it would be a good way of showing that I am thankful to God, and bringing the Cup to church was a way of showing him respect."

## Derek Plante

*Dallas Stars, 1999*

In the well-oiled Dallas Stars' championship machinery, Derek Plante was a spare part. He had been acquired from the Buffalo Sabres on March 23, 1999, as insurance against injury. He played in just six games during the playoffs, contributing one goal.

But when players were gathered in the Buffalo visitors' dressing room a couple of hours after winning the title, Plante had had an impact on the play. He spoke from the heart and touched everyone with his simple explanation of how much it meant to him to share in the championship experience.

"Even though I didn't play, I said it had been an honor for me to play with the Dallas Stars," Plante said. "It was an honor to be on the same team with those guys. The reason I didn't get to play was that this was a great team. And if I didn't play, it was fine with me as long as we won. I still felt like I was a part of it. And the guys had made me feel like I was part of it."

In retrospect, Plante said the Stars' celebration "was a blur." The highlight for him was bringing the Cup to his hometown of Cloquet, Minnesota. He slept with the Cup in his bed that night. Stars' winger Jamie Langenbrunner is from the same place. They took the Cup to the local hockey arena, and about 5,000 people showed up during the day to view it. A Duluth television station asked Plante to bring the Cup to the studio for a live appearance, and he happily obliged.

One of Plante's favorite moments came when the flight brought the Stars back to Dallas the next morning after they had captured the Cup on Buffalo ice. As they came down off the plane to the tarmac, Ed Belfour had the Stanley Cup. A huge crowd was cheering. "He was carrying the Cup like a sack of potatoes," Plante remembered. "He took the Cup over to the fans, and everyone was touching it and high-fiving. It was funny to see Eddie so excited. The people were excited. I never saw Eddie happier than that."

## Mike Modano
*Dallas Stars, 1999*

Immediately after Brett Hull scored the Cup-winning goal for the Dallas Stars in 1999, it was almost as if Mike Modano's career flashed before his eyes. Tears fell from his eyes, and his composure took a short leave of absence. He was overwhelmed by an indescribable blend of relief and jubilation. He had joined the Stars' organization as a potentially high-scoring No. 1 draft choice in 1988 and had endured a long climb to the summit. In the beginning, he had been a flashy open-ice player who looked as if he had the potential to win a scoring championship. By the time he reached his championship moment, he had been transformed into a different player. Somewhere in the process, Modano had been transformed into a warrior.

"Being with one organization the whole 11 years of my career maybe made it more special," Modano said. "All the trials and tribulations that I went through...and then being able to finish what I started, to have a say in the outcome...it's really hard to explain."

On the off day before the final game, Modano said he purposely spent some time by himself. "You visualize [winning the Cup]," Modano said. "When it comes, it feels like relief. The two months that we went through were probably the most physically and emotionally draining thing I've ever been a part of. I think that's why you see the emotion kind of pour through. When you have been pushed to the edge like that and then come out on top, it makes it that much more."

Modano said his Cup celebrations were tame in comparison to the excitement of the night when the Stars defeated the Sabres for the title in the triple-overtime thriller. He did get to take the Cup on Craig Kilborn's *Late Late Show* and host a family party at his home in Irving, Texas. He says his best moment was taking the Cup to the Children's Medical Center. "There is no trophy like this trophy," Modano said. "You bring it in, and the kids just light up."

His strangest Cup moment? "All the women kept flashing us [during the parade]," he said, laughing. "That's Dallas."

## Ken Hitchcock

*Coach, Dallas Stars, 1999*

Coach Ken Hitchcock's favorite moment from the night the Dallas Stars won the 1999 Stanley Cup championship came long after the champagne flow had been reduced to a trickle.

It was past 4:00 AM. The media had finished milking the players for all the emotion and tales of jubilation that they could muster. Wives, girlfriends, and family members had cleared the visitors' dressing room in Buffalo, leaving the players by themselves for the first time since Brett Hull had changed the course of franchise history by scoring the Cup-clinching goal against the Sabres.

"All of a sudden it just got quiet," Hitchcock remembered. "All that was left was us. Just players, coaches, other members of the organization."

Hitchcock believes it was general manager Bob Gainey who spoke first. Gainey is a soft-spoken, classy man who had won five Stanley Cup championships as a member of the Montreal Canadiens. Hitchcock remembers Gainey speaking eloquently about what the Stars had accomplished.

"It is a special feeling when you're basically in first place from start to finish," Hitchcock said. "It's special when you come out of the gate and play so well for so long and come out of it with the Stanley Cup championship."

That was Gainey's message, and then, one by one, players said their piece about what the Stanley Cup meant to them. Some had plenty to say, and some said very little. "But I can remember what people said that night almost verbatim," Hitchcock said. "The guy that broke me down was Derek Plante."

Plante was a spare player on the Stars; Hitchcock had only used him in six games during the playoffs. He hadn't played in the Stanley Cup Finals. "He just talked about how much it meant to him to be part of the championship," Hitchcock said. "It was very emotional."

The other special moment for Hitchcock came when he took the Stanley Cup to Kalamazoo, Michigan. Hitchcock had previously coached in the International Hockey League for the Kalamazoo Wings, and his wife and her children were from there. About 70 to 80 friends were there, and Hitchcock felt as if he were carrying the Holy Grail as he opened up the box and took the Stanley Cup out of his truck. "There was total silence," Hitchcock said. "This thing has such a special appeal that it invoked silence."

## Roman Turek

*Dallas Stars, 1999*

One indication of the NHL's popularity in the Czech Republic is the fact that, when Roman Turek took the Stanley Cup to Ceske Budejovice, he had difficulty trying to find time to drink even one beer out of the Cup.

More than 10,000 people showed up in the city square with the hope of glimpsing Turek with the Cup. Turek was the sixth Czech-born player to win the Cup, but the first to bring the Cup to Czech soil. A flight snafu caused a five-hour delay in the Cup's arrival and forced cancellation of the official public ceremony. Hall of Fame officials arrived in the Czech Republic, but the Stanley Cup didn't make the connection in Frankfurt, Germany. Turek was amused as the Cup handlers sweated out the arrival of 35 pounds of metal that is insured for $75,000. "They were nervous," Turek said. "They kept looking out the window and asking if it had arrived yet."

When the Cup finally arrived, a multitude of Czech hockey enthusiasts were still on hand, and everyone got their chance to be up close and personal with the Stanley Cup. Turek put it on display at the local hockey arena. "I can't tell you how many photographs were taken," Turek said, "but it seemed like a thousand or more."

Turek would lift the 35-pound Cup on demand, and by the end of the day he felt as if he had put in some hard work as a laborer. Several hundred residents of Turek's hometown of Strankonice gathered at their city hall to chant Turek's name and catch a glimpse of the world's most famous sports trophy and their hometown hero.

"Hockey is very big in the Czech Republic," Turek said. "People know what the Stanley Cup is."

Satellite dishes have brought the NHL into Czech living rooms with regularity, but it is the Czech players who really have turned this nation of 10 million into a hockey-crazed society. Dominik Hasek and Jaromir Jagr are national heroes, and the Czech Republic's triumph at the 1998 Olympic Games has pushed hockey to a higher point of reverence.

Many would have expected, maybe even hoped, that it would be Hasek who brought the Cup to the Czech Republic. Turek was honored to bring the Cup to his homeland, proud of his position as one of the world's top goaltenders. But perhaps there was a tinge of guilt to be celebrating a championship because he felt his contributions were limited. It had been Ed Belfour, not Turek, who had bested Hasek's Buffalo Sabres in the 1999 Stanley Cup Finals. Although Turek lost only three of 22 decisions in the 1998–1999 regular season, Belfour played every minute in the playoffs. There was no reason to switch, as Belfour had a 1.67 goals-against average.

"Of course I was happy we won the Cup, but it is very different when you watch from the bench," Turek said. "I didn't feel like I did much for us to win. Guys on the team told me not to think like that because I had won games in the regular season and worked hard. But I didn't play in the playoffs and I didn't make any big saves."

Turek's words came after he had been traded to the St. Louis Blues and had led that team to the President's Trophy in 1999–2000. He had been outstanding in the regular season, but he longed for a chance to take the Cup back to the Czech Republic under even better circumstances. Turek is a proud athlete, a player who once politely declined to appear on television after a game because he had given up three goals and didn't believe he had played well enough to warrant being interviewed.

Even as a backup on a championship team, Turek was so mobbed by fans that he remembered just having only one beer all day as he dealt with the demands of the fans. If he ever comes back to the Czech Republic as the star of a championship team, he probably won't have time to drink at all.

## Brad Bombardir

*New Jersey Devils, 2000*

A couple of minutes after the Devils had won the 2000 Stanley Cup and bedlam surrounded him on the ice, Devils coach Larry Robinson was rattling off the names of New Jersey players during a live ABC interview.

He wasn't mentioning key players like Martin Brodeur, Jason Arnott, or Scott Stevens. He named Steve Kelly, Kenny Sutton, Brad Bombardir, and others who hadn't played a minute in the Stanley Cup Finals. It was Robinson's acknowledgment that the triumph was aided by those in the background.

Bombardir had played 32 games in the regular season and wasn't in the postseason plans. But no one seemed to cherish the Stanley Cup experience more than he did. In the champagne-drenched Devils dressing room, Bombardir was truly enjoying the moment. "What do you do on a Saturday night?" Bombardir kept asking, even if no one was listening. "I drink from the Stanley Cup."

Not long after the event, he was one of the few Devils who already had an itinerary planned for his day with the Cup. "Gotta somehow have it where people can come see it, touch it, get pictures with it, kiss it, if that's what they choose to do," Bombardir told Kara Yorio of the *Asbury Park* (New Jersey) *Press*. "I'm going to take it out to my cabin where I grew up when I was a kid. They had a raft out in the water that we always played on. I want to take it out there with the sunset in the back."

## Martin Brodeur

*New Jersey Devils, 1995, 2000, and 2003*

The Surgeon General should put a label on the Stanley Cup to suggest that it's bad for Martin Brodeur's health. When he won his first Stanley Cup in 1995, he brought his first cigar to the podium for the Stanley Cup postgame press conference. When he arrived at the podium after winning the 2000 Stanley Cup, he had a cigar—different cigar, but same euphoria.

Although I witnessed his third championship, I didn't see his third Stanley Cup cigar. However, word is that he fired up another victory stogie after he captured his third title. According to cigaraficionado.com, Brodeur's interest in cigars didn't come until after he enjoyed his first Stanley Cup–winning cigar.

Brodeur called the victory cigar "the mark of a true champion," according to an article on the website. He was once quoted as saying that his sweat-drenched goalkeeping equipment would be ideal for humidifying his favorite cigar.

"I think you only realize how hard it is to win the Stanley Cup after you win it the second time," Brodeur said. "You just realize it took us five years to get back there. It's a great, great feeling to win."

In his second run to the Stanley Cup, Brodeur played brilliantly, giving up just six goals in the final five games of the Stanley Cup Finals against Dallas. The season undoubtedly wore him out, but after waiting five seasons for a championship, he celebrated robustly. Recovery came quickly for Brodeur. Two days later he took the Stanley Cup on the *Live! With Regis and Kathie Lee* show on ABC.

He also made big personal plans. First, he bartered for an extra day with the Cup so he could have a day with it in both New Jersey and Montreal. In New Jersey it would be shared with friends. In Montreal it was shared with friends and family. The family includes father Denis Brodeur, a former goaltender for the bronze medal–winning Canadian Olympic team of 1956. The elder Brodeur is better known as a highly respected professional sports photographer for the Montreal Canadiens and Expos. Two of his photos of Paul Henderson's famed goal at the 1972 Summit Series were shown on Canadian postage stamps. A hockey bond exists between father and son that goes beyond the conventional parental relationship.

Brodeur had another humorous reason for wanting to take the Cup back to Montreal: revenge. In 1995, during his Cup sojourn in Montreal, he organized a street hockey game with buddies. A chance to dance with the Cup was the prize. Brodeur's team lost. "I'm 2–0 on the ice, but 0–1 on the street," he told reporters.

In 2003 Brodeur again played superbly in the postseason, posting a 1.65 goals-against average and seven shutouts. New Jersey fans booed loudly when it was announced that Anaheim goalie Jean-Sebastien Giguere had been chosen as the winner of the Conn Smythe Trophy as the playoff MVP. Giguere had a 1.62 GAA, five shutouts, and seven overtime wins. The other members of losing teams in the Cup Finals to win the Conn Smythe were goaltender Ron Hextall of the Flyers in 1987, right wing Reggie Leach of the Flyers in 1976, goaltender Glenn Hall of the Blues in 1968, and Detroit Red Wings goalie Roger Crozier in 1966.

But Brodeur made it clear what his priorities were when he said, "I got the trophy that I wanted. I'm not worried about the Conn Smythe. He deserved it."

## Barry Smith
*Assistant/Associate Coach, Pittsburgh Penguins, 1991 and 1992*
*Detroit Red Wings, 1997, 1998, and 2002*

When Barry Smith thinks of the highlights of his NHL career, he instantly recalls the feeling he had sinking to the bottom of Mario Lemieux's pool after the Pittsburgh Penguins won the Cup in 1991.

"I just remember going over backwards with the Cup in my hand and looking up at the surface of the water," said Smith, who today coaches for the St. Petersburg team in Russia. "We had so many laughs that night. People were getting drenched. There was water everywhere. I got tossed into the pool right off the hop. Just being at Mario's house was special."

Smith has been on the coaching staff of two of the most talent-laden teams in the 1990s. He was part of two championship teams in Pittsburgh and three more in Detroit (including the 2002 team). The Buffalo Sabres have never won the Stanley Cup, but thanks to Smith and fellow Buffalo area resident Scotty Bowman, the city has hosted the Cup several times. Each time Smith has won, he has brought the Cup to his home on the beach. Part of Smith's celebration is to put the Cup on the back of his boat and tool along the beachfront. "Immediately people start yelling and hollering," Smith says.

Of all four of Smith's Cup associations, the one that he seems to feel best about was the Penguins' win in 1991. That was late coach Bob

Johnson's team, and Smith can't help feeling that the championship was predestined based on the events that followed.

Johnson was one of hockey's most likeable people, a gregarious man who never seemed to have a day that wasn't the best day of his life. When the Penguins had a bad practice, Smith would be upset, but Johnson would find a reason to exonerate his players.

"Barry," he would say, "it was just bad ice out there."

Smith smiles at the memories. "It was funny how that worked," Smith said. "It would only be bad ice on the right side, but not the left side."

No coach was ever more enthusiastic about the trappings of the game than Johnson. He would hold impromptu power-play meetings wherever he could find open spaces. He even held one once in a public bathroom. Sometimes during a meeting he would get people out of their chairs and then move the chairs around to demonstrate how he wanted players to move. He had coached college hockey at Wisconsin, and he was a teacher in his heart. But what made him a valuable pro coach was that he could also deal with the superstar player.

"When Mario came in to see Bob Johnson for the first time, Mario seemed nervous to see Bob Johnson, not the other way around," Smith said.

"Badger Bob," as he was known, was a gifted storyteller who often used his tales to get a point across to his players. When Lemieux was experiencing back difficulties, Johnson said to the media, "Did you ever go to the zoo? The lion is the king of the beasts, and every day he gets up and he stretches. We can learn from watching the animals."

Johnson also wasn't shy about praising his stars, and he publicly doted on his players like a proud father dotes upon his sons.

"He would walk through the room and say, 'Hey Barry, look, Mario is getting that massage. He's got tired muscles from working so hard. He's going to be reenergized tonight,'" Smith recalled, smiling.

Johnson coached the Calgary Flames from 1982 to 1987; he had exceptional teams, but he couldn't break free from the Edmonton dominance. He reached the Stanley Cup Finals in 1986, but the Canadiens and Patrick Roy denied him the prize. He left the Flames in 1987 to become executive director of USA Hockey, a job he expected to hold until his retirement. But the Penguins came calling, and Johnson decided he really hadn't lost his desire to coach.

"It was like he was getting one last kick of the can," Smith said. "It was really just a storybook ending to his life."

The Penguins swept the North Stars in the Finals, and yet Smith can remember that Johnson sweated out the final minutes of the game even though the Penguins had a 6–0 lead going into the third period. "We kept telling everyone to stay back, and Bob kept looking at the clock as if something was going to happen," Smith said.

After the Penguins won, the usually vocal Johnson was unusually silent. "He was so exuberant," Smith said. "He didn't have words to say."

Two months later, as Johnson prepared to coach Team USA in the World Cup, he was diagnosed with brain cancer. He died a few months later. "He was such a special man," Smith said. "Winning the Cup was a storybook ending."

## Dave Hannan

*Edmonton Oilers, 1988 • Colorado Avalanche, 1996*

When Dave Hannan was partying with the Stanley Cup at his suburban Pittsburgh home in 1996, he felt more like a security guard than an NHL champion. Hannan had the Stanley Cup for a day and a half after the Colorado Avalanche won. He was having a grand time until the Hall of Fame's assigned keeper of the Cup asked Hannan if he could leave the party early to visit with a friend he hadn't seen in a while. He made it clear he was putting the Cup's security in Hannan's hands.

"He said, 'You are one of the older players in the league, and I know I can trust you,'" Hannan said. "I didn't think anything about it until I looked around and saw people dragging the Cup around outside. And I began to think, *Wow, I've got to look after this Cup.* All I could think was, *I don't want to be the guy who loses this thing. I don't want my name in the paper as having lost the most treasured prize in sports history.*"

He started watching people at his party, sizing them up the way a store detective might eyeball potential shoplifters. He didn't want anyone walking off with Lord Stanley's mug. He didn't get peace even after returning home. "I locked all the windows and doors," Hannan said, laughing. "It was paranoia all around me."

When it was time to go to bed, he brought the Stanley Cup into his bedroom and placed it between him and his wife, Jinny. "She gave me one of those looks like, *You've got to be kidding me*," Hannan said. "But I really felt like I had to watch this thing."

The next morning Hannan and his wife even shined up the Cup before the Hall of Fame representative returned. Recalled Hannan, "I told him I thought I deserved half of his salary for being the security guard for the Cup."

All of Hannan's Stanley Cup memories are quite vivid, even though he admits that his Cup win with the Edmonton Oilers in 1988 was essentially a blur. He was dealt by the Pittsburgh Penguins as part of the Paul Coffey trade, and his championship season was the only season he spent with the Oilers. He played 12 games in the playoffs, although he didn't dress for the Cup-clincher. But the Oilers took care of Hannan. "When you win a Cup you always want someone who hasn't won before to be around," Hannan recalled. "Kevin [Lowe] got the Cup and brought it to me right away, and that was probably the defining moment of the Cup victory." Hannan remembered that he and Keith Acton were given the right to take the Stanley Cup to the team party in 1988 because they were first-time Cup winners.

Having waited eight years to win again with Colorado, Hannan better understood what it means to win. "You really realize how hard this trophy is to win," Hannan said. "Many great players in the National Hockey League never had a chance to win one of these, even though they had very successful careers. And would they all trade it for a Cup? I think they would."

The scene of the triumphant Colorado dressing room is also still fresh in Hannan's mind. He remembers his son, then six, sitting on top of the dressing stalls, watching the celebration. His father, Bill, got to gulp from the Cup.

Hannan still chuckles when he thinks about watching all the people trying to chug beverages out of the Cup as if they were magic potions. "It's a bulky thing to take a sip out of, even if you have someone hold the end of it," Hannan said. "Every time someone would try to drink out of it, they would spill all over their clothes."

## Alex Tanguay

*Colorado Avalanche, 2001*

Alex Tanguay could have been talking literally or figuratively when he said that, after he earned the right to lift the Stanley Cup for the first time, he "couldn't believe how heavy it was."

"Everyone tells you how heavy it is, but you don't realize how heavy until you lift it," he said. "It's really unbelievable."

The pressure in the Stanley Cup Finals is enormous. The pressure of Game 7 of the Finals is almost impossible to quantify. That's why Tanguay's two goals and one assist in Colorado's clinching win against the New Jersey Devils may be difficult to top in terms of Stanley Cup memories. "There is no better feeling than this," Tanguay said. "As a kid you always dream of being the one scoring the goals in the important times. But to actually do it is unreal."

Born in Ste. Justine, Quebec, Tanguay certainly understood the Stanley Cup's aura. Hockey is still a religious experience in his region. Children grow up wanting to become hockey heroes like Guy Lafleur, Gilbert Perreault, Mike Bossy, or Rocket Richard—to become another in a long line of French Canadian hockey heroes.

To be the offensive hero in a Stanley Cup Game 7 as a 21-year-old, second-year player is impossible to describe. Tanguay didn't have the words in French or English to explain what it meant to have his name linked forever with one of the best Game 7 performances in the Stanley Cup's long, illustrious history.

One of the missions of the Colorado Avalanche during the 2001 Stanley Cup race was to help Ray Bourque win a Cup after 22 years of trying. Bourque is another French Canadian hero, and Tanguay is certain that the added motivation of assisting in Bourque's quest can't be overstated. "I think winning it for Ray was a big deal for us because we truly believed he deserved it. He is a true Hall of Famer. One of the best defensemen of all time. We worked hard as a team to be able to accomplish this for ourselves and for Ray. I think seeing Ray being the first one, when Joe handed the Cup to Ray, we all had tears in our eyes. I think everybody in the hockey world had tears in their eyes. It doesn't get any better than seeing Ray Bourque carrying the Cup in Denver."

Tanguay also couldn't have been happier for goalkeeper Patrick Roy, who won his fourth Stanley Cup—the same number won by Terry Sawchuk. That's significant because the debate will forever rage about whether Roy or Sawchuk is the greatest goaltender of all time.

During Tanguay's rookie season, he lived in Roy's basement. "Growing up a Quebec Nordiques fan, I really didn't like Patrick [who played for Montreal]," Tanguay joked. "But I learned about this game from the best."

Tanguay comes from a town of 2,000 people and, at the moment of his greatest triumph, he just couldn't comprehend what the victory would mean to his community. Tanguay had a plan for his hometown celebration. "One of the things I'll do will be sharing the Cup with my friends," he said. "We will play golf in the morning, and whoever gets the best score will get to parade the Cup around town a little bit. Hopefully, it will be me parading the Cup around."

## Bob Hartley
*Coach, Colorado Avalanche, 2001*
Coach Bob Hartley pieced together windshield wipers long before he was fashioning the lineup that helped the Colorado Avalanche win the Stanley Cup championship in 2001. That's why the Stanley Cup went to the PPG Canada factory in Hawkesbury, Ontario, a small hamlet about an hour outside of Montreal and Ottawa. When Hartley won the Stanley Cup championship, he didn't forget his roots. "I would have been happy to stay there and work in the factory my whole life," Hartley recalled. "It would have been a good living. I don't remember exactly what I was making, but it was $14 to $15 per hour, and I was probably making $40,000 to $45,000 per year. My family lived there, and my wife's family. I would have been happy. I loved my job."

Hartley was a volunteer goaltender for the Hawkesbury junior team when the team president asked him to move up to be interim coach. "After the fourth game he said the kids want you as a coach, and I said forget about that," Hartley said.

But the more he coached, the more he loved coaching, and as he climbed higher in the hockey world through junior hockey and then the minor leagues, he never forgot his devotion to his hometown. He considers himself fortunate to have reached the level he has, and he really wanted to share the Cup with his community. Hartley belongs to Hawkesbury like the Kennedys belong to Massachusetts. When the Cup came to Hawkesbury, merchants dressed their storefronts in Avalanche colors with the winner getting a special prize.

It was a difficult decision to leave the factory, although the one year he both coached and worked there he says it almost killed him. "I would be resting in the same cemetery as my dad and my grandparents if I kept doing that," he quipped.

Hartley believes he learned the team concept working in the factory, everyone manning the oars to get the boat moving in the right direction. "I was raised to respect people and teamwork. I worked in a plant where there were 400 or 500 employees to work with. Now that I only have 20 to work with, life is pretty easy."

His philosophy? "I'm a big believer that you have to challenge yourself, not only as a coach, but as a person, as well," Hartley said. "My goal is to try to make the people around me better. I believe I grew up in this organization."

Hartley has effectively turned the media into "Hartley believers" by mixing cordiality with colorful and frequently humorous quotes. When a reporter brought up a past Colorado failure in the form of a question during the postseason, he playfully retorted, "I was waiting for a question like this from you. You're always in the past. You're still looking at Bill Buckner's [mistake] in 1986 instead of enjoying Pedro Martinez in 2001."

Hartley never played in the NHL, and he seems to have a "common man" approach to his status as a coach. When Hartley took the Cup back to Hawkesbury, it went fishing with him and his friends on the Ottawa River. It also went to the cemetery where many of his relatives are buried.

Although Hartley's love for his hometown is enormous, his reputation as a good neighbor is even greater. The night he returned home after winning the Stanley Cup, he found that his friends had decorated his home. "I came home at 4:30 in the morning, and they had banners all over my house," Hartley said. "I had a couple of foil Stanley Cups on my roof. As soon as we had taken the lead in Game 7, they started to build those Cups."

Hartley knew that he wanted to share the Cup with those special friends. "I always play street hockey with the kids in my neighborhood," he said. "Every week there are a couple of games." It made sense to Hartley that this tradition be continued in grand fashion. He handed out fliers to his neighbors announcing that there would be several street hockey games the next day and that the Stanley Cup would be the guest of honor. The police were summoned to close off the cul-de-sac. "I called it a Game 7 Stanley Cup playoff game," Hartley said.

More than 200 people of all ages showed up to play. Hartley, a former junior goaltender, assumed his position between the pipes. He had three games going at the same time. "After the games, I put apple juice in the Cup, and the kids drank right from it," Hartley said. "Obviously, we had more than apple juice for the adults."

Hartley wanted it to be a kid's grand moment. "You play lots of Stanley Cup games in the street when you are a kid," he said. "Growing up close to Montreal, that's what we always did. When we came back from the arena, we would line up 10 or 12 guys and we would do that for another three or four hours." It was the memory of his childhood games that prompted Hartley to celebrate with street hockey. "I thought this is something that my neighbors would remember," he said.

Hartley, a polite man who ends his press conferences with "Have a good day," reveled in the Cup's aura as much as anyone. Known for his love of landscaping, he snapped pictures of the Cup around his pond and garden.

Hartley does commercials for Lakewood Fordland, and he wanted to surprise the dealership by showing up with the Cup. Imagine what commuters thought as they saw Hartley tooling down I-25 with the Stanley Cup resting in the backseat of his Mustang convertible. "We were lucky there were no accidents," Hartley said. "People were yelling, honking. It was so much fun."

When Hartley thought the Cup was spending too much time in a press conference, he told his assistant coaches, "We have to move that Cup around."

"So I just went out and kidnapped that Cup," Hartley said. "I brought it back to our office, then a major celebration started again. Hundreds of pictures were taken that night."

Did Hartley have any special speeches prepared for victory night? "I wanted to keep a simple approach," Hartley said. "Play for the win, don't play for the Cup. Play for the win. We know what the reward will be. I told them that Stanley would be waiting for us."

Hartley said the Avalanche's championship run—which included two Game 7s—seemed like a "big love story where everything unfolded the right way. If we would have wanted to write a book about the Stanley Cup, I don't think we could have made up a better script."

During the last 10 or 15 seconds of that Game 7, Hartley said he kept his eyes "only on Ray Bourque. I wanted to see how he would react because he was such an unbelievable story for the team. I feel fortunate to have spent 15 months with that classy gentleman."

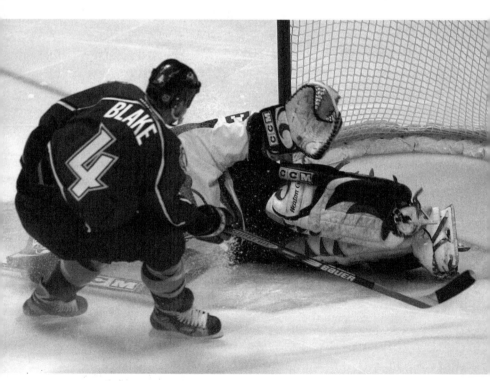

*Rob Blake of the Colorado Avalanche scores on New Jersey Devils goaltender Martin Brodeur in the first period of Game 4 of the Stanley Cup Finals on June 2, 2001, in East Rutherford, New Jersey.*

# Rob Blake

*Colorado Avalanche, 2001*

On July 14, 2001, signs draped in store windows throughout Simcoe, Ontario, shouted the town's feeling about Rob Blake's decision to bring the Cup back to his hometown. "You Make Simcoe Proud" was the simple message on the many placards.

Blake's wife was six months pregnant with the couple's first child. It was not the best of times to be flying in from the West Coast. But Blake had promised he would someday bring the Stanley Cup to Simcoe, and he is a man of his word.

When Blake returned to his Canadian roots, he saw telephone poles around the community standing at attention with handmade signs that read, "Home of Rob Blake, Stanley Cup Champion."

Blake's first Stanley Cup championship wasn't unexpected—not after he was traded to Colorado in March. While toiling for the Los Angeles Kings for 12 seasons, the Stanley Cup was a hope; when he got to Colorado, it became an expectation.

All the talk in Colorado was about Bourque's need to win a Stanley Cup, but Blake's drive to win wasn't any less passionate. Like Bourque, Blake had been a Norris Trophy winner and an All-Star, but he had not been a champion.

When Blake finally earned his championship, Simcoe celebrated his accomplishment with the excitement of a political convention. About 1,400 people attended a Stanley Cup celebratory dance, and 2,000 came to a rally in town. They greeted Blake with a grand parade, putting him on a float with the area's other Stanley Cup champions: Red Kelly (Detroit, 1950, 1952, 1954, and 1955; and Toronto, 1962, 1963, 1964, and 1967), Chico Maki (Chicago, 1961), and Rick Wamsley (Calgary, 1989).

At one point, Blake commanded the parade to stop when he saw a group of kids in wheelchairs. He hopped off the float, took the Cup to them, and signed autographs.

Perhaps the symbol of the day was Blake's younger brother, Rob, putting the Stanley Cup on top of the combine on the family farm. "This is a way of saying thanks to everyone," Blake told the Canadian press. "The response was overwhelming."

A couple of weeks before Blake's day in Simcoe, he signed a long-term deal to stay with Colorado. He accepted less money than he would have received had he tested the free-agent marketplace. Word was that the Toronto Maple Leafs and the New York Rangers would have given him more—maybe $1 million more per season.

But Blake said hockey was about winning, not about the money. In the summer of 2001, he believed he had a better opportunity to win again with the Avalanche than he had elsewhere.

However, Blake has never returned to the Stanley Cup Finals. He went from Colorado to Los Angeles and then signed with the San Jose Sharks in the summer of 2008 because he believed they had the best chance of winning the Stanley Cup in 2009.

## Dave Andreychuk

*Tampa Bay Lightning, 2004*

During the 2004 NHL playoffs, the No. 1–ranked Tampa Bay Lightning embraced the motto that they needed to seize their championship opportunity because they might never have another.

"And I was the living proof," said former Lightning captain Dave Andreychuk. Andreychuk had played 1,515 regular-season games with six different teams over 22 seasons without even advancing to the Stanley Cup Finals. "We had a lot of young guys, like Vinny Lecavalier, Brad Richards, and [Martin] St. Louis, and they were young guys who think they are going to be back there every year, and I could tell them that wasn't the case," Andreychuk said.

The Lightning were the NHL's top team wire-to-wire in 2004. And the 40-year-old Andreychuk not only scored 21 goals but was an inspirational leader.

Andreychuk's quest to win a Stanley Cup became a subplot of Tampa Bay's postseason march to the Finals. In 2000 the Boston Bruins had traded Andreychuk and Raymond Bourque, two non–Cup winners, to Colorado, giving them both an opportunity to win before they retired.

The Avalanche failed to win in the 2000 playoffs, but they did win in 2001, and Bourque, in his 22nd season, ended the longest championship wait in NHL history. Counting regular- and postseason, Bourque had played 1,826 NHL games before winning the Stanley Cup.

*The Tampa Bay Lightning's Dave Andreychuk (left) waves to the crowd as he rides with the Stanley Cup and Mickey Mouse during the team's parade at Disney's Magic Kingdom in Florida in June 2004.*

But Andreychuk hadn't stayed with Colorado. He had started his career with Buffalo in 1982–1983 and still lived there in the off-season. He re-signed with Buffalo in the summer of 2000, and the Sabres had been ousted in the second round while the Avalanche were winning a Stanley Cup for Bourque. He signed with Tampa Bay in 2001.

"I had pretty much come to the conclusion that if a championship was going to happen, it was going to happen," Andreychuk said. "But it wasn't going to be the end of the world if I didn't win the Stanley Cup."

But as the Lightning kept advancing in the playoffs, Andreychuk began to believe this was the best opportunity he'd ever had to win.

"I had a sense that something special was going to happen," Andreychuk said. "I had a lot of people following me because I had played a long time, and when you get that close, you don't feel the sense of urgency, but they do."

Most NHLers end up playing in cities far away from their hometown, but Andreychuk played his first 15 seasons within an hour of his hometown of Buffalo. His high school buddies were still his buddies, and he remained very close to his family. "I had nieces and nephews taking a month off of school to be part of it," Andreychuk said.

The Lightning had to go to a Game 7 in the Eastern Conference Finals against Philadelphia and another Game 7 against Calgary in the Finals to give Andreychuk his first Stanley Cup.

In Andreychuk's office he has a photo of 30 friends and family members, including his two sisters, Sandy and Karen, surrounding him on the ice after the Lightning clinched the Cup. "It was like having another team picture when I got the call that it was my time to go on the ice," Andreychuk said.

Andreychuk was still in a captaincy role immediately after the game, making sure every player and their families were accommodated. He said it didn't sink in that he won until a few days later. He actually had to watch a video to see what he did with the Stanley Cup after it was presented to him by commissioner Gary Bettman.

"You go over this as a kid, but when it happens, it's almost like time stops because you are never really sure what you are doing," Andreychuk said. "Apparently, I tried to jump but I was so tired that I only got a quarter-inch off the ice. I lifted it up, did a little dance, and wanted to hand it off right away, but Tim Taylor told me I was supposed to skate around the ice with it."

Andreychuk contributed one goal and 13 assists to the Lightning's championship effort, but he will mostly be remembered for his leadership. He chose to play with the Lightning before anyone believed they could be a successful team and helped them create their identity. He decreed that no one should walk on the Lightning logo that was emblazoned on the carpeting in their new dressing room.

"When you travel around on different teams, you pick up stuff from everybody, and I got that from Patrick Roy in Colorado," Andreychuk said. "Patrick was on one side of the dressing room, and he walked around the logo to go on the ice every time…it was about us respecting that it mattered what was on the front of the jersey, and not the back."

As captain, Andreychuk ended up in charge of the Stanley Cup for longer periods than other players. He hosted a party that night, and then later he took the Cup home to Hamilton and Buffalo, starting each day with a trip to children's hospitals.

"The Hamilton day was almost like a wedding because we rented a hall, sent out invitations, and had everyone there, from cousins to people who lived on the same street with me," Andreychuk said. "I was able to sit in my bedroom, the one I grew up in, with the Stanley Cup and my mom and dad, and take pictures."

In Buffalo, Andreychuk ate chicken wings out of the Cup.

"It was a day I never wanted to end," Andreychuk said. "People ask me, 'Why Buffalo?' And I say I went there as an 18-year-old kid, and I spent half my life there. I still go to Buffalo for the summers."

Andreychuk also went with the Stanley Cup to Disney World for a parade. Then there was a party at Tim Taylor's house, and Andreychuk remembers that because of a conversation he had with former Major League Baseball standout Wade Boggs, who lived in the Tampa area and knew many of the Lightning players.

Boggs was fascinated by the Stanley Cup's history.

"He was amazed that the Cup went to every player who had won," Andreychuk said. "He was in awe. He said when he won the World Series with the New York Yankees…he remembers what the trophy looked like, but he didn't think he touched it."

After the Penguins' incident, the Hockey Hall of Fame decreed that there would be no swimming with the Stanley Cup. But the Lightning were celebrating the first championship in franchise history, and the rules momentarily were thrown overboard during the euphoric celebration at Andreychuk's house the night they won the Cup.

"Andre Roy is always the life of the party, and he decided to jump into my pool for a swim with his suit on," Andreychuk recalled. Soon other Lightning players were in the pool in business attire, and before long the Cup was handed to them. "We have some awesome photos with the Stanley illegally in my pool," Andreychuk said.

It didn't take long for the Lightning to learn a physics lesson about a weighted mass in a body of water. "When it got to the bottom and it filled up with water, it was not easy to get out—there is no doubt about that," Andreychuk said, laughing. Andreychuk owns a photograph of many of the Lightning players underwater straining to push the Stanley Cup to the surface.

The Andreychuk home is located on a golf course, and the celebration lasted long enough that golfers were stopping by the next morning to see what the celebration was about.

Andreychuk believed he had gotten away with their Cup swimming escapade until he had his official visit with the Stanley Cup later that summer in Buffalo. Cup keeper Walt Neubrand of the Hockey Hall of Fame was the man assigned to look after the Cup, and he had done his homework. At 2:00 AM, Neubrand informed Andreychuk that he wanted to get some sleep because there would be another party the following night at Craig Ramsey's house.

"The Cup isn't going to go in the pool is it?" Neubrand asked.

"No, of course not," Andreychuk said.

"Well, I was just at Marty St. Louis' house," Neubrand said. "And I saw the pictures of the Cup in your pool in Florida."

"Busted," Andreychuk confirmed.

The Lightning were done in by dozens of incriminating photographs.

# chapter 9

# Back to Mario's Pool

Although Bryan Trottier, Steve Yzerman, and others have slept with the Stanley Cup through the years, the difference when Sidney Crosby spooned with Lord Stanley's chalice is that we have visual evidence that it happened.

Camera phones and the Internet have upped the ante for Stanley Cup celebrations.

The Penguins won the Stanley Cup by defeating the Red Wings 2–1 in a dramatic Game 7 in Detroit on Friday, June 12, 2009. They celebrated with family until 2:00 AM in the visitors' dressing room at Joe Louis Arena and then chartered back to Pittsburgh. Players then traveled by limousines to Mario Lemieux's house, where they partied and watched the sun rising behind the glistening Stanley Cup.

Crosby lives in Lemieux's house, and at some point, the worn out Penguins captain collapsed on his bed next to the Stanley Cup. By late that night, a photograph of Crosby sleeping with the Stanley Cup was posted on the Internet. Emails of the image were being distributed all over the world.

As players now realize, there is no such thing as a private celebration anymore. Also appearing shortly thereafter on Facebook was visual proof that the Stanley Cup had indeed made a return engagement to Lemieux's pool.

On Sunday, Lemieux held a team party to celebrate the victory, and 75 photos of that event, including images of players and guests frolicking with the Stanley Cup in the pool, were everywhere on the Web. One of the most memorable photos was of 6'7" defenseman Hal Gill swimming in the pool with the Stanley Cup and several children.

The good news from the Hockey Hall of Fame's perspective was that the Stanley Cup didn't end up at the bottom of Lemieux's pool, where it would have formed a suction. "We have veteran guys who knew not to let that happen," joked Penguins vice president of communication Tom McMillan.

With all due respect to previous owners who have won the Stanley Cup, an invite to celebrate the Stanley Cup at Lemieux's house is more historically significant than an owner's party would normally be.

Lemieux had twice previously won a Stanley Cup as a Pittsburgh player. He's one of the most popular athletes in Pittsburgh history. He saved the Penguins as a player, and then he rescued it out of bankruptcy as an owner. In the wild postgame celebration on the Detroit ice, McMillan said he was fearful that Lemieux wasn't going to get to raise the Stanley Cup as an owner for the first time. "He deserved that moment, and you know Mario, he wasn't going to ask for it," McMillan said.

But veteran Bill Guerin, always known as one of the league's classiest players, handed the Stanley Cup to the bearded Lemieux, who raised it to the applause and cheers of players around him. "Then he gave it to Sid, and it was unbelievable," McMillan said. "The symbolism of that moment wasn't lost."

In Canada, Crosby has owned the popularity of a rock star since he was 16. Compared to Wayne Gretzky, Crosby arrived in the NHL with impossible expectations. He was the league's boy wonder. Every reporter wrote about him, and every television camera was trained on him. But somehow, amid relentless pressure, Crosby, at age 21, was able to lead his team to a championship in only his fourth NHL season. Even Gretzky was 23, in his fifth NHL season, when he captained the Oilers to a title in 1984.

After Crosby had raised the Stanley Cup for the first time, he met the media with a bottle of champagne in his hand. When asked what he thought as he raised the Cup, Crosby said, "It was heavier than I thought." Then he gave the serious answer, saying, "It was everything I dreamed it would be. I feel lucky to be a part of this group."

It had taken Crosby just over 46 months from the time he was drafted No. 1 in 2005 to win his first championship. "It's not easy to be in the spotlight like he was at a young age," Pittsburgh coach Dan Bylsma said. "There is a lot of focus. There's lots of scrutiny. There's lots of demands.... This erases a lot of questions."

One the ice, no one was happier than Penguins general manager Ray Shero. He is the son of the late Fred Shero, the legendary coach who had guided the Philadelphia Flyers to back-to-back Stanley Cup championships in 1974 and 1975.

Before Game 6 of the 1974 Finals, Fred Shero told his players, "Win together today, and we walk together forever." Those words are now considered perhaps the best description of what it means to work together to win a Stanley Cup.

Ray Shero, winning his first Cup in only his third season on the job, understood his dad's sentiments better than most. "All the players, coaches, trainers, we'll all be on the Cup forever," Ray Shero said a few minutes after the team won. "We'll have some great lasting memories. They'll never take the victory away from us."

Although there were many poignant moments during the on-ice celebration, McMillan said one of his favorite memories was the sight of Penguins players joining in a rousing chorus of "We Are the Champions" and "Sweet Caroline" in the victorious dressing room.

One poignant moment for people inside the Penguins organization came when Eddie Johnston, a member of Pittsburgh's management team, received his time to lift the Stanley Cup. He won the Stanley Cup as a player with the Boston Bruins in 1972 but hadn't won the Cup in his 25 years with the Penguins. When the Penguins won in 1991 and 1992, Johnston was managing the Hartford Whalers. But in 1984 Johnston was the Pittsburgh Penguins' general manager who drafted Lemieux.

"Talk about going a long time between Cups," McMillan said. "E.J. waited a long time. He's a grandfather figure that everyone loves. It was great to to see him cap off his Pittsburgh career with a Stanley Cup."

Johnston officially retired from Penguins management after the 2008–2009 season, although he still consults with the team. "He was the last goalie to play every game in a season, and he played with Bobby Orr, and he played without a mask," McMillan said. "He is not a Hall of Famer, but hockey is built on the shoulders of guys like him."

Penguins coach Dan Bylsma views NHL playoffs as a story in search of a hero. The Penguins had many heroes, but none greater than Maxime Talbot. Only a 12-goal scorer in the regular season, Talbot scored his seventh and eighth goals of the playoffs to give Pittsburgh the victory over Detroit in Game 7. "If your team is playing well enough, then everyone has the opportunity to put on the cape," Bylsma said. "Max put on the cape [in Game 7]."

But the Conn Smythe Trophy went to Evgeni Malkin, the team's leading scorer. The Smythe Trophy isn't supposed to go home with the player, but Malkin brought it home on the Penguins' charter because he wanted to show it to his parents. His parents, Vladimir and Natalia, are superstitious and wouldn't travel to Detroit because, when they went for Games 1, 2, and 5, the Penguins lost. "I saw Mr. Malkin in the morning, and he said, 'No go to Detroit, bad luck,'" McMillan recalled.

The party at Lemieux's house was two days after the Cup celebration, and it was a lavish, catered event. Some of the photographs showed the inside of Lemieux's mansion, including his wine cellar. "In typical Mario fashion there were no speeches," McMillan said. "It was just a very elegant party." Apparently, the Stanley Cup went into the pool elegantly, as well. Otherwise, there would have been a photo of someone throwing it.

The Penguins' victory was made sweeter by the fact that the Steelers also owned the Lombardi Trophy. Since the Philadelphia Phillies had also won the World Series, representatives from all three teams took their trophies to Harrisburg to show off for lawmakers at the state's capital. During the tour, the Penguins' delegation was actually taunted by a Philadelphia Flyers fan who worked at the capitol.

The Penguins' delegation, of course, had the last word because they could simply point to the Cup and remind the Flyers fan that they had it.

One of the hot T-shirts to appear in the Steel City after the Penguins won the Stanley Cup in 2009 was emblazoned with the words: "ON THE ICE OR ON THE GRASS, PITTSBURGH TEAMS WILL KICK YOUR ASS."

# Kyle Quincey, Defender of Cup Honor

On October 9, 2008, the honor of the Stanley Cup was defended by a player who doesn't quite have the proper credentials even to hoist it up. While the Red Wings were raising the Stanley Cup championship banner before a game against Toronto, the NHL decided to launch the regular season with a "Face-off Rocks" celebration that featured the British heavy metal band Def Leppard.

Popular Red Wings player Darren McCarty, who was injured, was asked to participate in the event by driving the Stanley Cup onto the Fox Theater stage on a motorcycle. Defenseman Kyle Quincey was not scheduled to play that night, and McCarty asked him to tag along and walk behind the motorcycle to add a second layer of security for the Cup, which would be securely attached to a cart on the back of the bike.

"My job was to take the bolt off and then hand it to Darren," Quincey said.

He did exactly that, and then McCarty hoisted the Cup and handed it to Def Leppard vocalist Joe Elliott, who also raised it high. Then Elliott committed what could be called the ultimate hockey turnover. When placing the Stanley Cup on a stand, Elliott turned it upside down, with the bowl on the bottom.

McCarty was leaving the stage and didn't see Elliott's breach of Cup etiquette, but Quincey noticed and was mortified by the sight. "I was kind of in shock," Quincey said. "It's so disrespectful. To see it upside down was really weird. It's like someone trampling on your symbol or throwing your flag on the ground."

Immediately, Quincey used his hands to gesture to Elliott that he had blundered. "He looked at me and said, 'Whatever, no big deal,'" Quincey recalled.

It was a big deal for Quincey, who wasn't going to let British rockers defile Lord Stanley's Cup. He trotted across the stage and replaced the Stanley Cup on its stand in its traditional pose.

"Well, never mind," Elliott said. "We're soccer boys—what do we know?"

Red Wings defenseman Chris Chelios was miffed when he heard about the incident, saying the NHL should have picked a North American band that appreciated the importance of the Stanley Cup. Appearing on WCSX radio in Detroit, he charged that Elliott had defiled the Cup on purpose. "We knew he did," Chelios said. "We talked to people at the show, and the guy was being real rude to everybody. He was in a bad mood when they got there, so for whatever reason he didn't want to be there. And that's his way of showing it and taking it out on the NHL."

Stanley Cup keeper Walt Neubrand wasn't there for the episode, but he talked to other Hockey Hall of Fame officials who also believed that Elliott's act was purposeful.

On Def Leppard's website, Elliott said, "I will, as always, take full responsibility for what happened because I have big pucks. However, someone at the NHL should have known better and informed me first instead of keeping the Stanley Cup under lock and key until the last minute. The practice run the day before with a coffeemaker went swimmingly because it, like every other sporting cup I've ever seen, was wider at the top than the base. Ironic isn't it that after that night's gig, an NHL insider told me that long ago the Stanley Cup was also designed to be put down that way!!!"

Quincey's charge across the stage to defend the Cup's honor certainly deserves a special mention among the historic tales of the Cup's travels. What makes the story better is that Quincey doesn't own full membership in the society of Stanley Cup winners.

He played only six regular-season games and didn't appear in the playoffs for the Detroit team, even though he had played 13 playoff games the season before. Quincey qualified to receive a championship ring, and he got to spend his day with the Stanley Cup, but his name isn't engraved with other Red Wings on the Stanley Cup. Players must play 41 games or appear in the Stanley Cup Finals to earn that honor, although teams have successfully petitioned for non-qualifying players to be added.

Quincey said he gave Elliott the benefit of the doubt because perhaps he didn't know. "But, really, how could you not know?" Quincey said. "Chelios told me I should have hit him." If Quincey would have hit him, then Quincey's name should have been engraved on the Cup on the basis that it might have been one of the most meaningful hits in Stanley Cup history.

Who deserves to be on the Stanley Cup more than a man who defends its honor?

# appendix

# Stanley Cup Timeline

**1892:** Lord Stanley, governor-general of Canada, announces he will donate a trophy to designate Canada's national champion.

**1893:** Montreal AAA becomes the first winner of the Cup.

**1902:** The ring beneath the bowl, where names were etched, is completed filled.

**1907:** The Montreal Wanderers become the first team to engrave the names of all of their players, in addition to the team name, on the Cup. Prior to this season, only team names were engraved on the Cup's bowl.

**1907:** An unidentified man absconds with the Stanley Cup and holds it for ransom. However, the champion Montreal Wanderers have no interest in paying any amount for its return. The Cup is returned without payment.

**1908:** The Wanderers become the first team not to engrave their championship on the bowl.

**1924:** Although the formal engraving of names on the Stanley Cup began in 1907, it didn't become an annual event until 1924.

**1925:** The Stanley Cup unofficially becomes the NHL championship trophy.

**1938:** The Chicago Blackhawks finish the regular season with a losing record and then win the Stanley Cup title. No sub-.500 team has won the title since. The Blackhawks coach that season is Bill Stewart, who becomes the first American-trained coach to win the Stanley Cup.

**1948:**  The NHL remodels the Stanley Cup into a two-piece trophy with a wider base. All of the winning players whose names were never put on the Cup are engraved on it at this time.

**1949:**  The NHL and the Stanley Cup trustee sign an agreement giving the league jurisdiction over the awarding of the Cup (but not ownership).

**1952:**  Detroit's Terry Sawchuk sets NHL record when he gives up just two goals in a four-game sweep against Montreal. Tom Johnson and Elmer Lach score the only goals against Sawchuk in the series.

**1954:**  Marguerite Norris, president of the Detroit Red Wings, is the first woman to have her name engraved on the Stanley Cup.

**1955:**  Detroit Red Wings captain Ted Lindsay holds up the Cup for fans to see and then skates over along the boards so fans can get a closer look.

**1958:**  The modern one-piece Stanley Cup is introduced. The silver from the old barrel is retired to the Hall of Fame.

**1961:**  The Chicago Blackhawks win their last Stanley Cup, which means the franchise has the league's longest championship drought.

**1963:**  Construction of the Presentation Stanley Cup is completed, and that trophy is now the Cup seen on the ice when winners celebrate.

**1969:**  The original Stanley Cup bowl is retired to the Hall of Fame. This means that there are actually three Stanley Cup bowls (see 1992 entry).

**1973:**  The Montreal Canadiens win the Stanley Cup, and Henri Richard establishes the new NHL record of having his name engraved in the cup 11 times as a player.

**1971:**  After Montreal wins the Stanley Cup at Chicago Stadium, Canadiens' captain Jean Beliveau skates around the ice with the Cup over his head. The Canadiens follow him. This is the start of the traditional victory lap.

**1977:**  A Hall of Fame employee thwarts an elaborate plan to steal the Cup. Seven men with tools flee the scene, but police discover plans and photos of the Hall in a car parked nearby.

1979:   Montreal Canadiens star Guy Lafleur "steals" the Stanley Cup and takes it to Thurso, Quebec, where he entertains family and friends.

1990:   Petr Klima scores for Edmonton at 55:13 of overtime to give Edmonton a 3–2 win against Boston in the longest Stanley Cup Finals in NHL history.

1992:   The Stanley Cup Finals finish in June for the first time, when the Pittsburgh Penguins defeat Chicago 6–5 on June 1 to win their second consecutive NHL title.

1992:   A duplicate Stanley Cup is produced at a cost of $75,000. In a meeting of the NHL, the Hall of Fame, and the Stanley Cup trustees, it's agreed that the players should always receive the original as a tribute to the work they put in to earn it.

1995:   NHL commissioner Gary Bettman decrees that every player, trainer, coach, and member of management from the Stanley Cup championship team should get at least a day with the Cup. Players had been able to spend some time with the Cup unofficially before; however, at this point the passing of the Cup becomes organized, assuring that no one will be left out. Part of the agreement is that a member of the Hall of Fame must accompany the Cup on its many stops.

1996:   Colorado's Peter Forsberg becomes the first player to take the Stanley Cup to Europe. He takes it to his native Sweden. The Cup had gone to Finland and Germany in 1994, but not with a player.

1996:   Avalanche player Adam Deadmarsh becomes the first NHL player to have his name corrected on the Cup. The engraver had inadvertently listed him as "Deadmarch."

1997:   The Cup goes to Russia for the first time. Detroit Red Wings Slava Fetisov, Slava Kozlov, and Igor Larionov take it to Red Square, among other stops in Moscow.

1998:   The Red Wings win the Stanley Cup, giving coach Scotty Bowman his eighth Stanley Cup championship as a coach. This ties him with Toe Blake for the NHL record.

2002:   The Red Wings' Dominik Hasek becomes the first European starting goalie to win a Stanley Cup. This first was guaranteed since the Wings' opponent in the Finals was the Carolina Hurricanes, whose starting goalie was Latvian Arturs Irbe.

2004: When the Tampa Bay Lightning win the NHL title, the name of backup goalie John Grahame is added to the Stanley Cup. His mother, Charlotte, had her name engraved on the Stanley Cup in 2001 because she was the senior director of Hockey Administration for the Colorado Avalanche when they won the title. The Grahames are the only mother-son combination on the Stanley Cup.

2007: From May 2–6, the Stanley Cup made its first visit to a combat zone. The trip was organized by the league, Hall of Fame, NHL Alumni, and Canadian Department of Defense. It was put on display for Canadian and NATO troops. The Cup briefly came under rocket attack on May 3, but emerged without any damage.

2007: The Anaheim Ducks become the first modern-day West Coast team to win the Stanley Cup. Counting the pre–World War II era, the Ducks were the third West Coast team to win the Cup, joining the 1917 Seattle Metropolitans and the 1925 Victoria (British Columbia) Cougars. Those two teams won before the NHL took charge of the tournament. Owner Jack Kent Cooke brought the NHL to California 40 years ago with the Los Angeles Kings, who reached the Finals once, in 1993, but have never won the Cup.

2008: Detroit defenseman Nicklas Lidstrom becomes the first European-born captain and Dan Cleary the first player from Newfoundland to win a Stanley Cup.